THE EVERYTHING DOG BOOK

Choosing, caring for, and living with your new best friend; so complete you'll think a dog wrote it!

Carlo DeVito
with Amy Ammen

Adams Media Corporation
Holbrook, Massachusetts

For my wife, Dominique. And to Exley, Chelsea, Storm, Cheri, Pepi, Bentley, Red, Benji, Max, Burton, Timothy, and Jo. They have all taught me a great deal about dogs, and even more about being a better human being.

An Everything Series Book. The Everything Series is a trademark of Adams Media Corporation.

Published by Adams Media Corporation
260 Center Street, Holbrook, MA 02343

ISBN: 1-58062-144-9

Printed in the United States of America.

J I H G F E D C B

Library of Congress Cataloging-in-Publication Data
DeVito, Carlo
The everything dog book / by Carlo DeVito with Amy Ammen.
p.   cm.
Includes index.
ISBN 1-58062-144-9
1. Dogs. I. Ammen, Amy. II. Title. III. Series.
SF426.D46   1999
636.7'088'7—dc21   99-20531
CIP

This publication is designed to provide accurate and authoritative information with regard to the subject matter covered. It is sold with the understanding that the publisher is not engaged in rendering legal, accounting, or other professional advice. If legal advice or other expert assistance is required, the services of a competent professional person should be sought.
— From a *Declaration of Principles* jointly adopted by a Committee of the American Bar Association and a Committee of Publishers and Associations

Illustrations by Barry Littmann

This book is available at quantity discounts for bulk purchases.
For information, call 1-800-872-5627 (in Massachusetts, call 781-767-8100).

Visit our home page at http://www.adamsmedia.com

Contents

Chapter 5: Advanced Training 175

Chapter 6: Your Best Friend 211

Chapter 7: Your Dog's Health and Fitness 231

Chapter 8: Your Older Dog 259

Chapter 9: Canine Resources 269

Index 289

Introduction

Bentley was the answer to a sixth-grader's dreams. He was a confidant, a play pal, someone to talk to late at night. He was never judgmental, always loyal: someone who would definitely sneak down stairs with you for a late night snack, and one who would fight for space on the bed with you—covers and all. In short, he was my best friend. Bentley was a godsend who arrived at my door at what just happened to be three days before my twelfth birthday. Bentley was a Dalmatian.

He had an extremely square head for a Dalmatian, and a deep broad chest. And of course he had a tremendous number of spots. He had one large circle around his eye. My grandmother used to say to him, "Bentley, you smudged your mascara again." With his red collar and wonderful, bouncy gait, he was what every child envisioned a Dalmatian to be. He loved attention, food, sleeping and running.

My family and I have many great memories of Bentley. There was the Saturday when the entire family went food shopping and left him alone in one room. I can proudly say that he did not go to the bathroom while we were gone at all. Instead, he rewarded us by tearing up the entire kitchen floor. Then, there was the time we came home and the kitchen table looked like the *Titanic* going down to its watery grave—he had gnawed one of the legs entirely off. There was also the time my parents were entertaining out-of-town clients. During the dinner, Bentley clawed his way into the pantry and ate a whole cake, as well as assorted pastries. I remember the shriek my mother gave. I flew down the stairs only to find her chasing the dog around the table, his face covered in chocolate. He thought it was a game.

Of course, I have less provocative memories of Bentley. Like the complaints from our next-door neighbors, who often gave him treats only to find out that he had dug up their flower beds. Or the time he jumped out of a moving convertible.

He was not all bad, of course. There was the time he protected my little brother from a German Shepherd who had

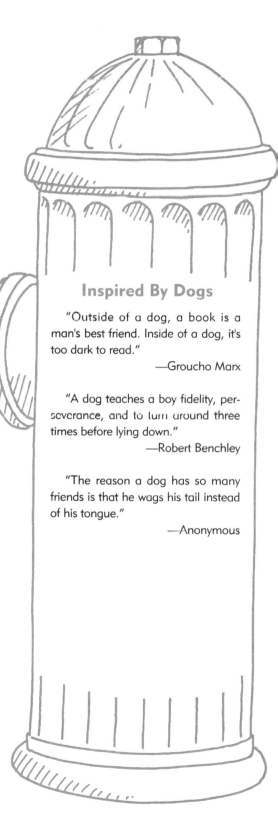

Inspired By Dogs

"Outside of a dog, a book is a man's best friend. Inside of a dog, it's too dark to read."
—Groucho Marx

"A dog teaches a boy fidelity, perseverance, and to turn around three times before lying down."
—Robert Benchley

"The reason a dog has so many friends is that he wags his tail instead of his tongue."
—Anonymous

roamed into our yard. The two did epic battle and Bentley came back bloodied. His twenty-three stitches were soon revenged as the German Shepherd came by yet again less than a year later. After the second bout was over, we kept wiping and wiping his coat, looking for the source of all the blood, until none could be found. In a scene from a John Irving novel, Bentley only afterward spit out a piece of his opponent's ear.

But most of my memories were of Bentley's love of food and his deep desire to either run or sleep. He could be outside and hear the refrigerator door open. He loved to sleep near the fire and insisted on lying on the living-room floor in the middle of every holiday. He stole all kinds of unattended food from coffee tables and counters. I never saw him resist anything that was remotely edible.

I even took Bentley to college with me one semester. I lived in an old fifth-floor walk up that had little heat and no insulation. Even with the windows closed and locked, the drapes and blinds would clatter in winter. In these months, after I was asleep, Bentley would sneak onto the bed and get the inside position against the wall. There he would curl up and keep us both warm, if not a little uncomfortable. Many a night I filled my knapsack at the cafeteria and went home to feed my waiting friend. He was a constant attendee at tennis matches and baseball games. For that semester, he was a well-known personality on campus.

Throughout the family's photo albums, Bentley is everywhere. There are many more stories I have left out. When the old pictures are brought out, stories about him abound. Everyone in our family has Bentley stories. We all laugh. That's how we've come to know that he was not only my best friend—he was my sister's, my brother's, and my parents' best friend as well.

Every family who has had a dog has these same types of stories. While dogs come in a variety of physical packages, they are all big where it counts—personality. In the character department, they are all colossal. People who are lucky enough to open up their lives and let in a friend as true and loving as a dog find a bond that transcends the verbal. It does not have the intimacy of a human relationship, but it doesn't have its deceits and disappointments, either. Dogs do not know how to lie. There is no exchange of ideas—unless that idea is the inherent goodness of cookies or treats. But there is something in the magically expressive eyes of a dog that is difficult to explain to someone who does not understand. If you have a dog, you already know what I mean. If you're thinking of getting one, you're in for the experience of a lifetime.

My parents thought they were dog people just because they owned a dog. They never bought a book to try and understand what Bentley needed. For example, they didn't understand that much of Bentley's worst behavior stemmed from his not getting enough exercise when he was young. They didn't understand the importance of training or obedience. Looking back, Bentley made all of our lives much better by his company, but we might not have been as good to him as we thought. If we hadn't had understanding neighbors and a lot of patience ourselves, Bentley might have been one of many dogs who end up sentenced to death just for being dogs.

It would be nice if dogs didn't require instruction booklets, but they do. There are lots of things that you need to know, not only for your dog's sake, but to strengthen the bond between you. Training is key, and that's why Amy Ammen wrote the training chapters. She's an amazing trainer who has trained countless pets privately, as well as teaching in large groups. She's also done training videos.

Dog owners also need to know about their breed's histories and traits, grooming requirements, nutritional needs, basic health-care, how to prepare their home and family for a dog, and much more. I am lucky to have met many dog professionals in my life since I lost Bentley. Thanks to them I understand that dog ownership is more than just feeding an animal and taking him to the vet when he's sick. It's more than just enjoying the unconditional love dogs give. It's about being partners as well as being friends.

Chapter One

DOGS AND WHERE THEY CAME FROM

A History of Dogs and People

The history of dogs is so closely woven in with the history of people that historians and archaeologists cannot agree on when or how they were introduced. Prehistoric people may have found many good uses for dogs. Once domesticated, dogs were used as early warning detection devices against human or animal intruders. They would defend people's caves and camps as their own, and so they must have been excellent protection as well as an alert system.

Obviously, the greatest use early people had for their canine companions was hunting. Once the dog was part of the human family, and once humans were part of the pack, hunting together became a valuable common interest. There is also conjecture concerning how far back humans used dogs to guard livestock. Of course, as a dog fancier, one must wonder in the end, what attracted dogs to people? According to dog experts there were mainly three things—food, fire (for heat in winter), and community.

Lloyd M. Wendt, a noted historian of the human/dog connection who wrote the very detailed book *Dogs* believes that the relationship between early humans and domesticated dogs can first be traced back 100,000 years to northern Africa and the Middle East. Remains found suggest a communal burial or death, rather than a violent end. Carbon dating has put the most recent findings at 92,000 years ago. He also noted that as little as 10,000 years ago, Algerians were drawing hunting scenes on cave walls, depicting the hunt, with dogs on leashes. Historians place the working aspect of the human/dog relationship at approximately 80,000 years ago, with the advent of the spear. Spears gave humans a weapon to fend off aggressive animals as well as something to kill them with. It was probably about this time that humans and dogs began hunting together in earnest.

It is important to note that the image of a human walking with his or her dog would look nothing like what we might picture it today. Humans have evolved since they first reached out in friendship to dogs. And back then, while dogs might have been mutts, they were more closely related to a type of fox or jackal than the dogs we know today. Much like humans, domesticated dogs have changed so much in some instances that they are classed separately from those dogs today that remain wild. The pets we know today are classed by experts as *Canis familiaris*. It's important to know that we've both grown up a bit.

The first domesticated dogs bred in captivity appear to have come from nomadic Berber tribes. While the Egyptians used their dogs for hunting and guarding livestock, the warlords of the Middle East had different plans. The Egyptians were safe from other warring neighbors with sea to one side and desert to another, but the small and large kingdoms and fiefdoms of the Middle East were much more in conflict with each other. The Persians, Assyrians, Hittites, Sumerians, and Babylonians all favored large fighting dogs that were believed to have originally come from India.

As humans became more adept at navigation on the sea, they also began to seek dogs that were optimal for specific tasks. Great wolflike animals were bred for hunting wolves, bears, and lions in Abyssinia and Persia. The largest and best of the herding dogs came from Tibet. And the fastest hunting greyhounds came from Egypt.

The Egyptians

Of course, the dog achieved its first great fame among modern people in Egypt. Dogs played an important part in everyday life—so much so that they were incorporated into the religion. The god Anubis was portrayed as a dog or as a strange mixture of a human's body with a dog's head. It was not uncommon to have the form of a dog sculpted to rest on the sarcophagus of a deceased king to deter grave robbers, and as a symbol of a guide who would lead the entombed through the afterlife. The Egyptians so loved their dogs that theirs was the first civilization that had a law to punish humans who were cruel to dogs.

The Greeks and Romans

Alexander the Great and later the Roman emperors were also fond of dogs. Because the Greeks and Romans traded with the Egyptians, dogs became popular with Hellenic aristocracy. However, the Greeks used dogs for a variety of purposes. Unlike the Egyptians, who prospered in semi-isolation, the Greeks and the Romans were products of the very heavily populated and mercantile-minded

Inspired By Dogs

"A dog is the only thing on earth that loves you more than you love yourself."

—Josh Billings

"You think dogs will not be in heaven? I tell you, they will be there long before any of us."

—Robert Louis Stevenson

Mediterranean and Middle Eastern cultures. Life was competitive and land came at great cost. Learning from the Persians and their other warlike neighbors, the Greeks began to use two dogs. One was large and massive in build, with a large, broad face, and was known as the Molossian. The other was also large, but with a rather pointed snout, and was somewhat fast and sleeker. This one was known as the Laconian Hound. Aristotle was a fan of both dogs, saying that the Laconian female was gentler and smarter, but by no means fit for war, and that the Molossian was the dog of choice.

The Molossian was named for the tribe that had made it well-known, which came out of northern Greece. The Molassian of Alexander the Great's time is the ancestor of today's Mastiff. This became for centuries the ultimate dog of war—large, strong, fearless, and smart. The Greeks and then the Romans used these beasts in war for something like a cavalry charge. The Laconian Hound was developed, it is believed, in Sparta. It was fast and brutal, but of a sleeker build than the traditional Mastiff.

The first literary classic pairing of a man and his dog comes from the Greeks. Dating back to one of the first classic pieces of literature known and studied for centuries, *The Odyssey* features the story of Odysseus, warrior of the Trojan War, attempting the long, treacherous, and adventurous journey home. After many years away from his farm and kingdom, the hero of the story is not recognized by those people who knew him long ago. Despite his claims, he is only believed when his faithful hound, old, decrepit and flea-ridden, crawls to his master, for whom he has been waiting. The dog then dies, wagging his tail, happy at his master's feet.

If dog was man's best friend in Greece, another dog was the mother of Rome. According to myth, two men fought over the founding of Rome: Romulus and Remus, who both had been raised by a wolf, suckling on her milk. It was the Romans who first outfitted their war dogs with thick leather collars, studded with sharp metal blades to keep other attacking dogs off of them. Dogs were instrumental in Rome's rise. As its famous roads were built and expanded, guard posts all along the way were manned by small militia and hosts of guard dogs. The roads were kept safe for Roman use. The Romans also used their large dogs as beasts of burden. It was not unusual to see dogs, along with cattle, oxen, horses and ponies, pulling carts of all sizes from all different parts of the empire.

The Middle Ages and the Renaissance

In the period after the fall of the Roman Empire, the bubonic plague, or Black Death, was one of the galvanizing events. It was during this time that the dog acquired many of its more negative lore. During the plague, in which fleas transported the deadly disease, historian Mary Elizabeth Thurston points out in her book *The Lost History of the Canine Race* that the dog, "with its inborn resistance to the plague bacillus," was now on its own. Most livestock was killed by the disease—cattle, sheep, chickens and others. People were killing each other over food. Few people during this period kept pets. Ownerless, dogs ran wild, usually in packs, eating corpses and killing in groups.

During feudal times, the aristocracy assumed ownership of many fertile lands, especially the great forests in which many animals were still abundant, as well as many natural resources. The hunt, during these times, became very ritualized and many different dogs were used for different kinds of game. Lords and barons had different dogs to take down deer, bears, bulls, wolves, large fowl, and foxes, and they had other dogs for small game, mostly vermin. Others were bred for specific duties, such as tracking, coursing, and retrieving on land and in water.

Thurston points out that Henry I of England had a kennel of 200 dogs for huntsmen to train, care for, and deploy. As the aristocracy grew, so did their land claims. And unless you were someone of rank, you could not claim game from a claimed preserve.

It was not until after the fall of the French king in the late 1700s, during the French Revolution, that ordinary people were allowed to hunt in the largest and most heavily stocked game forests. In the early 1800s many lands across Europe were opened up in an attempt to dissuade the masses from overthrowing various monarchies. These policies were part of larger political agendas, which all worked to varying degrees. However, one thing was an absolute success—hunting became popular to the extreme.

The different species we are so familiar with today are the result of the continuing quest during this time to find the perfect dog. In many cases throughout history, people have bred dogs

The Lap Dog

It is important to note here that it was at this time that a different kind of dog grew in popularity: the lap dog. Up until now, the majority of dogs were owned by people who used them as beasts of burden or for hunting. Most dogs served a purpose. It was during this time that smaller dogs, mainly seen as women's dogs, came into vogue, especially in the aristocracy. There are many portraits of women from this period who have smaller dogs around them. These were mainly considered companion dogs.

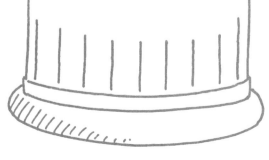

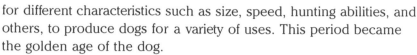

for different characteristics such as size, speed, hunting abilities, and others, to produce dogs for a variety of uses. This period became the golden age of the dog.

During Victorian times, the dog reached an all-time high status. Your choice of dog conveyed whether you were a sportsman or a true lady. Dogs helped people fulfill their aspirations toward a higher station in life. Indeed, it was in this period that many dog classifications began. It was also a time in which many new dog breeds were bred by varying groups, especially hunters. In the 1700s and 1800s, many of the sporting breeds, such as the German Shorthair Pointer, Wirehaired Pointer, Weimaraner, and other hunting dogs, were bred because middle-class Europeans had more time for hunting as recreation, and they wanted one dog to perform a series of functions that the European aristocracy could previously afford to keep several breeds to do. Likewise, smaller, toy breeds also became more popular, and many breeds which were hitherto unknown came to the fore.

In the end, what resulted was a friendship that had grown to proportions like no other relationship between humans and animals. For centuries, the dog has been more popular than any other pet. From *The Call of the Wild* to the newest version of *101 Dalmatians*, humans' love of their canine companions has been celebrated in literature, song, art, folklore, and popular culture.

Today's World of Dogs

In today's world, for every kind of lifestyle people lead, there is a different kind of dog. There are tiny dogs and giant dogs, hairless and shaggy, pedigreed and mutt. And there are many organizations out there that are very helpful in understanding what dogs are all about and are willing to help you.

Different clubs have different aims, but they all share several things in common. First, they are very much into promoting dogs, and shining the best possible light on the breeds they favor or the agenda they promote. Second, they are indeed intended to help people understand dogs better. Although many of the most popular organizations have political reasons for agreeing or disagreeing with each other, the one thing they certainly share is their love of our canine friends.

Many of these clubs offer many pamphlets on choosing, training, spaying, pet healthcare and many other things that go along with responsible pet ownership. They offer many valuable tools, some of

which are free, to make you a good fit with your dog. They are also doing everything they can to encourage pet owners to be more considerate of their non-pet-owning neighbors. No one wants to live near a dog that doesn't mind its master—who runs around jumping up on people and bothering them. While you might think your "puppy" is the best, cutest, cuddliest, friendliest little animal ever to grace the face of the earth, there is always some one out there who sees your dog for the slobbering, dirty, ill-mannered beast he or she really is. Good manners go a long way, especially in close-knit communities.

All of these different kinds of organizations are broken up into two categories: breed registries and animal advocacy groups. Breed registries are more concerned with breed standards and quality, while animal advocacy groups are aimed more at the prevention of cruelty and sheltering strays.

Registries

The American Kennel Club

The most famous organization that represents purebred dogs in the United States (and arguably the world) is the American Kennel Club. Established in 1884 to advance the interests of purebred dogs, today the American Kennel Club recognizes more than 140 breeds in seven groups (Sporting, Non-Sporting, Working, Herding, Terrier, Hound, and Toy). It is a nonprofit organization whose members are not individual dog owners, but breed clubs. Each member club (and there are currently about 500 of them) elects a delegate to represent the club at AKC meetings. The delegates vote on the rules of the sport of dogs—they are the legislative body of the American Kennel Club. The delegates elect the AKC's twelve-member Board of Directors, who are responsible for the overall and daily management of the organization.

Most people are familiar with the prestigious Westminster Kennel Club show that's televised from Madison Square Garden every February. Westminster is one of the member clubs of the AKC—one of the oldest, too. Besides the hundreds of member clubs, there are nearly 5,000 affiliated clubs that conduct AKC events (dog shows and other events) following AKC rules of conduct. Believe it or not, purebred dog fanciers participate in more than 3,000 dog shows a year, as well as more than 5,000 performance events.

The AKC oversees the establishment of recognized breeds in the United States, and also enforces the standards by which breeds are judged. To carry out its many functions, the AKC maintains offices in New York City (where it was founded) and Raleigh, North Carolina. It has several divisions: Registration, of course, but also Judges' Education, Performance Events, Publications, and more. The AKC maintains a reference library of more than 15,000 books, including editions of some of the earliest books ever published on dogs.

What does all this mean to you? It means that when you buy a purebred puppy and register it, you are joining a very large and time-honored family of people who are crazy about dogs. If you want, you can look up fifty generations of your Golden Retriever's ancestors. That's what being purebred means—not that your puppy is some kind of elite dog, but rather, that all the caretakers of his family before you wanted to breed the same kind of dog over and over. The AKC's purpose is to preserve the integrity of its registry of purebred dogs, to sanction events that promote the purpose and function of purebred dogs, and to ultimately protect and ensure the continuation of the sport. The AKC works very hard to make sure that the dogs it registers and awards show points, championships, and performance titles to are the best examples of their breed. However, the AKC is quick to point out that having an "AKC registered dog" does not necessarily mean your dog will be free of health problems, or that it is of championship quality. All it means is that your dog's parents are registered purebreds, and that those dogs' parents are registered purebreds, and so on.

With this in mind, do you need to or should you register your purebred puppy with the AKC? If you bought the dog from a responsible breeder, they will probably encourage you to register the dog. This doesn't mean you can make a lot of money in future breeding. It means the breeder's interested in recording the offspring of his or her animals. Breeders often sell puppies with contracts stating that you must spay or neuter a puppy that won't be shown.

If you bought your puppy from a pet shop or a friend, the shop or individual can supply the registration form (which they must if they're selling you a purebred!). It's fun to pick out a "registered" name for your dog. You'll probably end up calling him something like Spot, but you can tell everyone his "real" name is Jones's Greatness Personified, and you can show them his papers.

Never forget the family and the network you are joining by registering your puppy with the AKC. Don't abuse registering or owning a purebred dog. Be proud of your dog's heritage and your dog's health.

Other Breed Registries in the United States

The AKC is not the only registry organization in the United States or the world. There are many others, with varying philosophies and programs.

The United Kennel Club. The United Kennel Club was founded in 1898 by Chauncey Z. Bennett. The UKC registers more than a quarter-million dogs each year. Their largest number of registrations are for American Pit Bull Terriers. Those two important facts make the UKC the second oldest and second largest all-breed dog registry in the United States. They are located in Kalamazoo, Michigan.

The UKC, like the AKC, sponsors events of many kinds, from dog shows to a host of performance events. The UKC is made up of 1,200 different clubs that oversee 10,000 licensed annual dog events. Many of their events are very easy to enter and compete in, promoting owners to show and compete with their dogs, as opposed to hiring professional trainers or handlers.

UKC offers something called the P.A.D.™ (Pups And Degrees) performance pedigree. This is basically a tracking system which records all the puppies a registered dog has produced and follows those puppies and their performance in the ring. The UKC also sponsors a program for DNA profiling of your puppy, in association with PE Zoogen, a DNA testing firm.

Lesser-Known Registries. The AKC and the UKC only recognize 144 and 188, breeds respectively. And, believe it or not, there are people out there buying dogs that don't have established dog clubs and organizations behind them. These people find it very hard to compete for pure-breed championships. For example, neither the AKC nor the UKC register the Dogo Argentino. Sometimes, smaller clubs fill these voids. The American Rare Breed Association (ARBA) and the American Mixed Breed Obedience Registry (AMBOR) allow members to join with their dogs and compete in various sponsored events.

AKC Activities

The AKC oversees a wide array of events in which you can participate with your purebred. These include dog shows and many other events, from competitive obedience and field trials to the practical Canine Good Citizen program. Shows are for intact dogs only, but most other events welcome spayed and neutered dogs. You can learn more about these events in Part 6 of this book.

The American Kennel Club publishes a monthly magazine and many public education materials to inform the public. To learn even more about the AKC, you can contact Customer Service Department, AKC, 5580 Centerview Dr., Raleigh, NC 27606-3394; (919) 233-9767. You can also visit the AKC on the World Wide Web at www.akc.org.

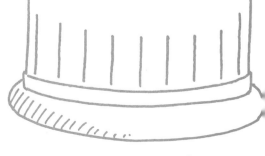

The Kennel Club

The first dog show was held in England on June 28–29, 1859, in the Town Hall at Newcastle-on-Tyne. More than sixty pointers and setters were entered. The winner of the show was not recorded. However, thus began a series of shows and events that needed to be legislated and overseen.

In 1870 Mr. S. E. Shirley formed what was then called the National Dog Club Committee. It was later agreed that twelve gentlemen meet at No. 2 Albert Mansions, Victoria Street, London, on April 4, 1873, to further discuss canine regulation. This meeting marked the founding of The Kennel Club.

There are 188 breeds currently eligible for registration with The Kennel Club. The breeds are identified by groups according to their origins; the six groups are Hound, Gundog, Terrier, Utility, Working, and Toy.

One of the earliest undertakings of the Kennel Club was the compilation of a Stud Book, containing the records of shows from 1859–1873. The Committee formulated a code of ten rules relating to dog shows. It was announced that societies that adopted this code of rules for their shows would be eligible for the Stud Book.

The Canadian Kennel Club

Much like the AKC, the CKC is the primary registering and overseer of the sport of purebred dogs in Canada. Many Canadians who want to compete in the United States register their dogs in both clubs. Much like the AKC, the Canadian Kennel Club is devoted to encouraging, guiding and advancing the interests of purebred dogs and their responsible owners and breeders in Canada.

The FCI

The Federation Cynologique Internationale is very much like the AKC of Europe. The FCI is not so much a club as a governing body that oversees many different clubs. Many of the clubs that belong are the national dog clubs of Western Europe, including Italy, Germany, France, and Spain, among others. This club sponsors two of the world's largest dog shows: The European Dog Show and the World Dog Show.

Pet Advocacy Groups

The American Society for the Prevention of Cruelty to Animals

The American Society for the Prevention of Cruelty to Animals is one of the most active pro-pet groups in the world. A nonprofit company, the ASPCA sponsors countless numbers of groups and events to protect animals' and pet owners' rights. The ASPCA has attempted to reduce pain, fear, and suffering in animals through humane law enforcement, legislative advocacy, education, and hands-on animal care.

The ASPCA was founded in 1866 by a diplomat named Henry Bergh, who served in the U.S. delegation to Russia. Bergh modeled the ASPCA on England's Royal SPCA. The ASPCA managed to get the nation's first anti-cruelty laws passed in the state of New York in its first year. The ASPCA provided ambulance service to horses in New York City two years before the first hospital provided them for humans. In seven short years, twenty-five states, a number of territories, and Canada had used the ASPCA as a model for their own humane organizations.

What's More Modern Than Surfing for Dogs on the Web?

There is no better way to have fun exploring all the ways people relate to their dogs today than by browsing sites on the World Wide Web. So numerous are a dog lover's options that there's even a book on the subject, *Dogs on the Web*, by Audrey Pavia and Betsy Sikora Siino (MIS Press, 1997). Here's a mere sampling of what you can check out:

World Wide Woof: www.worldwoof.com
American Veterinary Medical Association: www.avma.org
Hawaiiana Canine School: www.jakenmax.com/~hawaiiana/hcshmpg.htm
The Marin Humane Society: www.marin-humane.org
The Dog Agility Page: www.dogpatch.org/agility.html
The Virtual Dog Show: www.dogshow.com
DOGZ!: www.dogz.com
Snoopy's Doghouse: www.unitedmedia.com/comics/peanuts
International Appeal: www.bestdogs.com
Carla's Toy Dog Home Page: www.magna.com.au/~gclarke/carla/homec.html

Have fun!

Today, the ASPCA supplies a number of different services to pet and animal lovers all across the country. They are perhaps best known for helping shelter strays and foster adoptions. Their foster care program encourages sympathetic homes to help animals who are "too young, sick or aggressive to be offered for adoption right away a chance to have a long and healthy life by placing them in temporary homes."

People often confuse the New York-based ASPCA with other SPCAs around the country. There are Societies for the Prevention of Cruelty to Animals (SPCAs) in many states. The Massachusetts and San Francisco SPCAs are particularly active in promoting animal welfare through adoption and public education.

The Humane Society of the United States

The Humane Society of the United States (HSUS) is another of the nation's largest animal-protection organizations. While the ASPCA is more focused on pets, especially dogs and cats, the Humane Society has a much wider scope. HSUS promotes the "humane treatment of animals and to foster respect, understanding, and compassion for all creatures." The HSUS uses such venues as the legal system, education, and legislation to ensure the protection of animals of all kinds.

The HSUS was founded in 1954 and currently has nine major offices in the United States. Unlike the ASPCA, the HSUS does not have any affiliate shelters. The HSUS mainly concerns itself with wildlife protection, companion animals, and animal research violations. However, they do sponsor many events for pet owners and do encourage pet rescue (adoption). Some of the events they sponsor include free spaying clinics for pet owners of insufficient means.

The American Humane Association

Based in Englewood, Colorado, and founded in 1877, the American Humane Association (AHA) is a welfare organization involved in assisting both animals and children. These days the AHA oversees the treatment of animals on movie and television sets and is working to establish standards for dog trainers, among many other things.

About Breeds

There are many different breeds from around the world. For the purposes of this introduction to some of those breeds, their habits, and their characteristics, we are going to reference the American Kennel Club's classification of groups and breeds. Many kennel clubs the world over use a similar system.

The AKC breaks down all the different breeds into groups to make understanding the big picture a little easier. The breeds are grouped by key features in personality and breeding. There are seven groups of purebred dogs classified by the American Kennel Club:

Sporting	Working	Herding
Hound	Non-Sporting	Toy
Terrier		

The American Kennel Club also has a Miscellaneous Class, a sort of "holding" group for breeds that have not met all the criteria for full registration (of which there are many).

You may have a purebred dog or be considering getting a purebred, or you may have a mixed breed. Either way, your dog will behave in ways that have been bred into him over the centuries by people who wanted a breed to perform a certain function. If you wonder why your retriever is always bringing you something in his mouth when you come home, it's because every cell in his body is programmed to bring in downed birds to earn his keep. When he brings you a favorite toy, he's doing the next best thing.

This section is intended to help you better understand your dog, or to help you shop for the kind of dog you think would best suit your lifestyle—one that's a diehard loyalist, one that will run and play all day, one that wants to curl up on your lap for hours. Reading about the traits and the histories of the five most popular breeds in each of the seven AKC groups will do this for you. But remember, every dog is an individual. That's why it's important to talk to other owners of the kind of dog you have or are interested in.

Sporting Dogs

The Sporting Group is made up of some of the oldest breeds registered by the AKC. Many of the dogs in this category were bred for hunting. Specifically, they were bred for one or two of the following purposes: to "point," retrieve, or "flush" game birds. That is why the Sporting Group is broken down into pointers, retrievers, and setters. The sporting group is home to many of the AKC's most popular breeds, including the Labrador Retriever, the Golden Retriever, the Cocker Spaniel, and the English Springer Spaniel. These were dogs bred for specific purposes, and most are still doing the jobs they were bred for. While many people who buy these dogs will never need them to do anything but be the family pet, these dogs, when given the opportunity, will begin to automatically use their hunting instincts, pointing and retrieving with abandon. These traits can be some of the most enjoyable aspects of owning a sporting dog. It's wonderful to see your Weimaraner go on point while running a hedgerow; it's fun to have your retriever tirelessly retrieve a tennis ball from a lake or the ocean; it's reassuring to have your spaniel go back and forth in front of you on a walk (this is called quartering in the hunt field). But be forewarned: your dog is a dog, and one day he may come back with not just a ball or toy, but with fresh kill.

Aside from that, the sporting breeds are renowned for their outgoing personalities. Many of them, suited to the right families, make wonderful family pets. They also make good watch dogs (as opposed to guard dogs). They are known to be sociable, but are not known to be overly aggressive, and will always let you know when someone is approaching.

It is important to keep in mind that the early breeders of these dogs wanted them to be able to hunt all day, and bred them for strength and stamina. The better the dog worked, and the longer, the more highly prized it was. While that's great news if you're a hunter, it's particularly important to remember when you buy one of these breeds. They tend to be very active, in most cases. And you should ask the breeder about the parents of your soon-to-be pet so you know about their temperaments and exercise needs, as well as about any health problems that might run in the family.

The Complete AKC Sporting Group

American Water Spaniel
Brittany
Chesapeake Bay Retriever
Clumber Spaniel
Cocker Spaniel
Curly-Coated Retriever
English Cocker Spaniel
English Setter
English Springer Spaniel
Field Spaniel
Flat-Coated Retriever
German Shorthaired Pointer
German Wirehaired Pointer
Golden Retriever
Gordon Setter
Irish Setter
Irish Water Spaniel
Labrador Retriever
Pointer
Sussex Spaniel
Vizsla
Weimaraner
Welsh Springer Spaniel
Wirehaired Pointing Griffon

Golden Retriever

Color:	Yellow to deep golden color
Eyes:	Brown
Body type:	Medium; strong; webbed feet
Temperament:	Very trainable; friendly
Activity level:	Somewhat high early on, but settle down after first year

The Golden Retriever dates back to the mid-1800s, to Inverness-Shire, Scotland, where they were first bred at the estate of Lord Tweedmouth. It is suspected that one of the main breeds used in developing the Golden was the Tweed Water Spaniel, as well as a smaller Newfoundland and some Irish Setter. However, Lord Tweedmouth didn't buy his first Yellow Retriever until 1865, when it is thought he bred him with his fledgling breed.

The dogs were bred for upland game hunting. They were bred to be hearty, as they were used all year round. The Scottish weather not being kind to man or beast, the hunters needed a dog that could negotiate the tough terrain, especially along the bitter cold and damp seacoast, and still flush and retrieve game.

A Golden Retriever was first shown at the Crystal Palace in London in 1908. Because of the dog's instant popularity with visiting sportsmen, Goldens were imported into the United States before the turn of the century. However, they were not an AKC recognized breed until 1925.

The Golden is a dog that was bred to be tough and strong. Don't let the happy, silly face fool you. While they are more than happy to sit around the house and wrestle on the floor with you, they are also adept in the field. They possess great energy as puppies, but settle into adulthood easily. They are very trainable and very good-natured. They are excellent with children and are one of the most popular breeds in all of dogdom for a good reason.

The Golden Retriever is generally light yellow to deep golden honey in color. The coat tends to get a little deeper in color after the first year. They stand about 23 to 24 inches at the withers, with females slightly

Golden Retriever

shorter. They have brown eyes. Their coat should be long and either flat or wavy. They need to be brushed properly, or their coats form thick mats that are difficult to brush out.

Labrador Retriever

Colors:	Solid yellow, solid black or solid brown
Eyes:	Hazel to brown
Body type:	Medium; strong; webbed feet
Temperament:	Very trainable; friendly
Activity level:	Active at a young age, but settle in the first two years

The first Labrador Retrievers were noted in journals dating back to 1822, in which they were described as an admirable group of "small water dogs" used for hunting and retrieving fowl in cold weather. They were short-haired and smooth-coated, and while they did not have great noses, they had many more admirable qualities. But the truth be known, Labradors did not originate in Labrador—they originated in Newfoundland!

Because of a heavy tax levied by the British government on the Newfoundland area, many breeders gave up their hunting dogs, and the breeders of these dogs became fewer and fewer. Eventually, it was English breeders who took a fancy to the breed and made it quite popular. In fact, while the Kennel Club first recognized the breed in 1903, from dogs whose pedigrees could be traced back as far 1878, the American Kennel Club did not recognize the breed until 1917. And the first registered Labrador Retriever in the AKC was Broklehirst Nell, a female imported from Scottish breeders!

The Labrador Retriever has been the most popular breed in the United States for some time, and with good reason. They are excellent family dogs that love the water and love to work. Sportsmen, especially waterfowl hunters, have prized these dogs for a great part of this century for their

Labrador Retriever

patience and ability to swim in icy autumn and winter waters to retrieve fowl from rivers, lakes, and ponds.

They are not tall dogs, averaging less than 23 inches at the withers, and tend to weigh around 60 pounds. They come in three solid colors—yellow, black, and brown. The brown Labrador is known as a chocolate Lab. No wonder so many chocolate Labs are called Hershey, after the candy bar! While they are quite active puppies, Labs make excellent family pets as they mature. They tend to be very sociable, make good watch dogs, and are very good with children

Cocker Spaniel

Cocker Spaniel

Color:	Black; any solid color other than black; parti-color; or tan points
Eyes:	Brown
Body type:	Compact; strong
Temperament:	Trainable; friendly
Activity level:	Active at a young age, but settle in after the first year

The Cocker Spaniel is one of the nine spaniels currently in the Sporting Group. While the spaniel family can trace its roots back to the 14th century, it has divided over the last five centuries. The original *Spanyell* was more or less a Spanish dog that, over the years, was bred for different purposes. There are even spaniels in the Toy Group.

The word Cocker is thought to be an outgrowth of the breed's exceptional ability to flush woodcock. In the beginning they were known as a "cocker" or as a "cocking spaniel."

Even today, the Cocker Spaniel is an excellent hunter. A Cocker should cover the ground in front of a hunter, no farther than the range of his shot. A hunter must always be ready, because a good Cocker works quickly. Once he flushes the game, the Cocker waits for the hunter to bring it down, watching where it falls. When given the command by the hunter, the Cocker then retrieves the downed game. Cockers retrieve on land and in water.

The Cocker Spaniel was recognized by the (English) Kennel Club in 1892. The AKC had already recognized the breed in 1878.

However, while the "cocker" was gaining acceptance in England, it was also growing in popularity in the United States. American breeders developed the Cocker Spaniel into a smaller, more profusely coated, boxier dog than English breeders, and a split was soon apparent. Consequently, the breeds became separated into American Cocker Spaniels and English Cocker Spaniels. In the United States, we call the American Cocker simply the Cocker Spaniel; in England, the English call our English Cocker Spaniel the Cocker Spaniel.

With a boxy head, heavy brow, short, upturned nose, and merry disposition, the Cocker Spaniel is one of the most popular dogs the AKC has registered over the past twenty years. This is because the dog is also an excellent show competitor and a great family pet. Because he is the smallest of all the sporting breeds, he is also considered by many a lap dog. A great all-around pet, Cockers love attention and are very trainable.

They come in four varieties of colors: solid black, any other solid color other than black (ASCOB), Parti-Color, and Tan Points. They should be no taller than about 15½ inches in height, and weigh no more than approximately 28 pounds. While they are not speed demons, Cocker should have no problem keeping up a pretty good average speed regardless of the ruggedness of the terrain. They are lean-looking dogs, with a forward chest and lines that narrow toward the powerful hindquarters. Their coat is long and luxurious when combed as a pet or for show competition.

English Springer Spaniel

Color:	Black and white; liver and white
Eyes:	Brown
Body type:	Small; strong; agile
Temperament:	Trainable; friendly
Activity level:	High energy at a young age; require activity

Where the Cocker tends to be more of a pet these days, the English Springer is still a popular hunter. It is interesting to note that back in the 1880s, the Cockers and Springers were taken from the same litters. The larger dogs from a litter were grouped together with like-sized dogs and called springers. An English Springer Spaniel was deemed so because he weighed more than 28 pounds. Today, of course, Springers are considered a separate breed.

Springers can be liver and white or black and white in their markings. They have a longer muzzle than a Cocker and are taller. They should not be more than 20 inches in height, and have a fine, wavy coat with feathering on the chest, legs and stomach.

Because of their overall size and speed, Springers became very solid and popular hunters. The breed was acknowledged by the Kennel Club as a separate breed by 1902 and by the AKC in 1927. They are excellent flushing dogs, "springing" game in the opened field or in thick cover. Again, they should never be beyond the range of the hunter's gun, and should wait for instruction after the game has risen.

They are high-energy dogs and are fond of working or any kind of exercise. They will need your attention and are best suited for families that don't mind going for extra walks. Springers are very affectionate and make good house pets. As watch dogs or as companions, they are smart and alert.

English Springer Spaniel

German Shorthaired Pointer

Color:	Solid liver; liver and white; liver and flecking
Eyes:	Hazel, brown
Body type:	Medium; strong; webbed feet
Temperament:	Trainable; friendly
Activity level:	High energy; need physical exercise

The German Shorthaired Pointer was an attempt by German sportsmen to breed the all-in-one hunting dog. He is a product of the late 1800s, the zenith of the Victorian sportsman. The German Shorthair was bred to have the energy to hunt all day, be able to swim strongly to retrieve water fowl, have an excellent nose to find game (especially larger birds like quail and pheasant), and to point and flush. He was the ultimate dog!

By all accounts the German breeders pulled it off. There are bits of Spanish Pointer, Bloodhound, and Foxhound, among others, in his makeup. His versatility is what makes him popular, especially with people who hunt. He can be used to hunt upland game, as well as navigate the cold waters of duck hunting. And this dog loves to work.

The Shorthair is usually either solid liver colored, or white and liver, or liver with flecking. A Shorthair should not be any taller than 25 inches and should weigh no more than 70 pounds. In the United States and Australia the dogs have docked tails, though that is no longer practiced in the UK. The tails were originally docked because they were long and skinny and were prone to break easily, thus keeping the dog from working. He is lean with a broad chest and lines that narrow perceptibly at the powerful hindquarters.

These are fast dogs, whose speeds can exceed many other breeds. Many hunters like to hunt with these dogs on horseback. If you want this dog as just a pet, be prepared to take up jogging, hiking, or some other outdoor activity. These dogs are high energy and will require your attention to help spend some of that energy every day. Shorthairs are good watch dogs and arc good with children. They make very good family pets.

German Shorthaired Pointer

Hounds

The Hound Group has in it some of the dogs whose ancestors were humans' earliest companions and assistants. Alexander the Great hunted with hounds. This group also offers the widest range in size of any group. The smallest hound is the Dachshund, which is the only dog in this group that is neither a sight- nor a scenthound, but rather was bred to hunt smaller game "to ground," going gamely into burrows and dens for small mammals. The largest dog in the group is the giant Irish Wolfhound. So then, why are these dogs grouped together?

Hounds generally are grouped together because they will actually hunt down prey and either corner it or kill it. They will not wait for the hunter, but will let the hunter know where they are by various types of barking. Hound people make a distinction between "barking" (meaning just your average dog bark) and "baying" or "tonguing." These terms refer to the different types of barking when a hound is on the trail, hot behind some fast-moving game. As the dog follows the tracks it lets out what I have heard some hound owners refer to as a "song."

I know a foxhunter who had several hounds at home. One day she found a note on her door from an annoyed neighbor that asked if she could keep her dogs from barking so much. The hunter replied with the following: "Number one, they are hounds, not dogs. Secondly, they do not bark, they tongue."

Hounds are generally categorized into two distinct groups. The first are the scenthounds. These are the trackers who hunt with their noses. The best known of these are Bloodhounds and Foxhounds. The other group are sighthounds. The Afghan, the Pharaoh Hound, and the Irish Wolfhound fall into this second category. All of these dogs had very specific uses, and many dogs date back either to the feudal hunts or to ancient Egypt. The Irish Wolfhound hunted wolves; the Harrier and the Petit Basset Griffon Vendeen hunted rabbit; the Otterhound hunted otter; the Scottish Deerhound hunted deer; and the Rhodesian Ridgeback hunted lions.

The most popular hounds (by AKC registrations) are the Beagle, Dachshund, Basset Hound, Bloodhound, and Rhodesian Ridgeback. Most hounds have loud barks and are very vocal. However, there are many popular dogs in this group. They all tend to be social, as many of these dogs hunted in packs. Like the sporting dogs, these animals tended to be bred for stamina. Some of them, the Foxhounds especially, need exercise to be happy pets. Others are less demanding.

Beagle

Beagle

Color:	Mixture of white, tan, and black
Eyes:	Brown
Body type:	Small; strong
Temperament:	Trainable; friendly
Activity level:	High energy; need exercise

In long-ago England, back in the days of King Arthur, hounds were bred for hunting. But no one knows the actual history of the Beagle. Many English lords kept packs of hounds for hunting, and the Beagle was eventually established among them. The hounds were separated while puppies according to their size. The larger

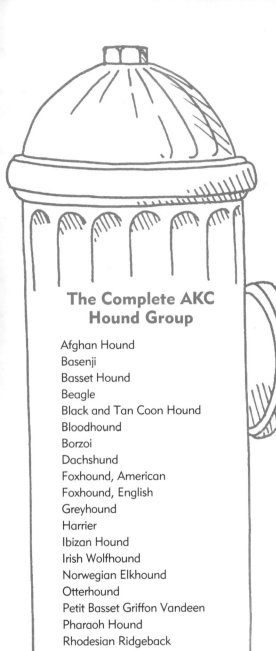

The Complete AKC Hound Group

Afghan Hound
Basenji
Basset Hound
Beagle
Black and Tan Coon Hound
Bloodhound
Borzoi
Dachshund
Foxhound, American
Foxhound, English
Greyhound
Harrier
Ibizan Hound
Irish Wolfhound
Norwegian Elkhound
Otterhound
Petit Basset Griffon Vandeen
Pharaoh Hound
Rhodesian Ridgeback
Saluki
Scottish Deerhound
Whippet

hounds were used for larger game—everything from foxes to deer. The smaller hounds were used for rabbits. This is the origin of the Beagle. Many experts believe that the modern Beagle can be traced back by lineage to the mid-1800s, to the hounds of Parson Honeywood of Essex. The first Beagle was officially registered with the AKC in 1885. More recently, the Beagle has been famous as the model for the world's best-known pet dog, Charlie Brown's Snoopy.

Even today, the AKC splits Beagles into two competition classes: Beagles under 13 inches in height at the withers, and Beagles between 13 and 15 inches in height at the withers. The Beagle is still one of the most popular breeds around the world. They are sturdy, lovable dogs. While they are very friendly and look rather huggable, they can be very courageous. These are great little dogs that need daily outdoor exercise. They also love people and like being part of the family.

They shouldn't be taller than 15 inches and should have a smooth coat of mixed colors. They should have warm, expressive brown eyes. They are very sturdily built and have energy to spare. And for a little dog, they have a deep, echoing bark when alerted by anything.

Dachshund

Color:	Variety of solids and mixtures; blacks, browns, red; coats come in smooth, long-haired, and wirehaired
Eyes:	Dark brown eyes, almost black
Body type:	Small; low to the ground; long body; standard and miniature sizes
Temperament:	Active; friendly
Activity level:	Moderate

The Dachshund is certainly one of the most recognizable of all dogs. Best known for its length and shortness, the Dachshund has always been a dog that lends itself to musings from cartoonists. This deft little hunter was originally bred to hunt badgers and rabbits. Mostly, because of its unique size and shape, it was used to hunt burrowing animals, actually forcing its way into the ground and bringing back the killed animal.

However, the Dachshund in America has almost always been a pet. The Dachshund dates back several centuries, in various incarnations. One of our most enduring breeds, it was originally bred in Germany. The name literally translated means "badger-dog." The Dachshund we know today was bred for somewhat smaller game. However, few Dachshunds still actively hunt in the United States today.

The Dachshund is an alert dog, able to run a field with its nose to the ground. However, because of his size and lovable nature, the Dachshund is one of America's favorite house pets. Great for an apartment or a home, the Dachshund loves being a part of the family.

Dachshund

Dachshunds come in three different varieties and two sizes: smooth coat, wirehaired and longhaired, and standard or miniature. They should always have a long body, short legs, and dark brown eyes. Standards generally weigh 16 to 32 pounds, miniatures 11 pounds and under.

Basset Hound

Color:	Usually a mixture of tan, white, black
Eyes:	Dark brown
Body type:	Medium; strong
Temperament:	Trainable; friendly
Activity level:	Laid back; needs some exercise

Like the Dachshund, the Basset Hound is another of the most easily recognized dogs. However, the Basset Hound is a much larger dog, and Bassets are still known to hunt. The Basset is a slower hunter than the Beagle. He plods endlessly but happily, confident that his prey will be cornered. Of French origin, the breed was popular for centuries in France and Belgium. Usually, these dogs were hunted in packs, and this is still the case in the United States to this day. George Washington, who was a great fancier of hounds, was given Bassets by the Marquis de

Basset Hound

Lafayette. It has been said that the Basset Hound has the second best nose in all of dogdom, behind only that of the Bloodhound. The Basset Hound was first registered with the AKC in 1885.

The Basset has long been a favorite of the media. A Basset was on the cover of TIME magazine in the late 1920s to celebrate the Westminster Kennel Club's show in New York. Bassets were made popular in such television shows as *The People's Choice* in the 1950s and *Coach* in the 1990s. Perhaps the best-known Basset is "Fred Basset," the cartoon figure drawn by Graham. The Basset Hound has also been the "pitch man" (if you'll pardon the expression) for Hush Puppy Shoes for many years.

The Basset is a friendly, ambling dog. Speed is not his game. He shouldn't be taller than 15 inches at the withers, but make no mistake, Bassets are sizable dogs and are quite powerful. The Basset is a smooth-coated dog that loves being outdoors, but is just as happy in the house with family and friends. His rather droopy, sad eyes are well known and make him even more lovable.

Bloodhound

Color:	Black and tan; red and tan; tawny; all may have a small amount of white or flecking
Eyes:	Hazel to yellow
Body type:	Large; strong
Temperament:	Trainable; friendly
Activity level:	Laid back; needs some exercise

Like the Basset Hound, the Bloodhound is a well-known dog because of his characteristically sad-looking, very jowly face. But don't let that face fool you. The Bloodhound is as solid a dog as there is. One of the oldest dogs known to man, the Bloodhound has the most acute sense of smell known to canines, which has always made him a valuable friend.

Through the centuries Bloodhounds have been kept by feudal lords, monasteries, European gentry, and, in the United States, by law enforcement officials. Bloodhounds are notorious trackers, able to follow the scent of lost people—including convicts on the run—over hundreds of miles. One scent of the person's clothing is enough for the Bloodhound to go about his business. Contrary to

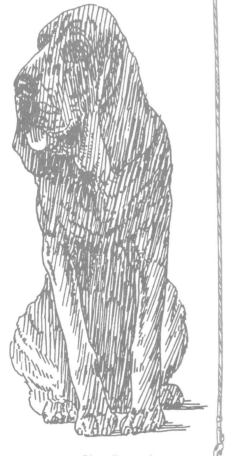

Bloodhound

popular opinion, Bloodhounds, unless otherwise trained, do not attack their quarry. They simply track the scent until they find the missing person.

In the United States the Bloodhound has been involved in thousands of arrests in the past 90 years, as well as finding countless lost persons. Many today double as house pets and Search and Rescue dogs. Bloodhounds are smart dogs who are quick to learn, but may be obstinate. They are very loving and good-natured. They are big dogs, and very strong, and they are persistent when on a scent. They can weigh up to 110 pounds, and they inspire loyalty from their owners that's as big and intense as they are.

Rhodesian Ridgeback

Color:	Light wheaten to red wheaten
Eyes:	Hazel
Body type:	Large; strong
Temperament:	Trainable; friendly
Activity level:	Laid back; needs some exercise

The Rhodesian Ridgeback is so named because it has a ridge of hair growing forward along the spine of its back. This dog was bred from different breeds brought by European settlers (Danes, Mastiffs, Bloodhounds, etc.) and mixed with a half-wild, half-domesticated dog used for hunting by the native Hottentot peoples of Africa. The Boer farmers needed this new breed of dog for hunting as well as to protect their land from wild animals. The Ridgeback could survive the hot, humid African midday, as well as weather its cold nights. For the Boer farmer, he was the all-purpose dog, rugged enough to serve his master in a variety of ways.

In the late 1800s, the Rhodesian Ridgeback was introduced to the top big

Rhodesian Ridgeback

game hunters of the day. The Ridgeback found instant fame with them, as they used the dogs to hunt lion from horseback. The dog came to be known after that time as the African Lion Hound. Once they became popular and made their way to different parts of the world, people found that this great lion hunter also made an excellent pet and family companion. Ridgebacks are very intelligent and easy to train. Because of their short coat, they are easy to maintain; they have friendly and lovable personalities. They are devoted to their families and are good watch dogs. They should be 25 to 27 inches in height at the withers and weigh approximately 70 to 80 pounds.

Working Group

Most of the dogs in the Working Group were bred for specific jobs. Many of these date back to the Romans, where guarding valuables such as property and family was paramount. However, there were other jobs to be done. The Greater Swiss Mountain Dog was used to drive cattle and was the most popular dog in the Alps until about 50 years ago. The Portuguese Water Dog was the fisherman's dog, used to retrieve items, or people, that had fallen overboard or to carry messages from one boat to another. The Newfoundland was bred for hauling in huge fishing nets laden with fresh fish. Saint Bernards were rescue dogs, saving lives throughout the Alps. And, of course, the Alaskan Malamute and the Siberian Husky were sled dogs, pulling people and their families back and forth across frozen tundras.

There are many popular dogs in this group, most notably the Rottweiler, Doberman Pinscher, Akita, and Mastiff, which were bred primarily as guard dogs. They are powerful dogs, and when properly trained and socialized, they make invaluable friends. These dogs will risk life and limb to protect their families and are a great source of pride and love. However, there are many people who have given these dogs a bad name. Because they are large, powerful dogs, if they are not properly trained and socialized with other dogs, they can become a menace. It is not in their nature—it is in the nature of the people who buy these dogs and then train them to be that way.

The Rottweiler is the best example of this kind of training. Rottweilers, by nature, are very sociable dogs. They are even cuddly and fun-loving, like big teddy bears. But they need to be socialized at a young age and given proper obedience training. Take that same dog, don't socialize him, encourage his aggressive behavior, and give him the kind of training that uninformed people perceive is right for guard dogs, and you have a dog that is a danger not only to himself, but to his own master as well. These dogs desire love and affection. If you discourage their aggressive behavior at a young age, you will have an excellent pet who is great with children and a wonderful guard dog. Encourage his negative traits and you will have a dog that is a constant danger to anyone—friend or foe. These dogs are not "gangstas." They're trained by irresponsible, immature thugs into ticking time bombs, giving those people a false sense of power.

If it weren't for the fact that some of these thugs with dogs give this group in particular a bad name, what is being said here goes for all dogs. All of these dogs can be very good family pets. It's a matter of socializing your dog with other dogs at an early age, and with humans as well. Do this, and you will have a loving, devoted family pet that is in fact wonderful with children.

Rottweiler

Color:	Black and rust or tan
Eyes:	Brown
Body type:	Large; strong
Temperament:	Trainable; friendly
Activity level:	Laid back; needs some exercise

The Rottweiler has a long and difficult history to trace. We know that the Romans first used the Rottweiler in their conquest of Europe. While the Romans had first encountered the Mastiff in Britain, where Caesar wrote quite admiringly about the fighting dog, the Rottweiler had a less romantic, but still important role in the Roman conquest. Since the Romans lacked refrigeration, they needed to keep their beef on the hoof and moving. The Rottweiler was this dog. He was extremely strong, of a large, but not too large size (90–120 pounds), and very, very smart. A stout, rugged dog, he could herd cattle over various types of terrain during long marches. And being compact and quick, he could race to the fight if any intruder, human or animal, tried to intervene.

It has been surmised that the Rottweiler and the Great Pyrenees were both Roman cattle dogs that were tokens left behind by the

Rottweiler

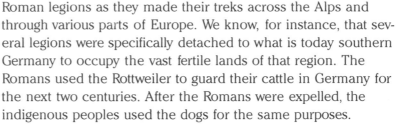

The Complete AKC Working Group

Akita
Alaskan Malamute
Bernese Mountain Dog
Boxer
Bullmastiff
Doberman Pinscher
Giant Schnauzer
Great Dane
Great Pyrenees
Greater Swiss Mountain Dog
Komondor
Kuvaz
Mastiff
Newfoundland
Portuguese Water Dog
Rottweiler
Saint Bernard
Samoyed
Siberian Husky
Standard Schnauzer

Roman legions as they made their treks across the Alps and through various parts of Europe. We know, for instance, that several legions were specifically detached to what is today southern Germany to occupy the vast fertile lands of that region. The Romans used the Rottweiler to guard their cattle in Germany for the next two centuries. After the Romans were expelled, the indigenous peoples used the dogs for the same purposes.

The Rottweiler actually takes its name from Rottweil, a town in western Germany. There the dog was known as a drover of cattle for centuries. Rottweil was a cattle center and earned the Rottweiler another name—the Rottweil Butcher's Dog. It has been alleged that the Rottweiler almost became extinct in the late 1880s, but this cannot be proved. We do know that when many of their original jobs were curtailed by laws forbidding droving, and by the advent of the railroad, Rottweilers found themselves in great number and little demand. The breed indeed dwindled quickly.

However, by the turn of the century the Rottweiler had found employment in law enforcement. There, again, the dog distinguished himself as a smart, compact, able helper. Admitted to the AKC Stud Book in 1931, today the Rottweiler has become quite popular; his playfulness and his deep desire to guard home and hearth have made him invaluable to families around the world. He is the second most popular dog in America, behind the Labrador Retriever.

While the Rottweiler should be an alert dog, he should not be an anxious or nervous dog. Many Rottweilers are very calm, and their eyes should show a certain sense of calm and happiness. They are very much family dogs, and revel in attention and playfulness. If trained properly from birth, they are excellent with children and excellent natural guard dogs.

They are relatively big dogs. They can grow as high as 27 inches at the shoulder and weigh up to 120 pounds. They should have a broad head and no fat. Being shorthaired dogs with a flat coat, they should appear compactly built, with wide chests and lean lines. While they might like to sleep for long periods of the day, and don't run as much as you might expect, they are capable of great bursts of speed and have tremendously powerful jaws.

Siberian Husky

Color:	All colors from pure white to black
Eyes:	Brown or blue, or one of each
Body type:	Medium; strong
Temperament:	Trainable; friendly
Activity level:	Active; needs some exercise and obedience

The Siberian Husky first burst upon the American horizon in 1909 when a sled team entered the All Alaska Sweepstakes Race of that year. They were the only team of dogs that were not Alaskan Malamutes. The strange dogs were entered under the name Siberian Huskies. They were smaller than the Alaskan Malamute, as well as a little more wiry. Many "racing experts" sneered. But the team won the race that year. The next year, three more Husky teams entered, and they won all the top spots. Thus began was the Siberian Husky's fame in America.

The Siberian Husky is the product of the Chuckis people of Siberia. These dogs were first developed centuries ago. But they kept the bloodlines as pure as possible, so that the Siberians of today look very much like their ancient ancestors. The Husky was developed as a specific breed for a specific purpose—speed and durability. The Chuckis were a nomadic people, and hunters. To follow their game, they needed their dogs to be fleet of foot, rugged, and dependable. They were meant to haul small sleds over great distances in short periods of time—say, several days. This is opposed, of course, to the Alaskan Malamute, who was bred to move freight rather than people.

Siberian Huskies are strong dogs that require an alpha role model. These are dogs that were bred for pack life and are full of energy. They require regular exercise and grooming. Huskies all want to lead the pack and know their place in their own very complex society. You need to be loving, but firm.

The fact that they are bred from local Siberian dogs comes as no surprise, as the Siberian Husky looks like a tamed wolf. However, they are very playful and fun-loving. They have a thick, double layer

Siberian Husky

of fur, which requires lots of attention in the summer, unless you want to burn out a vacuum cleaner every other year. During the molting season, you'll be able to pull the fur out in little clumps. But don't. Use a very good brush, or better yet, a shedding blade. With their whitish coat, they should stand no higher than approximately 23½ inches and weigh no more than 60 pounds. The coat can range from pure white to a mix of other colors. The most common is a grayish black and white. They can have either brown or blue eyes; some have one of each.

Doberman Pinscher

Color:	Black and tan; red; fawn
Eyes:	Dark brown in black and tan; color appropriate to other colors
Body type:	Medium; strong
Temperament:	Very trainable; friendly
Activity level:	Needs some exercise; responds well to obedience

The Doberman Pinscher was first developed in Thüringen, Germany, by a local town watchman named Herr Karl Friedrich Louis Dobermann. Dobermann wanted a nimble, quick-thinking dog of action to accompany him on his rounds during the 1870s. The breed was a combination of all the qualities that Dobermann was looking for in the ultimate police dog. He had the strength and musculature of the Rottweiler; the compactness of the Pinscher; and traits of several other local breeds, including the Black and Tan Terrier.

The lines of the Doberman Pinscher are unmistakable. Sleek, tapered, and quick-moving, this alert dog is the ultimate guard/police dog. Properly trained, these dogs are the ultimate help to humans and their best friend. The Doberman has a fast, crisp gait and is capable of long bursts of speed. A highly intelligent dog, he can be trained to do a great number of tasks and can be trusted to think on his own. The breed distinguished itself as both a guard dog and messenger in many fields of battle, as well as a protector for individuals during peacetime.

The Doberman should be approximately 28 inches high at the shoulder. He should have a deep chest and sleek line to the hindquarters. He should not have any heaviness about him, but

Doberman Pinscher

Serious Statistics

The *New York Times* recently reported that a number of deaths each year result from a dog attack. These are more or less unusual cases, but the statistics bear repeating. There were approximate 300 deaths due to dog attacks between 1979 and 1997. Give or take, that's approximately 15 deaths a year over the last 18 years. The top five offenders had the highest rates of incidents:

Pit Bulls	57
Rottweilers	19
German Shepherds	17
Siberian Huskies	12
Alaskan Malamutes	12

The rest were over a wide range of breeds. Among reported attacks on children 0 to 9 years of age, 73% were made by a Rottweiler, Pit Bull, or German Shepherd.

What should the average pet owner make of these statistics? First, it is important to note that the Working Group has some of the biggest, strongest dogs in it. It should not be a surprise that this group's statistics are somewhat higher than the others. As well, many of the dogs in this group have been used as guard dogs, and as such, they are prized for their abilities in these instances. It's also important to remember that these are some of the most well-known and visible breeds, and that if someone isn't sure what kind of dog attacked them, they're bound to call it a pit bull or a shepherd.

It is important to teach your children to respect dogs at all times. It is important not to encourage violent or untoward gestures by children toward animals. You should not allow your children to hurt their pets or act violently toward them. Likewise, it is important not to let a child shower too much attention on an animal, lest it feel endangered because of suffocation, etc.

The profile of the child most likely to get bitten is a 5- to 9-year-old boy. This group accounts for more than 60% of all emergency room visits. A significant portion of these "attacks" occur during the summer months.

Don't let the facts scare you—but at the same time, be aware of them, and be respectful of your dog. Your dog is an animal who values your friendship. If a dog ever feels truly threatened or violated, it may attack. Treat your dog with respect and love, and properly train and socialize him, and more often than not he will return the favor.

should be lean and toned. His head should be carried alertly and his almond-shaped eyes keen. These are relatively active dogs, who require exercise and obedience.

Great Dane

Color:	Black; fawn; brindle and harlequin.
Eyes:	Preferably dark brown
Body type:	Very large; strong
Temperament:	Trainable; friendly
Activity level:	Laid back; needs some exercise

Here's the great thing about Great Danes—they aren't Danish at all! For more than a few centuries, this dog was known by a number of names, including the German Mastiff, the German Dog, or the German Boarhound. It is known that the French came up with this moniker of Great Dane. How the English latched onto it is unknown. However, one thing is known for sure: this giant of the canine world is one of the most impressive specimens out there.

Standing around 32 inches at the shoulder, the Great Dane is one of the largest dogs. Great Danes come in a variety of colors and are among the most fascinating domesticated animals. They were originally developed to hunt wild boar in the late Middle Ages. Some fanciers believe that early descriptions around the world mean that this dog is much older than previously thought. The fact that it is from the Mastiff family might confuse the issue somewhat. Regardless, nobility used this dog for some of the most dangerous and ferocious hunting of the time, and the dog made a name for itself by accomplishing these feats with power, speed, and deftness.

Today, few, if any, Great Danes are used for hunting boar. These magnificent beasts are now family pets. They are somewhat active dogs that do need a lot of space. If you have an apartment, you'd be sur-

Great Dane

prised by how little they move around; of course, you'd be sorry once they did. These dogs need room because they are so big. Room to run around outside would be nice, too, since a dog this big needs an equally big space to stretch out in. It's also important to have plenty of food on hand; these dogs require more than most, so you'd better keep stocked up.

Great Danes are large, tapered dogs, with heads held high and eyes alert. They have a bouncy, elegant gait. While they are indeed imposing physical specimens, they are in fact quite friendly, and love attention. One of the most famous Great Danes is, of course, Marmaduke, the classic cartoon character.

You do need to train these dogs when they are young. It is important to remember that these are big, powerful dogs, bred to do some very difficult tasks. An untrained Great Dane has the strength to pull even a big man a city block or two if he wants. It is important to make sure you have your Dane under control before he grows too large and strong.

Akita

Color:	Any and all colors, including white, brindle or pinto
Eyes:	Preferably dark brown
Body type:	Very large; strong
Temperament:	Trainable
Activity level:	Laid back; needs some exercise

The Akita is a magnificent dog whose intelligence, strength, and loyalty have been highly valued in Japanese culture for more than four centuries. The Akita was used to fulfill a number of tasks, not the least of which was hunting various large game such as bears, wild boars, and deer, as well as being a greatly prized guard dog. It was not uncommon for centuries for a Japanese mother to leave her home under the watchful eye of the family's Akita. Nor were there any shortage of stories about Akitas whose bravery on the hunt was spectacular, whether fighting off large game or retrieving fowl from the field with a soft mouth.

Originally, only the Emperor, his nobility, and his most favored citizens were allowed to own Akitas. Indeed, not only were Akitas

Akita

ranked by the type of color and leash they wore; they were also codified by a special language that was specific only to them. The culture even deemed it necessary for one family member to be chosen as the Akita's caretaker, which was a high honor within the family ranks. Knowing all of this, it is no wonder that the Akita is the national dog of Japan.

The Akita is a very heavily coated dog, with pointed, erect ears and almond shaped eyes. He stands between 26 and 28 inches in height at the shoulders and can weigh as much as any of the big dogs. He has a broad, thick head, and a body to match. This is one of the strongest dogs there is—and that's saying a lot in the Working Group.

The Akita was first introduced to the United States by Helen Keller, who had received an Akita as a gift from a city official during her visit to the Prefecture of Akita in 1937. Akitas became very popular after World War II. Many GIs coming home from the war in the Pacific had great tales about these large, powerful animals. The breed was not admitted to the AKC until 1972.

The Akita, because of his breeding and ancestry, is by nature a somewhat aggressive dog. They have a distrust of strangers and other animals. Akitas are sometimes known not to get along with other dogs, but good care, love, socializing, and obedience are all very important steps in keeping your Akita well-balanced and happy. Loyal and faithful, independent and fearless, the Akita is a dog who will find great comfort in his family, and whose family will find great comfort in him.

Saint Bernard

Color:	White with brown-yellow, red, or brindle
Eyes:	Preferably dark brown
Body type:	Very large; strong
Temperament:	Trainable; friendly
Activity level:	Laid back; needs some exercise

It is important to note right from the start that all the stories about Saint Bernards saving people in desolate winter landscapes are absolutely, undeniably true! The dogs were originally known as Alpine

Mastiffs and were short-haired until about a century ago. Their story begins in a small passage between the Swiss and Italian Alps, where a group of monks had a monastery that was used by Alpine travelers.

As far back as 1670, the dogs were employed by the monks of the Hospice of St. Bernard. These dogs were probably not as heavy as those we know today. It has been suggested that these dogs were some of the large mastiffs that had been used by the Roman legions and had bred with local dogs since then. The monks used the dogs not only to keep them company, but to accompany them when they went out to look for lost travelers. The dogs had strong noses and seemed to be able to track people even in the most treacherous conditions. Usually, the monks took out a group of these dogs, or just sent them out in roving bands. The dogs would find weary travelers and either guide them back or perform a rescue. When the dogs found a stranger who could no longer travel, they would immediately go about their business. Depending on the number, one or two might lie down next to a collapsed traveler (to provide body heat), and the others would go back to the hospice to get help and lead the monks back to the waiting dogs.

Saint Bernard

One dog, Barry, was known to have saved forty people in a ten-year period beginning in 1800. Thereafter, for a while, the dogs were called Barryhunds. They were also called Hospice Dogs. It was not until 1865 that the dog was officially recognized by the name they go by today.

In the late 1800s, the Saint Bernard line almost died, and the monks so famous for breeding them went outside for the first time to try and strengthen the breed. An early cross of the original Saint Bernard was with the Newfoundland. It was then that the long-haired version of the dog appeared. While it was initially thought that the longhaired dogs would be an improvement (it was hoped that they would be able to better weather the bad winters), it turned out that the shorthaired dogs fared better in the snow and ice, as it didn't mat their fur.

The Saint Bernard is usually somewhere between 28 and 34 inches tall and can weigh well upwards of 200 pounds. They are very large dogs, who, while they don't require great amounts of exercise, do need large amounts of space just to turn around. They come in longhair and shorthair versions. They are massive and extremely friendly and make excellent family pets.

Terriers

Talk about your basic Napoleonic complex. The dogs in this group are by turns tenacious, lovable, energetic, and downright funny. The terriers group is mostly made up of a number of wire-haired, smaller dogs that were originally bred to help land owners and gamekeepers keep undesirables off their properties—namely raccoons, foxes, rats, weasels, and badgers.

The word Terrier finds its root in the Latin word *terra*, which means earth. And that's what many of these dogs were used for. They were bred from way back to dig out animals that went to ground for cover or safety, then kill them or chase them out. They would bark and dig simultaneously, driving away vermin, or fighting their adversaries right there in the den's entrance. Indeed, many dogs in the Terrier group have short, strong tails that many a gamekeeper or huntsman used to pull the little fighter out when it seemed he might be getting the worse of the scrap, or when it seemed that the contest had been decided.

In the 1800s, dog fighting, though a cruel and inhumane sport, was popular. While Mastiffs and Bulldogs were the most prized in the area, breeders decided they needed a new dog, and so several new breeds were created in this period. Many were achieved by crossing certain breeds with terriers, which added fleet movement and tenacity to their part of the match. Usually married to them were brawn and size. The resulting breeds are no less lovable than any other breed of dog. Many of these dogs get lumped under the rubric "pit bull." The term Pit Bull refers to the time when two dogs were thrown into a pit and fought to the death, an abhorrent practice that is outlawed today.

For the most part, terriers are well suited to urban, suburban, or rural life. However, they are determined little dogs and will require training in many cases, to keep them on the straight and narrow. Like some of their larger brethren, these dogs need obedience and love, and they need a real leader to keep them from ruining the house or backyard.

Don't be fooled by the package. Just because these dogs are small doesn't mean they are all good apartment dogs. Many of these are very high-energy animals and require extensive exercise. Consult either this text or your breeder before making your decision.

Jack Russell Terrier

Color:	Mostly white, with brown, tan and/or black markings
Eyes:	Preferably dark
Body type:	Small to medium; very muscular; lean; strong
Temperament:	Trainable; friendly
Activity level:	Highly energetic; needs lots of exercise

If you are not the alpha dog or the pack leader, your Jack Russell will let you know. They have no problem filling that role. Few dogs are as well-liked and as misunderstood as the Jack Russell Terrier. The trendy, adorable, feisty little dogs have long been popular. Their popularity soared even higher with the success of Eddie, the canine character on the popular television show *Frasier*. However, while this sturdy, squat warrior is as huggable as can be, he is in reality a very strong-willed, incredibly energetic animal whose number-one aim is to dig into the earth and find something— preferably something living. He has his group's most famous attributes—ferocity, tenacity, willfulness, independence, and indefatigability—times two. He is an apartment dog only if his owner takes him out regularly and often.

Where did this scrappy dog come from? The Rev. Jack Russell was a prominent minister in England in the 1800s. He was also a foxhunter and dog breeder, as well as being an all-round infamous character, sometimes delaying funerals for days so they would not interfere with his hunting plans. But his breed of Fox Terriers was famous. Long after the Fox Terrier became more of a show dog than a hunter, the Jack Russell Terrier was the dog most in demand by huntsmen. The dog was bred to chase the baying pack all day, and was then employed to chase out or dig out the hated poacher fox. This required a dog with tremendous stamina and great fortitude. The Jack Russell Terrier has plenty of both.

Jack Russell Terrier

He is short and strong, with a personality that is second to none. He is sometimes less tolerant of other dogs, especially his own kind. Left alone all day, especially in an apartment or small house, the Jack Russell may get into trouble. He is mischievous when not employed doing something, or outside, left to his own devices.

Jack Russells need lots of attention and an owner with an active lifestyle. If you like to exercise, then the Jack Russell is for you. They need big helpings of love and obedience, especially if you want to keep them from being bored. Boredom is the Jack Russell's worst enemy. Loneliness is his second-worst enemy. Though they do like love and attention, they don't want to be smothered. If you have children, you'll have to work hard to make sure that the Jack Russell knows his place in the pack.

If properly trained and exercised, this breed is a wonderful, if rambunctious, companion animal, whose high energy and bright disposition will keep you smiling and exhausted for a long time.

American Staffordshire Terrier

Color:	Any solid color; parti; patched
Eyes:	Preferably dark
Body type:	Small to medium; very muscular; strong
Temperament:	Trainable; friendly
Activity level:	Laid back; needs some exercise

Few people who own these dogs even know their real name, let alone their real history. The Staffordshire Terrier originated in England in the 1800s. The dogs were a combination of the Bulldog and a terrier of unknown distinction. It is important to know, claims the American Staffordshire Terrier Club of America, that the Bulldogs of the 1800s were leaner and more agile than those we know today. The Bulldog of one or two centuries ago was actually used to bait bulls and was an aggressive, strong, and courageous dog.

It is true that the Staffordshire Terrier was bred by gamblers who wanted a good fighting dog. The Staffordshire Terrier combined the agility and intensity of a terrier with the courage and strength of the Bulldog. The result was a dog of smaller-than-medium build with exceptional strength and incredible tenacity. The American Staffordshire Terrier is a variation on that theme. The American Staffordshire Terrier allows for a wider range of size limits and generally does not discriminate by size, but rather by proportions. In general, though, the American

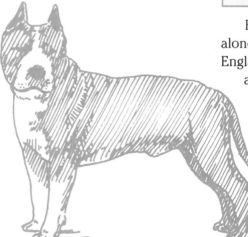

American Staffordshire Terrier

Staffordshire is larger than the Staffordshire Terrier, his English cousin.

Because the dogs in England were originally a mix of two breeds and were used for fighting, they were known by many names—Bull-and-Terrier Dogs, Pit Dogs, and Bull Terriers. The American Staffordshire was even known as the Yankee Terrier. Eventually the name that became prevalent was Pit Bull Terriers, and even that was finally shortened to just Pit Bulls.

It is important to state this unequivocally: The Pit Bull is a generic term applied to all the dogs of this category. However, the American Staffordshire Terrier is a specific breed, with specific characteristics. He is not the American Pit Bull Terrier, which is a close, but distinct, relative. Many Pit Bulls that are bought in the United States are not AmStaffs. Many have other dogs bred into them, and therefore vary in characteristics.

The American Staffordshire Terrier is a better dog than what he was bred for. The AmStaff has always been incredibly popular in the United States, and there remain many positive examples of these dogs from the past, despite their deplorable origins and reputation. Many were used by the U.S. Army, especially in the First World War. As pets they are relatively docile and do not require great amounts of exercise. They do need lots of obedience and socializing to help them become more accepting of others. They love family life and revel in its benefits. They are also exceptional guardians who are very alert, quick, and muscular and good at detecting strangers or intruders.

West Highland White Terrier

Color:	Solid white only
Eyes:	Preferably dark brown
Body type:	Small; compact
Temperament:	Trainable; friendly
Activity level:	Needs some exercise

Westies, as they are affectionately known, come from the large family of terriers that emanated from Scotland. Many believe that they were originally part of a breed that also included Scotties, Cairns, and Dandie Dinmonts. What we do know of this

The Complete AKC Terrier Group

Airedale Terrier
American Staffordshire Terrier
Australian Terrier
Bedlington Terrier
Border Terrier
Bull Terrier
Cairn Terrier
Dandie Dinmont Terrier
Fox Terrier
Irish Terrier
Jack Russell Terrier
Kerry Blue Terrier
Lakeland Terrier
Manchester Terrier
Miniature Bull Terrier
Miniature Schnauzer
Norfolk Terrier
Norwich Terrier
Scottish Terrier
Sealyham Terrier
Skye Terrier
Soft Coated Wheaten Terrier
Staffordshire Bull Terrier
Welsh Terrier
West Highland White Terrier

white, cuddly cutie is that he can be traced as far back as the late 1700s or early 1800s. The Westie was not always known as a West Highland White Terrier. Like many of their associated breeds, many of these were dogs who went to ground, chasing, cornering, and sometimes killing vermin and other small mammals. They were originally known as the Roseneath Terrier, named after a castle owned by the Duke of Argyle, where they can be traced back many years. This was the name under which they were registered with the AKC in 1908; the name was officially changed to West Highland White Terrier in 1909.

The Westie has a double coat which consists of soft, thick fur underneath and coarse hair on top. For the average pet owner, the Westie requires visits to the groomer to be seasonally clipped and properly groomed. To keep his coat clean, the dog needs to be combed or brushed regularly. They are hardy little dogs, with great spunk and vitality. They are very trainable. Like many smaller breeds, while they are courageous and loving, they make better watchdogs than guard dogs, and will always be first to alarm the rest of the house at approaching strangers. They are good in houses or apartments, but like many terriers, they may dig in yards and gardens.

West Highland White Terrier

Scottish Terrier

Color:	Gray, black, brindle or wheaten
Eyes:	Preferably dark brown
Body type:	Small; compact
Temperament:	Trainable; friendly
Activity level:	Needs some exercise

Like other terriers, the Scottie (as he is affectionately known) was born to hunt foxes, vermin, and other small animals. He dug into lairs and dens, ready to confront those he had chased down. It is contended that the Scottie is one of the oldest among the Terrier Group. Scotties are immediately recognizable by their short, squat stature, their long muzzle and their very bushy eyebrows. Their faces are very malleable and capable of great expression.

The Scottie was first shown in England in 1860. After a long period of debate, a standard was officially set in 1880 and has suffered only minor changes since. The first registered Scottie in America was Dake, who was registered with the AKC in 1884.

The Scottie tends to bond with one person in particular. One of the best-known cases was Franklin Delano Roosevelt's dog, Fala, who was incredibly fond of FDR. And President Roosevelt returned his dog's affection by bringing her on all of his travels.

Active, spry and tenacious, the Scottie is an excellent apartment or house pet. They need regular exercise, but not too much. Their coats are dense and require proper grooming by a professional. Also, regular brushing and combing will keep the coat shiny and clean for long periods of time. A Scottie should weigh no more than 22 pounds.

Scottish Terrier

Cairn Terrier

Color:	Any color except white
Eyes:	Preferably dark brown
Body type:	Small; compact
Temperament:	Trainable; friendly
Activity level:	Needs some exercise

Let's get this out of the way first: Yes, Toto from *The Wizard of Oz* was a Cairn Terrier. Now, here's the part you probably don't know. The Cairn Terrier is named after a pile of dark stones. Here's how it worked. Many Scottish farmers used the Cairn to dig into dens where farm predators sheltered and hid their stolen booty. Many times, these refuges were small piles of stones that the Scottish used as memorials to the dead, or as sign posts for travelers. These piles of rocks were called cairns. Thus, if you were a farmer, you used your Cairn Terrier to find foxes and other farm looters, and root them out of cairns where they might be hiding.

During the late 1800s, in England as well as in America, Cairns and Westies were interbred. That stopped when they began to be registered. The first Cairn Terrier was registered with the AKC in 1913. Many fanciers believe that the dog has not really changed its appearance in more than 150 years. The AKC advocates a breed

Cairn Terrier

standard that says that all male dogs must weigh 14 pounds; females must weigh 13.

The most enduring image of a Cairn, without a doubt, is Toto. Dorothy's peppy little accomplice was the ultimate Cairn. Agile, inquisitive, tenacious, and loyal, this friendly little dog was the epitome of what every Cairn represents to his or her owner. A good house dog and a good outdoor dog, the Cairn loves to cover untamed ground as well as curl up near his owner.

Airedale Terrier

Color:	Tan head and legs; black or dark gray body
Eyes:	Preferably dark brown
Body type:	Medium; muscular; wiry coat
Temperament:	Trainable; strong-willed; loves family
Activity level:	High energy; needs physical exercise

Some suspect that the Airedale is a cross between a terrier and an Otterhound. Regardless, at 23 inches at the shoulders (or withers) and at an average weight of approximately 40 to 50 pounds, he is the largest dog in the Terrier Group. He is quick, agile, strong, and smart. He is also aggressive and has been used to hunt big game around the world, most notably in Africa.

The Airedale gets his name from a valley in Scotland, where Yorkshiremen bred him for hunting. He was quicker than an Otterhound and bigger than a terrier, thereby combining what those sportsmen felt were the best attributes of each. They are still used as excellent police dogs all across Europe. They are swift, smart, and trainable, if not a little headstrong. Though training can sometimes be difficult, in the end you will be rewarded by this loyal, independent-thinking dog.

The Airedale looks like a large terrier, with his long, mustachioed muzzle, wiry coat, and curling tail. He has a deep chest which narrows dramatically toward solid hindquarters. Airedales are known to be very loyal and make excellent watch dogs. They are very good with children and wonderful protectors. They are suspicious of strangers and other animals. They also need lots of activity, because they are very high-energy dogs. We're not talking about a quick walk around the block. Put on your running shoes!

Airedale Terrier

Toy Group

The Toy Group is composed exclusively of some of the smallest dogs in the canine world. And also some of the cutest! Many of these cuddly little rascals have been bred purely for companionship and were never intended to be anything other than pets. Some of them come from very obscure backgrounds, but make no mistake—these are dogs.

The most amazing thing about little dogs is that they think just like big dogs. They mark territory; they are loving; they are protective; they are great watchdogs; and they will bite, too, if they feel threatened. The best thing about them is they get away with a lot more because of their size and cuteness, and guard their privileges jealously: they are usually welcome on the couch to sleep in your lap; they're usually allowed in public places and on transportation, where their larger cousins are absolutely forbidden; hotels even sometimes turn a blind eye to them. At the very least, they're so small, they're easier to hide!

Some of these dogs are so small that many centuries ago in Europe they were called sleeve dogs, because ladies of means hid the dogs in their sleeves! If that's not a companion dog, I don't know what is. There are stories about many of these breeds regarding loyalty. In other stories, one of these dogs keeps vigilant watch over his master, with shrill barking in the middle of the night to warn of approaching assassins.

Toy dogs tend to be smart and feisty. They can be trained easily for the most part and many do not require too much exercise. These are all good house and apartment dogs. They love attention and they expect to get it. They also require grooming, and they love that, too.

Yorkshire Terrier

Color:	Blue and tan
Eyes:	Preferably dark brown
Body type:	Tiny; spry
Temperament:	Trainable; strong-willed; loves family
Activity level:	Energetic; need some physical exercise (usually they can get enough running around the apartment, house, or backyard)

These are spirited little dogs. While they are considered little darlings by many because of their size, long, luxurious coat, and spunkiness, make no mistake, these animals consider themselves dogs—and even worse, they consider themselves terriers. They are tenacious and, while they love affection, you need to dole out love and obedience in equal measure, or else they will be more than happy to run your house for you. They love to investigate everything. They fit into practically anything. They are one of the smallest breeds of dogs, beside the Chihuahua.

These dogs became popular in Victorian England, but had a job at one time, too. They were the favorite dogs of weaving and clothing factories, where they chased rats and mice. Being terriers added to their ability—and desire—to perform this role. However, the Yorkie, as he is known, has long been a companion dog. The first record of one being born in the United States dates to 1872. Yorkies travel easily and like to be taken everywhere. The Yorkie likes the outdoors, but like all toy breeds, he should have a warm coat or sweater if you're out on a chilly morning.

These are excellent, alert family dogs that love to be part of the family and part of the fun. Their long coats require maintenance at least twice a week.

Yorkshire Terrier

Pomeranian

Color:	Red, orange, cream and sable, and brown and blue
Eyes:	Preferably dark brown
Body type:	Very small; thick, luxurious coat
Temperament:	Trainable; strong-willed; loves family
Activity level:	Laid back; needs some physical exercise

Pomeranians originally came from Iceland and were related to the sled dogs of that country. Later on, they became somewhat popular in Germany and took their name from the province of Pomerania. The most famous story about a Pomeranian comes from Queen Victoria, who was a great dog lover. She had been to Germany on a visit when she saw her first Pom (as they have affectionately come to be known) and brought one back with her

Pomeranian

to England. From then on, her affection for the breed grew. When she died, she had many of them, and she asked that her favorite dog, a Pom known as "Turi," be set beside her. She died with him at her side. The Pom was first registered with the AKC in 1888.

These furry little fireballs are aggressive and tenacious watchdogs and excellent companions. They sometimes can be wary of strangers or other animals and will not hesitate to act. They respond well to training and are very affectionate.

Like other spitz breeds, they have pointy ears and an appearance of foxiness, which also come from the reddish coat. The fur, a double layer of soft, dense undercoat and long, glistening overcoat, grooms easily with regular brushing.

Shih Tzu

Color:	Any solid, parti or patch
Eyes:	Preferably dark brown
Body type:	Very small; thick, luxurious coat
Temperament:	Trainable; loves family
Activity level:	Laid back; needs some physical exercise

The actual origin of these dog is somewhat obscure. It is alleged that they date as far back at the 7th century A.D. when they were given to the Chinese Emperor. However, the dogs may have come to the Court's notice as early as the 10th century or as late as the 1600s. Many sources quote the breed having come from Tibet.

Regardless, the Shih Tzu has been in the Imperial Dog Book for some time, and it is known that the dogs were bred there for at least 300 to 400 years. The dog was one of the favorite pets of the Ming Dynasty. It was known as the "lion dog." After the fall of the Emperors, many of the Court's most prized pets were slain for food or for political reasons. It is estimated that few remain in China today. They were first popular in Britain after the 1860s. They did not become popular in the United States until after World War II. The first Shih Tzu was registered with the AKC in 1969.

These are feisty little dogs with extremely long, beautiful coats. They are playful and loving.

Shih Tzu

Miniature Pinscher

Miniature Pinscher

Color:	Solid red; stag red (red with specific markings); black and rust; chocolate
Eyes:	Preferably dark brown
Body type:	Very small; well toned
Temperament:	Trainable; strong willed; loves family
Activity level:	Laid back; needs some physical exercise

The Miniature Pinscher is centuries old and can be traced as far back as the 1500s. However, the breed did not gain real interest in the United States until after the First World War. The Miniature Pinscher Club of America was founded in 1929, and interest in the breed blossomed from then on. The MinPin has consistently been one of the most popular of the Toy breeds. His nickname is the King of Toys because of his regal bearing and outgoing personality.

The Miniature Pinscher resembles the Doberman Pinscher in almost every way, keeping the same proportions, though he is not bred down from that dog. Like his larger cousin, he should be alert and active, with a great sense of affection and loyalty. The MinPin's flat, short, shiny coat makes him an easy dog to take care of. He also requires that you hand out obedience and love in equal measures. This dog has a distrust of strangers and other animals, as his high-pitched bark will frequently remind you. He loves to sit on the couch next to you or in your arms, or in those of a well-known friend.

Pug

Color:	Silver; fawn; black
Eyes:	Preferably dark brown
Body type:	Very small; muscular; spry
Temperament:	Trainable; strong-willed; loves family
Activity level:	Energetic; needs some physical exercise

The Pug is of Asian origin, that much we know for sure. Other than that, much of his original breeding is not known. What is known about the Pug could fill several books, for this is a most famous breed. The Pug first became well known in China before the advent of the modern calendar. The Buddhist monks of Tibet kept

Pug

The Special Bond Between Man and Dog

In Japan, at Tokyo's Shibuya railroad station, there is a large statue of an Akita named Hachiko. Annually, hundreds of people gather around this statue to pay tribute to this remarkable dog and celebrate his story.

Hachiko was the pet of a Tokyo University professor named Dr. Eisaburo Ueno. Hachiko accompanied Dr. Ueno to the station every day. There, Dr. Ueno would board the train and head to the University for work. And every afternoon, Hachiko would return to the station, waiting there to greet his beloved master.

One evening, Dr. Ueno did not return. He had died at the University, on an afternoon in May of 1925. The next day Hachiko returned to the station, again waiting for his master.

He came the next day, and the next, and the next. He returned and waited patiently, every day, for nine years, searching through the crowd for his lost master. No person or event could distract him from this self-appointed task. One night, in March 1934, Hachiko did not arrive for his evening vigil. He had passed on, and an entire nation mourned.

The story sparked not just national interest, but international fame. So widely known was the story of this one dog's devotion to his master that it was decided to erect a statue to the dog, in memory. Contributions poured in, not only from throughout Japan, but from all over the world. And yearly, the Japanese fete their stoic, loyal, and faithful friend.

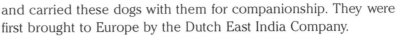

The Complete AKC Toy Group

Affenpinscher
Brussels Griffon
Cavalier King Charles Spaniel
Chihuahua
Chinese Crested
English Toy Spaniel
Italian Greyhound
Japanese Chin
Maltese
Manchester Terrier (Toy)
Miniature Pinscher
Papillon
Pekingese
Pomeranian
Poodle (Toy)
Pug
Shih Tzu
Silky Terrier
Yorkshire Terrier

and carried these dogs with them for companionship. They were first brought to Europe by the Dutch East India Company.

In the most famous story about Pugs, they saved the life of William, Prince of Orange, in 1572, as they woke up his camp before the Battle of Hermingny. The Pug became the official dog of the House of Orange, and his likeness was carved into William's tomb. Later, the breed was the favorite of Josephine, wife of Napoleon, Emperor of France. It was alleged that one of her dogs bit him as he entered her bedroom on the night of their wedding.

The Pug became especially popular after the English stormed the Chinese Imperial Palace in 1860 and brought back to England with them a large number of the small Toy dogs. They are very playful and very loyal. They love affection and need little grooming, as they have a thick, short coat. They are the largest of the toy breeds, weighing in around 13 pounds.

Maltese

Color:	White only
Eyes:	Preferably dark brown
Body type:	Very small; low to the ground; white flowing coat
Temperament:	Trainable; strong-willed; loves family
Activity level:	Energetic; needs some physical exercise

The Maltese has been living in the lap of luxury for more than 200 years and is used to being well treated. While the breed was probably developed from some kind of spaniel background, the Maltese actually comes from the Island of Malta, which is in the Mediterranean off the Italian coast. These furry little creatures have been loved for centuries, with their long white hair and their vivacious personalities. They have garnered press and attention their entire existence. Indeed, it was the Romans who first fell in love with the breed, and many Latin writings relate their popularity with the rich and famous of the day. They remained popular through the Renaissance and the

Maltese

Victorian era, as the Queen herself owned several of these wonderful companion dogs.

They are best known for their white, flowing coats, which must be well cared for if the Maltese is being shown. They should have a good gait and look like a little mop without a handle happily bouncing around the floor. They are active, but can get most of the exercise they need running around the apartment, house, or back yard. They love the outdoors, but this can pose a problem to those in show coat; most owners of pet Maltese keep their dogs clipped to make their life and their dog's a bit easier. Maltese are excellent watch dogs. They love being at the center of the family's attention and are very loving and playful in return.

Chihuahua

Color:	Any color, solid, marked or splashed
Eyes:	Preferably dark brown; light eyes are acceptable in lighter-coated dogs
Body type:	Tiniest dog; trim; fragile
Temperament:	Trainable; vivacious; loves family
Activity level:	Energetic; needs some physical exercise (but they can usually find it running around the house)

It has been surmised that the Chihuahua dates as far back as the 5th century, being a favorite of the Mayan Indians of Central and South America. However, we do know for sure that the predecessor of the Chihuahua was the Techichi, which was well known throughout Central America during the 9th century. This little dog was so popular that it was not unknown to find them mummified next to their masters at certain burial sites.

It is not known how, but it has been deduced that this Central American dog was bred with an Asian hairless breed, which reduced his size even more. The resultant dog became popular with high-ranking Aztecs, and some even assumed a religious importance in that culture.

Although this is the heritage of the Chihuahua, today's dog is even smaller than his ancestor, which is the result of American breeders' efforts. The average Chihuahua weighs no more than 4 pounds. He is the tiniest dog in dogdom. He is very perky and has many big-dog characteristics—but if the truth be known, he is a house dog and can be very fragile.

He is not recommended for a family with young children—not because of his personality, but rather because of his size and fragility. Generally speaking, Chihuahuas are not outdoor dogs. They can find plenty of exercise in the house and do not require great amounts of obedience training. You may, however, want to make sure house training is strictly enforced. Other than that, they are large-hearted toy dogs whose faces are made for television. With their small apple-shaped heads and their big, watery dark eyes, they can easily wiggle their way into even the hardest heart.

Chihuahuas come in two different varieties—smooth coat and long coat. The smooths looks even tinier than the long-coated Chihuahuas, because the fur isn't there to puff them out a bit. These dogs should be spry and alert and tapered toward the hindquarters. As with most shorthaired dogs, the smooths require little grooming. The long-coated dog should have a smooth feel to it, whether the coat is flat or wavy. Both varieties love family, but need to be socialized to accept strangers. They are very affectionate, loving, and loyal.

Chihuahua

Non-Sporting Group

These dogs have one thing in common—they all don't fit into any other category. While some of them were working or sporting dogs in previous lives, their jobs have been so long outmoded that they have primarily been companion dogs for almost a century, in some cases longer.

Other than that, let's be honest—this is a miscellaneous crowd as far as the AKC and other breeders are concerned. But in here you have some very popular if disparate dogs. You have the Poodle (originally one of Europe's finest hunting dogs); the Dalmatian (the ubiquitous coach dog); the Bulldog (used to bait bulls centuries ago); the Bichon Frise (a companion dog too big for the toy group); and many, many others.

All of the dogs in this group are very much worth looking at—especially so because the dog world lumped them together only because they couldn't pigeonhole these individualists!

Poodle (Standard and Miniature)

Color:	Solid blue, gray, silver, brown, café-au-lait, apricot, or creme
Eyes:	Preferably dark brown
Body type:	Trim; fragile
Temperament:	Trainable; vivacious; loves family
Activity level:	(Standard) Energetic; needs some physical exercise; (Miniature and Toy) Can usually find it running around the house

Standard Poodle

There are few dogs more world-renowned than the Poodle. Who doesn't know what one looks like—with their foppish clipping and their poofy heads? Clipped in some extreme pattern or simply shaved down, beneath all that curly coat is a very talented, very intelligent, very sporty dog.

Actually, for centuries, the Standard Poodle (the largest of three classifications of Poodles) was one of the most desirable hunting dogs in Europe. One of the most interesting things about Poodles is that they seem to have originated in Germany, but became so popular in France that they are more often associated with the later country.

As stated, the Poodle comes in three sizes—Standard (the largest, at 15 inches at the shoulders and taller), Miniature (between 10 and 15 inches in height at the shoulders), and Toy (10 inches in height at the shoulders, and less). Only the Standard and Miniature are in the Non-Sporting group; the Toy Poodle is in the Toy group. Other than that, all Poodles are essentially the same. They should have a curly, wiry topcoat and a slightly thicker undercoat.

The name Poodle comes from the German word *pudelin*, or *pudel*, which refers to their ability to swim. Poodles were regarded as some of the best water retrievers, bar none. They also found great fame in their abilities to hunt truffles—a very expensive delicacy, and a very rare find. They are friendly, intelligent, and fun-loving, and they assume a natural place at the center of family life.

The Miniature Poodle gained fame along with the Toy in France in the 1800s. Because of their high intelligence and desire to work and please, the Poodle found work in the many traveling circuses of

Miniature Poodle

When a Toy Is Not a Toy

If you are a parent, it is important that you consider the following before you undertake buying a toy breed. They are dogs, first and foremost—not toys. They are delicate little animals who do indeed require the respect of their masters and need their own safety ensured. Make sure your child is old enough to understand that this is an animal that will be easily injured if handled roughly, and may also bite if he thinks he's being cornered or mistreated.

Toy dogs do not always understand when little Johnny is running after them and wants to hug them a little too tightly. They feel threatened and they will bite, or they may suffer internal damage from an unknowing child. Many children want to hug a dog, but what they don't understand is that they are really squeezing and suffocating the animals. There is usually nothing intentional about their misguided attempt to communicate their love for their pet. They simple don't comprehend the dog's delicate nature.

All dogs love attention and hugs, but be sure your child already understands the difference between gentleness and play that is too rough. If you're not sure how your children would handle a Toy breed, you should consider something a little bigger that can take the tussle and playfulness of small children and play with them with confidence.

the time. Highly trainable, they were called on to perform well-rehearsed acrobatics. They achieved a high level of both precision and fame.

The Poodles are known for their coiffures. These originated during their time as prime hunters. The head, chest, and forefront were left shaggy, to provide warmth to the dog, especially in seasons when it was cold and he was called upon to retrieve game in frigid waters. Today, Poodles are generally groomed in one of three clippings: The Sporting clip; the English Saddle clip; and the Continental clip. The Sporting clip seems the least offensive to those not in the know. Generally considered more desirable for showing are the English Saddle clip and the Continental clip. The Continental is the most severe, with seven pompoms decorating what is essentially a half-shaven body. The Saddle clip leaves more fur on the body, but it has different sculpted rings, especially around the hindquarters.

Today, the Poodle isn't generally considered a hunter, and few use him for this sport. He is still sometimes used to find truffles, but mainly he is considered a very affectionate and understanding pet. The Miniature and the Toy are both excellent house pets that need some exercise. However, the Standards should get a little more: while the two smaller Poodles could live in an apartment with proper exercise, the Standard Poodle might feel confined. All Poodles need lots of exercise and love to run. Playful, energetic and loving, the Poodle, regardless of size, has a big heart and a sound disposition.

Dalmatian

Color:	White with black spots
Eyes:	Brown or blue
Body type:	Strong; trim; agile; speedy
Temperament:	Trainable; energetic; loves family
Activity level:	Highly energetic; needs lots of physical exercise

The Complete AKC Non-Sporting Group

American Eskimo Dog
Bichon Frise
Boston Terrier
Bulldog
Chinese Shar-Pei
Chow Chow
Dalmatian
Finnish Spitz
French Bulldog
Keeshound
Lhasa Apso
Poodle (Standard and Miniature)
Shipperke
Shiba Inu
Tibetan Spaniel
Tibetan Terrier

Certainly, the Dalmatian is one of the most affable dogs around. He is also one of the most easily recognizable. With his white coat and black spots, the Dalmatian is noticed no matter whom he travels with.

The Dalmatian takes its name from a region of eastern Europe, Dalmatia, in the former Yugoslavia. No one is really sure of his background. We know he traveled around somewhat with gypsies, and many mentions have been made of him going back for hundreds of years. The first Dalmatian registered with the AKC was in 1888.

While the Dalmatian may have obtained its greatest fame in Walt Disney's two classic renditions of *101 Dalmatians*, he was popular even before that. The Dalmatian was a coach dog. He ran near, ahead of, or beside a traveling horse-drawn coach, in the days before cars. He was used to herd away stray livestock, or as a warning for humans and other animals to beware of the oncoming coach. In other lands and times he has performed admirably as a retriever and as a ratter.

Because of their birth, breeding and training, Dalmatians are tireless and are not the most suitable dogs for all people. The Dalmatian is smart, gregarious, and loving, but he has an insatiable desire for activity and exercise. Owing to his former life, the Dalmatian can run a medium pace for long, long periods. This makes him an undesirable apartment dog, where he might go crazy with boredom. Some can become destructive as a result of inactivity. The Dalmatian needs plenty of exercise. If you do not lead an active lifestyle, then, as with some other dogs, this tremendous animal is not for you. However, if you have the desire to exercise and the room to keep him comfortable, he is an excellent companion who loves the activity of family life and being on good terms with its members, and who is an excellent watch dog. With their short, smooth coats, Dalmatians require little upkeep.

Dalmatian

Boston Terrier

Color:	Brindle or black with white markings
Eyes:	Preferably dark
Body type:	Small; muscular; agile
Temperament:	Trainable; loves family
Activity level:	Needs some physical exercise

Born and bred in the United States, the Boston Terrier gets its name from the city where it originated in the 1870s. The Boston Terrier is a cross between a Bulldog and a White Terrier. For many years it was known as the Bull Terrier and the Round Head, but was eventually changed to Boston Terrier in 1891, with the establishment of the Boston Terrier Club of America. The breed, after some disagreement, was finally admitted to the AKC in 1893.

There are three classes of Boston Terrier: 20 to 25 pounds; 15 to 20 pounds; and under 15 pounds. The Boston Terrier has a short-haired, smooth coat which is white and either black or brindle. They are squat dogs, like the Bulldog, but lean like a terrier. Their rather large, round, dark eyes are set widely apart. These dogs are very even tempered, very congenial, and make excellent watch dogs. They are as fearless as they are loving.

The Boston Terrier makes an excellent companion and is adaptable for life in an apartment or country home. Although his disposition is generally very amiable, he has the heart of a Bulldog and terrier, and he will fight furiously to defend himself. But he would rather spend a Saturday sleeping with you on the couch.

Bulldog

Color:	Solid white, red, fawn; well-defined patches (known as piebald)
Eyes:	Dark
Body type:	Heavyset; strong; squat
Temperament:	Trainable; lovable; loves family
Activity level:	Needs light physical exercise

Boston Terrier

The Bulldog of today is somewhat different from his ancestors. Bulldogs were originally bred for fighting. Their original work came in the form of "bullbaiting," which involved packs of these small dogs surrounding and taking down a maddened bull. It was wild, mean, and grotesque and was outlawed in 1778. In bullbaiting, the Bulldog would eventually pin the bull by the nose.

The Bulldog also gained fame in a time when dog fighting was legal and popular in England. The Bulldogs were among the most accomplished dogs in this field. They were somewhat leaner than the dog we know today and much more vicious. They were known for their tenacity and ferocity; they could sustain incredible injuries and continue to fight. To this day, the Bulldog's tenacious legend lives on, as he is the mascot of many school athletic programs as well as that of the United States Marine Corps.

After dog fighting was outlawed, there were a number of dog fanciers who decided to save the breed they had so come to admire, rather than see it go extinct because it had lost its original uses. Many years were spent breeding out the violence that had long been bred into them.

Today, the Bulldog is one of the friendliest of all canine companions. With his distinctive waddle and trademark folds of skin, this stout little fellow will tug with great determination—at your heart. He is good-natured, excellent with children, and friendly with other dogs. His coat is shorthaired and requires little maintenance, but his face needs to be cleaned several times a week in order to avoid infections.

He is good in an apartment or a country house. He requires only light exercise. The dog should weigh between 40 and 50 pounds.

Bulldog

Bichon Frise

Color:	White long hair
Eyes:	Dark
Body type:	Trim; fragile; quick
Temperament:	Trainable; energetic; loves family
Activity level:	Slightly energetic; needs some physical exercise

Pronounced "BEE-shon Free-ZAY," this is an exotic little breed whose history has been somewhat obscured by time. We do know that he is a descendant of the Barbet Water Spaniel. Bichon Frises are known to have come from the Mediterranean, though no one is sure exactly where. Over the centuries, the Bichon Frise has been known by four different names. It was the choice dog of fashionable society in many European countries at one time or another, including Italy, Spain, and France. Bichons became endangered after the French Revolution, as they were very much associated with the aristocracy. They did not come back into vogue until the 1930s on the continent, and were not recognized by the AKC until 1972.

These small dogs are quick, alert, and energetic. They are famous for the way they are groomed, which makes them look like a living powder puff. They are loving and playful, and a good family dog. They require more grooming than exercise, in order to avoid matting, but they don't shed much and are considered good pets for people with allergies.

Bichon Frise

Herding Group

The Herding Group is relatively new, having been established in 1983. Herding breeds were originally part of the Working Group, but when it became so large as to be unmanageable, the breeds were subtracted from it, and the Herding Group was established independently. Some of the oldest breeds we know of today got their first job guarding and managing humans' livestock.

Among all the dogs we've covered, these are some of the smartest, most trainable, and energetic of dogs. It is important to remember that these dogs have been bred to do a job, and it is in their genes to perform it. They herd. While you are walking down the street they will want to circle you—especially if you are with a friend, loved one, or family. The bigger the crowd, the more they want to shape you into a nice group.

The Herding Group tends to have some dogs who bark a lot—they are trying to communicate. These are dogs whose natural instincts are to communicate with one another and with people. Because they've been used through the centuries to guard sheep and cattle, they can nip and snarl to get their charges to move where they want them to.

The Complete AKC Herding Group

Australian Cattle Dog
Australian Shepherd
Bearded Collie
Belgian Malinnois
Belgian Sheepdog
Belgian Tervuren
Border Collie
Bouvier des Flandres
Briard
Collie
German Shepherd Dog
Old English Sheepdog
Puli
Shetland Sheepdog
Welsh Corgi, Cardigan
Welsh Corgi, Pembroke

These breeds are generally happiest in homes with large yards and should be given plenty to do. In general, they are very active, so you need to be able to keep them busy. These dogs really, really want to work; they have the bodies and minds to do jobs and do them well. That's why you find so many herding breeds in obedience, agility, herding, and flyball competitions.

They usually make excellent guard dogs. Herding dogs were meant to guard the sheep and cattle as well as herd them. They were an especially important part of keeping away other predators. Many of them are aggressive, ferocious fighters, who are strong and willful. Herding breeds have long been employed as police dogs as well. Some have even been trained as guide dogs for the blind. Not all of these dogs are for the novice owner. Indeed, many were developed to think on their own, or do the bidding of their human counterparts. With some of them, when you are unsure, either you will fill them with confusion, or they will make decisions for themselves. You need to be the lead dog—and they will follow. Many dogs in this breed will respond quickly and easily to obedience. In fact, they excel at it.

German Shepherd Dog

Color:	Tan and black; any other dark color
Eyes:	Dark
Body type:	Large; powerful; agile; noble; quick
Temperament:	Trainable; aggressive; energetic; loves family
Activity level:	Energetic; needs plenty of physical exercise

While the Germans developed the "everything" hunting dog with their Shorthaired Pointer, they were also developing another all-around working companion, the German Shepherd Dog. This big, tough, rangy animal is as smart and powerful as they come. While some might expect this breed to be one of the oldest in the world, it is surprisingly new. The first German Shepherd Dog club was founded in 1889.

The breed was developed using a number of older breeds of similar type. The dogs gained tremendous fame during the First World War, where countless troops on both sides gazed in astonishment as these dogs risked life and limb bringing messages back and forth between the trenches, as well as serving a number of other functions.

Today the German Shepherd Dog is the most versatile in the world. He serves as a police dog, guard dog, and a guide dog, and he excels at rescue as well. Shepherds also make excellent pets. They are sometimes slow in accepting children, but once they bond with a child, that child has a protector and friend for life.

The German Shepherd Dog is the most popular dog in the world and the most widely used working dog. Shepherds are intelligent and active—and above all, they are a herding dog. They have very strong personalities and expect a strong leader. Again, if you don't step up to the plate, they will. They are very conscious of their position. Obedience goes a long way in establishing pack leader status. Because of their herding instincts, they will always want to assert their position in the pack, especially with other dogs. They can get along well with other dogs, but they must be socialized at a young age, with people and dogs. They are generally suspicious of strangers.

The key to owning a German Shepherd Dog is knowing that they live to please their owners. They require lots of exercise and do not tire easily. They have tremendous stamina and require someone who will provide them with a number of tasks to confront them and keep them busy. They are powerful and quick, with an ability to concentrate. The dog is 24 to 26 inches at the shoulder and can weigh quite a bit. This dog should always be confident and fearless.

German Shepherd Dog

Shetland Sheepdog

Color:	Black, blue, merle and sable, ranging from golden through mahogany, marked with varying amounts of white and/or tan
Eyes:	Dark; blue or merle eyes permissible in blue merles only
Body type:	Moderately long; standing between 13 and 16" at the shoulder
Temperament:	Outgoing, friendly, highly trainable
Activity level:	Needs exercise, but not excessive

This is another breed of Scottish descent. The name "Shetland Sheepdog" already tells you something about him: he is as rugged as his home turf, the Shetland Islands. These islands are a rough place to live, battered as they are by wind and sea. Hence the Sheltie's small size and profuse coat. Everything on the Shetland Islands is small from being windblown over centuries.

Shelties look like miniature Collies, and Collie breeders did a lot to curtail confusion about the breeds by requesting that they not be recognized by the Kennel Club as Shetland Collies, but as Shetland Sheepdogs instead. Shelties were first recognized by the AKC in 1911, and today are the fifteenth most popular breed in the United States.

The breed is highly trainable and has long been a big winner in the obedience ring. It is also a gregarious animal whose good looks have earned it much praise in the breed ring. And its resemblance to Lassie, but in a small package, have made it popular with families, who love the dogs as pets. Shelties still retain their herding instincts and are watchful of children in their care.

Shetland Sheepdog

Collie

Color:	Sable and white; tri-color; white
Eyes:	Dark
Body type:	Trim; strong; quick; agile
Temperament:	Trainable; energetic; loves family
Activity level:	Energetic; needs physical exercise

The Collie of today is the one that has been used in the Scottish Highlands to guard and herd sheep for more than 100 years. He was made popular by the Lassie stories, movies, and television shows. Today he is more a house pet than a herder of sheep.

There are two kinds of Collie: the Rough Collie and the Smooth Collie. Lassie is an example of a Rough Collie. The Smooth-Coated Collie is the same dog, but with a hard, dense, flat coat with abundant undercoat. Both are very affectionate dogs with very good personalities. They get along well with other dogs and love to be part of the family.

The dogs first gained notoriety in the United States when Queen Victoria entered two of hers in the second Westminster Dog Show in 1878. Soon, J.P. Morgan established kennels to breed this noble guardian.

Not a very good apartment dog, the Collie loves exercise and companionship. Loving, devoted, but smart and independent, the Collie wants obedience training. This is a somewhat laid-back dog, compared to the rest of the Herding Group. They can range from 24 to 26 inches and weigh between 50 and 80 pounds.

Collie

Pembroke Welsh Corgi

Color:	Red, sable, fawn, black and tan with some white
Eyes:	Dark
Body type:	Small; low to the ground; thick
Temperament:	Trainable; energetic; loves family
Activity level:	Slightly energetic; needs some physical exercise

The difference between the Pembroke Welsh Corgi and the Cardigan Welsh Corgi is that the former has no tail while the latter has a full tail. Pembrokes are usually red or sable colored, while Cardigans are typically black. The Pembroke also has a slightly different build, seen most easily in the higher, more pointed ears. Of the two breeds, the Cardigan is by far the older. Both are probably descended from the same family as the Dachshund.

Corgis stand about 10 to 12 inches at the shoulder, but were bred for herding cattle. They did it well. That should tell you something about the character of the Corgi. Corgis were called "heelers," as they would scamper behind the bulls and nip at their legs to get them moving. Because they were so low to the ground, built somewhat like a pointy-eared Basset, they could easily get underfoot and could easily avoid getting kicked by angry cattle. Corgis were also used by farmers to stop strange cows from wandering into their pastures.

The Pembroke is an excellent watchdog and a great family dog. He requires only moderate exercise and can survive in a large apartment or a spacious house. He is a gentle dog who gets along well with others, and he can enjoy the rigors of either country or city life. He is a gregarious pet who gets along well with children. He has a short, heavy coat that comes in a variety of colors.

Pembroke Welsh Corgi

Australian Shepherd

Color:	Blue merle, black, red merle, red with patches of white
Eyes:	Various
Body type:	Small to medium; trim; rugged; quick
Temperament:	Trainable; energetic; loves family
Activity level:	Highly energetic; needs lots of physical exercise

It is alleged that the Australian Shepherd actually originated in the Pyrenees Mountains, in the Basque region that straddles Spain and France. Basque shepherds first immigrated to Australia and then to the United States in the 1800s. And with them, they brought their dogs. The little, quick, agile dogs were highly intelligent, easy to train, and tireless. Since they accompanied the shepherds from Australia, the dogs were misnamed Australian Shepherds.

The breed as we know it is not registered in Australia, probably because this breed was really bred and developed by sheep farmers in the Western United States; thus, the Australian Shepherd is really an American breed. These dogs have been used for various jobs all around the country.

Much like the Collie, the Australian Shepherd has a luxurious coat of many colors. They have thick, dense undercoats and coarse, long hairs on top. Much like the Border Collie, this dog requires lots of exercise and obedience training, though he makes a wonderful family pet. He is as smart and loving as they come and will work tirelessly, intelligently, and faithfully. That's why he's becoming more and more popular as an obedience and agility star.

Australian Shepherd

Other Breeds

Most certainly there are other breeds. We have only skimmed over the most popular breeds in the seven AKC-recognized groups.

A great many breeds in the world are not recognized by the AKC. This isn't because they're not good enough; it's because they don't have a large enough representation in the United States, or a well-organized breed club, or a proven stud book. The AKC does maintain a Miscellaneous Class, in which you'll find Havanese, Anatolian Shepherds, and Italian Spinonis, among others. These breeds are up-and-coming breeds, or breeds that want to participate in some AKC programs without gaining full recognition. Many breeds from all over the world are registered with other registries, or are still being developed.

About Pit Bulls and Wolf Hybrids

The American Pit Bull Terrier is a very close relation of the AKC-recognized American Staffordshire Terrier. The APBT is registered by the United Kennel Club and is a popular animal (whether registered or not). Unfortunately, like the Rottweiler or the Doberman in the past, the Pit Bull has gotten a bum rap as a vicious breed because of some of the people who use him as a guard dog.

If you want to truly understand the Pit Bull, there are many books written about this noble all-American. Generally speaking, Pit Bulls have large heads, strong jaws, and short, smooth coats with some kind of brindle coloring. They are sinewy and tough, and may weigh as much as 50 pounds. Improperly trained, they can become dangerous to their owners, their family, friends, or unknowing strangers.

If you are dead set on getting a Pit Bull, make sure you ask around about the person who is breeding and selling them. *Be careful.* These dogs are popular, and many irresponsible breeders are turning out unsound animals. You should talk to your local licensing bureau, as Pit Bulls are banned or outlawed in certain areas. If you are caught with one, you may be fined and your pet may be confiscated—a most unfortunate fate to befall so loyal a companion animal!

Wolf hybrids are dog–wolf crosses that are bred and kept as domesticated companion animals. In many cases, though, the concept doesn't work. Wolves have always resisted domestication, and the instinct in the wolf hybrid to return to a wild state is often very strong and can break an owner's heart (and

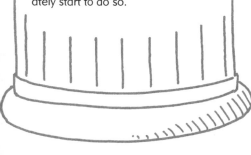

Wanted: Dog for Work on Golf Course

Recently, the Border Collie has found employment in the Eastern United States. Some golf-course groundskeepers came up with the idea of using the dogs to chase away migrating Canadian Geese that traditionally marred the courses with their large, plentiful droppings.

These medium-sized, intense herders are much desired by kids today because of the popularity of the movie *Babe*. These are very smart working dogs. And if you have any doubt about the strength of breeding and genes, all you have to do is see a Border Collie, no matter the age, be introduced to sheep for the first time. Even if they've never herded in their life, they will immediately start to do so.

get him into serious legal trouble if the wolf/dog damages property or people).

Dog–wolf hybrids are quick, powerful, and incredibly resourceful. They are also very independent-minded, usually being a mix of wolf and spitz or herding breeds. What none of our backyard Frankensteins have figured out, though, is that breeding a wolf with a dog doesn't blend the best of both animals. The breeders want the strength and tenacity of the wolf with the obedience and domestication of the dog. They want the ultimate guard dog with unparalleled strength and the ability to take orders. Unfortunately, most often it's the strongest characteristics of the wolf that result. Although these hybrids are incredibly cute puppies, they usually grow up to be more than most people can handle. They tend to revert, rather than progress. Dogs bred as the ultimate guard dogs instead find amazing means of escape and then become predators.

Many wolf-dog stories end very badly. There are three typical scenarios:

1. The wolf–dog escapes and runs off into the wild. Chances are very good he will not be accepted in any wild packs and may be considered game himself.
2. The wolf–dog attacks a family member or a stranger for no apparent reason. Sometimes it is a child. He is humanely put down.
3. The wolf–dog escapes and hangs around the suburbs. He picks off other small domesticated animals or small livestock. Eventually he is subdued by animal control and brought into an animal shelter. He is then usually put down, because few if any animal shelters will allow any potential pet owner to take on one of these animals. Sometimes, sadly, these escaped dogs are shot by rangers or police.

Are they bad animals? No, but they are not really pets. The best-case scenarios include being chained or penned up in a kennel, far from family, which means a life of never-ending loneliness for an animal that very much wants to be part of the pack.

If this doesn't stop you from obtaining one, then read ahead. If you are thinking of buying or adopting a dog–wolf hybrid, speak to the "breeder." Ask for references from people who have taken their dogs previously. Call your local veterinarian and ask about local dog–wolf hybrids. Ask him or her about their success rates and about reputable hybrid fanciers in your area. In many instances, you should talk to your local licensing bureau, as wolf–dogs are banned or outlawed in some areas. If you are caught with one, your pet may be confiscated and you may be fined.

These animals are usually very wily, but are not good at obedience. They are very difficult to house-train and are sometimes dangerous with children. In short, these are not good pets!

Chapter Two

CHOOSING YOUR DOG

Questions You Should Ask Before You Get a Dog

There is nothing better than coming home from a hard day's work to a tail-wagging, sloppy-tongued mop of a dog who can't wait to greet you. Dogs are bouncy and loving and wonderful—there's no getting around it, they're wonderful companions. They are fun, friendly, and love attention. They love to play, go for long walks, and be mischievous.

But know going in that dogs are a tremendous amount of responsibility. It's fun to cuddle up with a dog while watching television, or take him hiking and running; it's fun to play with a dog at the beach, in a park, or in the snow. But dogs also require forethought and attention, even on days when we would rather think only of ourselves.

Every year, thousands of dogs are left homeless and are sheltered in dog pounds and rescue homes all across the country. Often this is no fault of the dog's. When the cute puppy turns eight months old and starts showing an ornery streak, that can be the last straw. When an over-obliging owner suddenly finds himself with a dog who growls when he's told to get off the bed, well, the dog may become a casualty. People give up their dogs because they didn't fully understand doggy behavior and all the things that need to be done to keep a dog healthy and well-behaved. They find out that Dalmatians require too much exercise; they didn't know St. Bernards grew *that* big!; those tiny Maltese are mischievous balls of fire. Suddenly Rover finds himself at the shelter with a haunted look on his face, cowering at the back of his pen, as countless strangers pass by and he remains alone. In a day when razors, pens, diapers, and even spouses are disposable, dogs are no exceptions. Unfortunately, they pay for being disposable with their lives. In fact, every year, thousands of dogs are put down because of neglect or homelessness.

A big reason this happens is that many people don't think before they add a dog to

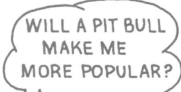

WILL A PIT BULL MAKE ME MORE POPULAR?

their lives. Don't let this happen to you! Ask yourself some important questions before you go running out to get the dog your kids are screaming for or that you think will fill the gap in your life: What kind of life do you lead? How much room do you have, and what kind of house do you live in? What kind of attention do you think you can offer the animal? Will someone be home all day to housetrain and socialize a puppy? Do you have a fenced yard? How old are your children? Does everyone in the family want a dog, or are you caving in to one demanding child? Do you want an active dog, a laid-back dog, a big dog, a small dog, a hairy dog, a hairless dog, a slobbery dog, a neat dog? With more than 140 AKC-recognized breeds to choose from, and plenty of mixed breeds, you can really pinpoint the kind of dog that will suit your lifestyle.

So take this time to think about what you and your family want. Be responsible, and enjoy the comfort, love, and happiness that owning a dog can bring for a long time to come.

Narrowing Your Selection

Lifestyle

I'm not talking about *Martha Stewart* or *Better Homes & Gardens* style. You can't pick out a dog because you think he'll look good with your sofa, or he'll go well with your English garden. You don't pick out a dog that matches your Ralph Lauren outfit or goes with your rugged Levis and Timberlands. This is not how you pick your dog. A dog is not a designer emblem. It's an animal with a mind of its own and a sense of humor all its own. It's like having another person in the house!

When I talk about lifestyle, I'm talking about what you do every day. What is your idea of fun? Rollerblading? Riding your bike? Watching a movie or sports on television? Going hiking? Going on little day trips in the car? Going to the park or beach and lying out in the sun? Do you work? Part-time? Full-time? Are you one of those career sociopaths who puts in 70 hours a week? Do you like to come home, shower, and go back out to dinner and the movies or your favorite bar? Are you obsessively neat? Are you allergic to pets? You have to ask yourself these

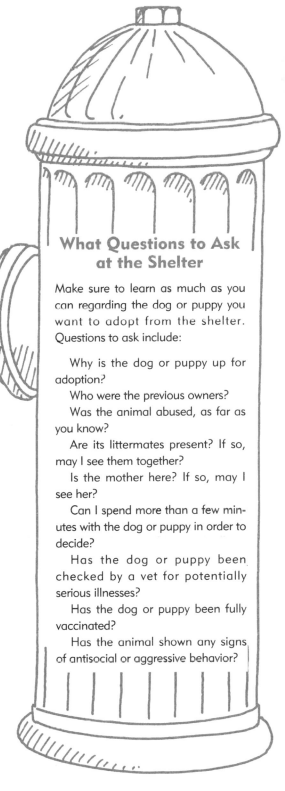

What Questions to Ask at the Shelter

Make sure to learn as much as you can regarding the dog or puppy you want to adopt from the shelter. Questions to ask include:

Why is the dog or puppy up for adoption?

Who were the previous owners?

Was the animal abused, as far as you know?

Are its littermates present? If so, may I see them together?

Is the mother here? If so, may I see her?

Can I spend more than a few minutes with the dog or puppy in order to decide?

Has the dog or puppy been checked by a vet for potentially serious illnesses?

Has the dog or puppy been fully vaccinated?

Has the animal shown any signs of antisocial or aggressive behavior?

kinds of questions when you are choosing a dog so that you can pick the dog that's best for you.

You're Cramping My Style

It's important to think about your life before you buy your dog, so that six months later poor Fido isn't back out on the street looking for a new job. You don't want to be coming home and cursing your happy little pooch, just because he's at home drawing breath, keeping you from meeting your soulmate at tonight's hottest party. Many times people who don't think about what kind of dog they really want are at cross purposes with their dog. You don't want a pet that's going to cramp your style. And of course, you don't want to pick a dog whose life you're going to make miserable.

If you're an in-line skater, you want to know that when you come home, you can suit up, put a leash on Rover, and bring him along. You want a dog who shares in that fun. You need an athletic dog who has the stamina and explosive energy to keep up with you. You don't want some sedentary hound who's panting after the first half-mile. Likewise, if you like going for an evening stroll, you don't want some drooling half-lunatic pulling you around the block like a crazed demon. You want a good dog who shares your pace and enjoyment of the evening air.

Maybe you need a dog who can keep up with your children and whom you can trust to watch over them. You need your dog to be, not a substitute parent or some kind of living, unbreakable toy, but a companion and playmate for your kids to share in their well-behaved fun.

Going to Dog Shows

The best way to find out about the idiosyncrasies of various breeds, and to really get a good look at them, is to go to dog shows. You'll find representatives of just about all the AKC breeds at a dog show, and best of all, you'll find their breeders, the people who understand them best. Not only that, because you'll get to look around and talk to so many people, you may leave with a completely different idea about what kind of dog you want than you had before you went to the show.

Good Names for Your Dog

Alley	Hamlet	Pepper
Augie	Helen	Phaser
Billy	Hercules	Rock
Bogart	Homer	Rudy
Bon Bon	Hunter	Sarge
Booboo	Jake	Sheba
Brook	Jello	Silvia
Buck	Jet	Sophie
Camille	Kate	Spock
Cheetah	Kirk	Spot
Chief	Louisa	Tarzan
Clinton	Madonna	Unus
Colgate	Moe	Vapor
Delilah	Mozart	Wendy
Derrida	Mud	Zappa
Electra	Nicki	Zelda
Fido	Ollie	Zippy
Fuzzy	Patches	Zoe

For example, you may think a Beagle will suit everyone in your family fine. He'll be small enough for the kids, solid enough to be played with, active enough to go on family outings, and not so big you feel he'll take over your small house. When you go to the dog show intent on meeting some local breeders and finding out if they have puppies available, you may see the Beagles in the ring and decide that something about them doesn't appeal to you at all. They always have their noses to the ground; they bark at other dogs too often; they seem aloof. And just as you feel your heart sink, your son tugs your sleeve and says, "Look, what's that?" and you fall in love with a West Highland White Terrier.

Seeing is believing, and being able to talk to breeders is invaluable. Breeders are used to dealing with people in the same situation as you. Also, they are concerned that the dogs they breed find the right homes for them. A Husky breeder would not recommend that one of her pups go to a home in which the primary caretaker was wheelchair-bound. That wouldn't be fair to the person, and it wouldn't be fair to the dog.

How do you find dog shows to attend? Call the veterinary offices in or near your town. They should know the names of breeders who can tell you if shows are coming up in the area. You can call the American Kennel Club and ask for show information. The AKC's customer service number is (919) 233-9767. You can also find show information on the AKC's Web page, www.akc.org. Good luck and have fun!

Talking to Breeders

As mentioned earlier, breeders are your best source of information about a dog you are interested in. After all, these folks are passionate about their breed! They've lived with it, some for several decades, and can tell you the breed's positive and negative qualities.

Breeders will interview you, too, which will help you decide if the breed is truly right for you. A breeder may ask you how often you like to go hiking, say, or how often you travel. You may realize you're not the sportsperson you thought you were, or that your schedule is tighter than you thought. Then again, you may be relieved to hear that a breed you thought was too active actually doesn't need as much exercise as you thought, and the breeder has helped you figure out how to fit in a good workout for the dog without compromising your daily habits.

Another great thing about talking to breeders is that you will get a good sense of who you want to get your puppy (or older dog) from. The person who's especially helpful, or with whom you "click," or whose dogs seem the most well-behaved and mellow of the lot you've spoken with—this is the person from whom you want to acquire your new family member. You should feel comfortable calling your breeder at any time during your dog's life to ask him or her about any kind of problems you're having. If your pup's chewing is getting out of control, or if housetraining isn't working, or if your adult dog suddenly goes lame, it's nice to know there's someone you can call who not only knows the breed, but knows your dog personally.

A responsible breeder will tell you all about your potential puppy's or older dog's past—what the parents and siblings are like, whether there's working stock in the bloodlines, what kind of traits he's been breeding away from (or for), particular health problems to look out for, and much more. In fact, a breeder who doesn't want to inform you of all these things, particularly health records for breeds prone to hip dysplasia or other genetic conditions, is one to stay away from—he's probably got something to hide.

Responsible breeders want their puppies or older dogs to find homes in which they'll be loved and cared for as real family members for the duration of their lives. Many of them will put in writing that if for any reason you can't keep the dog any longer, you'll contact them first before surrendering the dog to a shelter. Doesn't this sound like the kind of grandma or grandpa you want for your dog?

Talking to Veterinarians

Studies prove that veterinarians are the first ones most pet owners turn to for help with a variety of problems, from health to behavior. And because they're on the "front lines" of dealing with various breeds and their owners, they can give you some solid advice about general traits of some breeds.

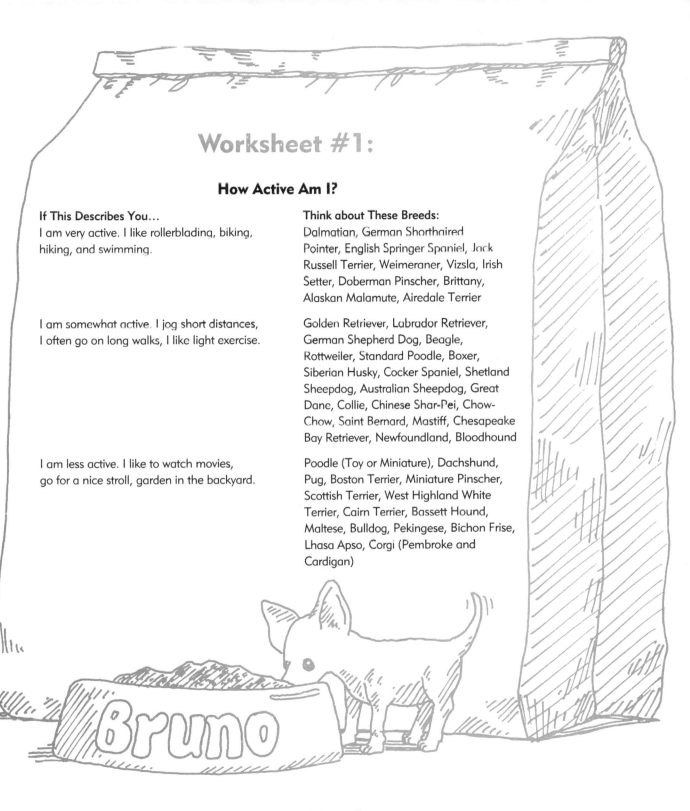

Worksheet #1:

How Active Am I?

If This Describes You…

I am very active. I like rollerblading, biking, hiking, and swimming.

Think about These Breeds:

Dalmatian, German Shorthaired Pointer, English Springer Spaniel, Jack Russell Terrier, Weimeraner, Vizsla, Irish Setter, Doberman Pinscher, Brittany, Alaskan Malamute, Airedale Terrier

I am somewhat active. I jog short distances, I often go on long walks, I like light exercise.

Golden Retriever, Labrador Retriever, German Shepherd Dog, Beagle, Rottweiler, Standard Poodle, Boxer, Siberian Husky, Cocker Spaniel, Shetland Sheepdog, Australian Sheepdog, Great Dane, Collie, Chinese Shar-Pei, Chow-Chow, Saint Bernard, Mastiff, Chesapeake Bay Retriever, Newfoundland, Bloodhound

I am less active. I like to watch movies, go for a nice stroll, garden in the backyard.

Poodle (Toy or Miniature), Dachshund, Pug, Boston Terrier, Miniature Pinscher, Scottish Terrier, West Highland White Terrier, Cairn Terrier, Bassett Hound, Maltese, Bulldog, Pekingese, Bichon Frise, Lhasa Apso, Corgi (Pembroke and Cardigan)

The veterinarians at the clinic nearest you may know that Labrador Retrievers are being overbred in the area, and they're seeing a lot of chewing, digging, and nervous behavior problems. They may be able to tell you that 70 percent of all German Shepherds they see develop hip dysplasia. They may also tell you that Bichon Frises make ideal family pets. It's important to remember that even though they see a lot of different dogs, they are not experts on all breeds.

What is important is that once you've chosen your puppy or dog, you need to establish a relationship with a veterinarian you can trust completely. If a veterinarian makes you feel silly about asking a basic question, or doesn't seem to want to spend much time examining your animal, keep shopping until you find someone you can discuss anything with. It's the same scenario as shopping for a breeder—this is someone you'll trust your dog's life with.

Talking to Friends

You may spend months reading books, going to dog shows, exploring the wide world of dogs to find just the one for you, and suddenly a friend will tell you they know someone whose dog just had a litter and she needs good homes for the puppies. You ignore all your instincts, go see the litter, fall in love, and come home with a puppy whose genetic background is a mystery to you, that will grow to look like something you've never seen before, and that's three times bigger than you ever imagined. Does that mean you're going to suffer with the wrong dog for the rest of its life? Maybe. But then again, maybe not. Animals are adaptable, and luckily, people are, too. It may not have been the smartest move on your part, but if you vow to be a responsible dog owner and walk, feed, exercise, groom, and look after your dog's health, the two of you will do just fine.

Purebred or Mixed Breed

There is a lot of information written about purebreds because, as I hope you've learned here, they've been selectively bred to look and act in particular ways. This should make choosing a dog to join your family simpler. But it can also make it seem quite complicated! There are so many choices; so much to do; so many things to think about. After investigating all the breeds, you may find that none especially does it for you.

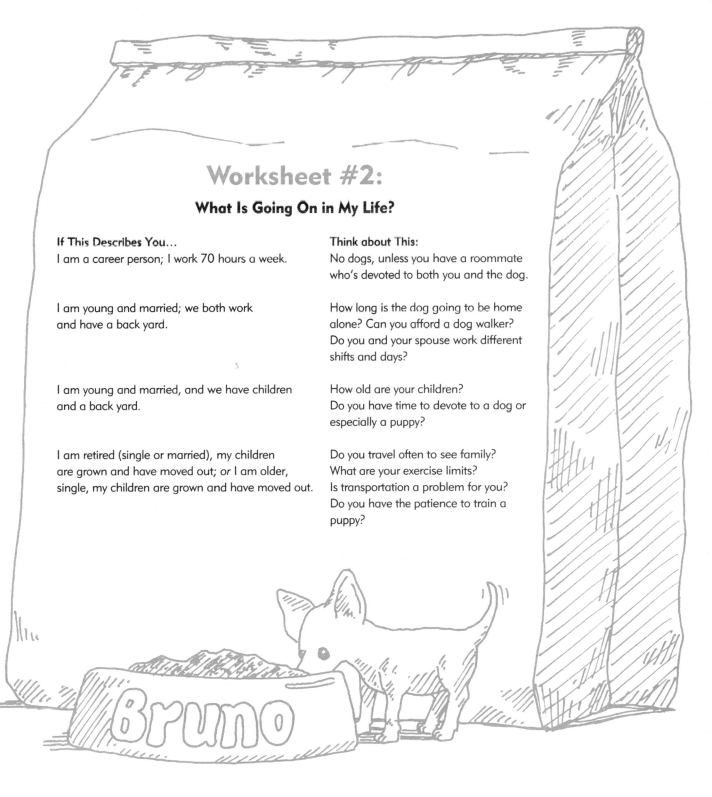

Worksheet #2:

What Is Going On in My Life?

If This Describes You...
I am a career person; I work 70 hours a week.

Think about This:
No dogs, unless you have a roommate who's devoted to both you and the dog.

If This Describes You...
I am young and married; we both work and have a back yard.

Think about This:
How long is the dog going to be home alone? Can you afford a dog walker? Do you and your spouse work different shifts and days?

If This Describes You...
I am young and married, and we have children and a back yard.

Think about This:
How old are your children? Do you have time to devote to a dog or especially a puppy?

If This Describes You...
I am retired (single or married), my children are grown and have moved out; or I am older, single, my children are grown and have moved out.

Think about This:
Do you travel often to see family? What are your exercise limits? Is transportation a problem for you? Do you have the patience to train a puppy?

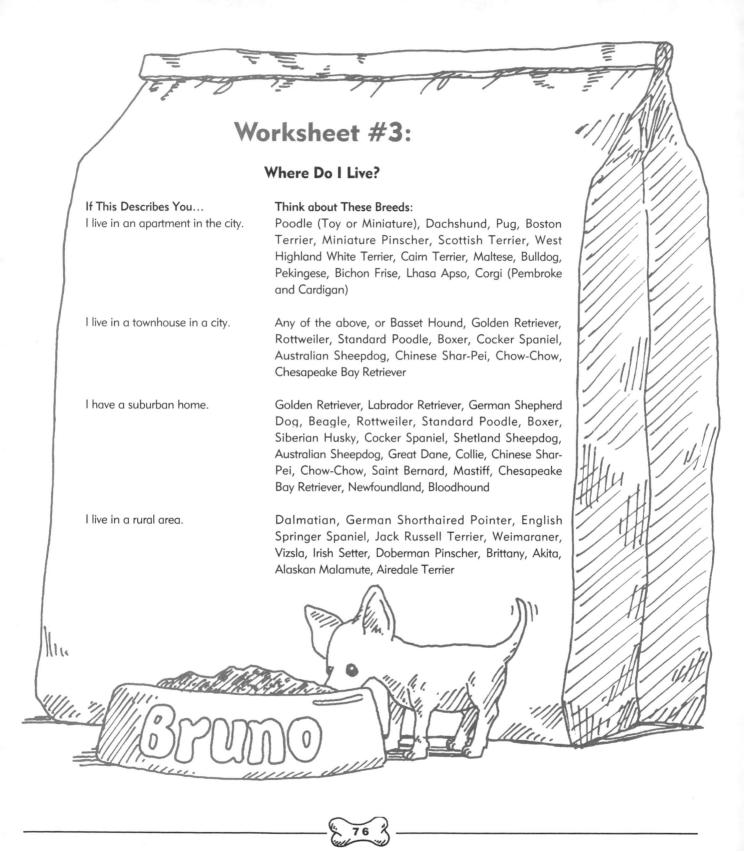

Worksheet #3:

Where Do I Live?

If This Describes You...

I live in an apartment in the city.

I live in a townhouse in a city.

I have a suburban home.

I live in a rural area.

Think about These Breeds:

Poodle (Toy or Miniature), Dachshund, Pug, Boston Terrier, Miniature Pinscher, Scottish Terrier, West Highland White Terrier, Cairn Terrier, Maltese, Bulldog, Pekingese, Bichon Frise, Lhasa Apso, Corgi (Pembroke and Cardigan)

Any of the above, or Basset Hound, Golden Retriever, Rottweiler, Standard Poodle, Boxer, Cocker Spaniel, Australian Sheepdog, Chinese Shar-Pei, Chow-Chow, Chesapeake Bay Retriever

Golden Retriever, Labrador Retriever, German Shepherd Dog, Beagle, Rottweiler, Standard Poodle, Boxer, Siberian Husky, Cocker Spaniel, Shetland Sheepdog, Australian Sheepdog, Great Dane, Collie, Chinese Shar-Pei, Chow-Chow, Saint Bernard, Mastiff, Chesapeake Bay Retriever, Newfoundland, Bloodhound

Dalmatian, German Shorthaired Pointer, English Springer Spaniel, Jack Russell Terrier, Weimaraner, Vizsla, Irish Setter, Doberman Pinscher, Brittany, Akita, Alaskan Malamute, Airedale Terrier

If you're worn out on the purebred route, or it simply doesn't matter that much to you how much you know about your dog's genetic makeup, you may want to adopt a mixed-breed dog. Yes, a mutt! These may not be the most beautiful dogs you've ever seen, and you may never be sure whether their instincts are coming from retriever blood or terrier blood or perhaps a bit of everything—but like their purebred cousins, mixed breeds can make superlative pets.

Mixed-breed dogs often marry the best traits of the dogs they're descended from. It is fun to try to guess what breeds went into making your dog. In some cases you'll know—if your Lab bred the Australian Cattle Dog next door by mistake—but in many cases you won't know at all. I had friends who had a Saint Bernard/Flat-Coated Retriever cross. The dog had the general build of the Saint Bernard, with the Saint Bernard's coloring. However, the hair on the dog was like the flat hair of the Flat Coat. Also, the dog was smaller than the Saint Bernard but bigger than the Flat Coat. He was gentle and friendly and loved going in the water. He had webbed feet. Because we knew about his parents, we knew why the dog loved the things he did. The British magazine *Dogs Today* runs a monthly contest for its readership to try to guess the parentage of a mixed-breed dog. It's fun to see what people guess—and what the actual mix is—when next month's issue comes in.

In the end, neither a purebred or a mixed breed is going to be a better dog than the other. Both are just dogs. The important considerations are, again, how well your lifestyle accommodates your dog's basic needs. If he's a big hairy purebred or a big hairy mix and you're a neat freak who lives in a fifth-floor walkup, things might not work out. Whether you choose purebred or mixed, you have to realistically assess the amount of time and energy you have to take care of your dog the way he deserves (and needs) to be taken care of. Remember, while quality breeding is important to keep the various breeds alive, dogs, unlike humans, don't differentiate between breed and non-breed. Dogs only care that you are their primary caregiver and leader. It's only people who differentiate between purebred and mutt.

Puppy or Adult

This is a question most people don't stop to think about, but should. Most of the time when people think of getting a dog, they

think about getting a puppy. They think of the cute ball of fluff running around the house making the family laugh. They want to nurture and raise the dog from a pup.

Do You Really Want a Puppy?

But think about it: Do you really want a puppy? Is a puppy the best fit with your family's lifestyle? Having a puppy is like having a 2-year-old in the house. Puppies want to get into everything, and they use their mouths to explore. They need to chew, and if you don't supply a variety of toys, they'll chew what's available. Puppies need to be kept on very strict schedules in order to be housetrained. That means taking the puppy out first thing in the morning, several times during the day, and last thing at night. It means monitoring the puppy during the day to try to prevent accidents from happening. It means making a real commitment to training and socializing, because when your puppy gets big and he doesn't know what's expected of him, he'll make the rules. It may be cute to have your puppy curl up on the couch with you or sleep in your bed or jump up on you to greet you, but then don't be surprised if you meet with resistance when your pup's grown up and you don't want him doing those things anymore.

What Older Dogs Have to Offer

When you get an older dog, you obviously miss those early days of playfulness and cuteness. But you do get other things in return. Older dogs are generally calmer; they're usually housetrained; they're more set in their ways; and people report that they seem grateful to be in a new home in which they're loved and appreciated.

There's also the feel-good part of getting an older dog, because whether you adopt one from a shelter or a purebred rescue group or just take one in from a neighbor, you are essentially saving that dog's life. Yes, you are inheriting behaviors that the dog has learned from its previous owners or circumstances, but contrary to the old saying, you can teach an old dog new tricks. And if you approach getting an older dog as conscientiously as you would approach getting a puppy, you're sure to find one whose temperament suits you, for better or worse.

Adopting an older dog doesn't mean going to the dog pound and rescuing a mangy mutt on death row (though those who do are

Your Puppy's Age

Studies have found that the first eight to ten weeks are a critical period in a puppy's life. Besides needing to nurse from his mother to receive nutrients and protective antibodies (until he gets his shots), puppies develop their personalities during these first few weeks. They learn crucial lessons about being a dog from their mother and littermates. As they grow, they become part of a pack, and a sort of pecking order is established among the litter. This may make you feel sorry for the "runt" of the litter who's always the last to suckle from mom's teats or who seems to be bullied by his littermates, but there's nothing you can do about it. This is life for a dog and each pup assumes his rightful place in the pack hierarchy.

Responsible breeders understand the dynamics of early puppyhood and use the information they gain from watching and handling the puppies to help pair them to their future owners. If a family has active, assertive children who may intimidate a lesser-ranked pup, the breeder may want to pair that family with the "alpha" puppy, who can take care of himself. Similarly, an alpha pup in a reserved, quiet family may grow to dominate them.

Puppies need to be with their mother and littermates for at least eight weeks. Some breeders hold on to them for as long as 12 weeks. This is especially the case in a litter with several show-potential pups. Anyone who encourages you to take a puppy younger than eight weeks old is not allowing enough time for the pup to develop fully. Puppies this young risk developing a whole array of behavior problems as a result.

blessed). There are many older dogs available, both purebred (through breed-supported rescue groups as well as the local shelters) and mixed-breed, that are physically and mentally sound. The obvious thing about taking in an older dog is that you're making a difference in a dog's life. But the thing you need to consider is: Is an adult dog going to make a difference in your life?

My wife and I took in an older dog who had belonged to a woman who moved and couldn't take the dog with her. We both worked, and we knew we couldn't devote the time necessary to bring up a puppy properly. Also, since the new dog was going to be a friend for our five-year-old dog, we felt there might be too much of an age difference. We wanted a dog Exley could play with right away and who was at a similar life stage. We wanted a dog who was housetrained, who didn't bark (much), and who would fit in with our routine fairly quickly. We found Chelsea at our local SPCA, and she seemed to meet our basic requirements. She was five years old. For the first few days we had her, she was timid and unsure of what to do. She was perfectly housetrained and responded to "sit," "stay," and "down." She sat by our front door for days, patiently looking out onto the street as if she was waiting for someone to come pick her up. Except to eat and sleep, she did not stray from the door. She was quiet and sort of sulky. She was obviously still mourning the loss of her previous owner. After a couple of weeks, though, she started to come into her own. Today, she runs the house. She is a giant, shedding, pushy broad of a dog, who is more than happy to put her nose into anything. She is playful, alert and active. She was easy to assimilate into our busy lives and has provided our other dog with a playmate and friend. We definitely inherited a shy dog, but without a mean bone in her body. With all the people coming in and out of our house, she now comes warily but surely up to greet strangers without barking at them. We couldn't imagine life without her.

Where to Get Your Dog

Breeders

Certainly, you would think, this is like asking a Chevrolet salesman if he himself would buy a Chevrolet. What do you think he's going to tell you? "Oh, no, I think you're much more a Honda type. Honda's down the road." But if you get a good breeder, he or she may indeed tell you just that.

When I started looking into buying my first dog as an adult, I naturally considered the types of dogs I had had growing up. This is what we all do. I decided to talk to some dog professionals. I happened to be working for a company at the time that had a pet division. Some of the people who worked in it were dog show judges as well as breeders themselves. I talked to those professionals, and they helped guide me to several breeds and then pointed me in the direction of some qualified breeders. Unfortunately, not everyone has the opportunity to tap into this kind of resource. Researching not only helped me find the dog I wanted, but also made me question my selection and then work the right questions through in my head, to understand whether my final decision was correct.

I eventually went to Nancy Campbell, a German Shorthaired Pointer breeder who also ran the rescue and fostered several homeless dogs. She asked me more questions than I asked her. I thought I already knew it all. She was talking with concern in her voice, and I feigned knowledge and confidence in my decision. Then she really started asking me about all kinds of things. How big was my apartment? How often do I exercise? How late do I work? How long does it take me to get home? And then she said NO!

You can imagine my surprise! She felt that I was not prepared to take a puppy into my home and raise it properly. I had a career and often worked late. Although I had people who would be able to walk a dog, she felt that I wouldn't be there enough to socialize the dog. In short, she would never sell me a puppy and strongly urged me to reconsider my desire to get a dog.

Not being one to take no for an answer, I called her back several days later and told her I had thought it through, come up with some realistic answers and wanted to discuss it with her again. She said she thought it would be a bad idea for me to try raising a puppy at this time in my life, but urged me to think about taking on a dog from the German Shorthair Rescue program. She argued that the dog would not have to be housetrained, and that he was a little older and could handle being alone for periods of time better than a puppy. She also strongly

Puppies vs. Adults: Pros and Cons

Puppies
Pros:
- Cute
- Playful
- Cuddly
- Bonding between you and your dog establishes pack position early

Cons:
- Needs to be housetrained, socialized, and obedience trained
- Has to work through chewing and adolescent stages

Adults
Pros:
- Easily (if not already) housetrained
- Doesn't usually require lots of training
- Playful, active
- Good for working singles and couples

Cons:
- Miss the cute puppy stage
- May inherit someone else's problems

Your Purebred Dog's Papers

Many times you'll hear breeders say they have all the papers for the dog. This can seem confusing to someone who doesn't know what those papers are for or what they mean. A responsible breeder should give you two pieces of paper with the sale of a puppy: a pedigree and a registration form. The pedigree tells you the dog's family background and usually goes back five generations. The pedigree is optional, but most breeders include it.

The registration form must be turned over to you the very day you purchase or acquire your puppy. This form allows you to officially register your dog with the American Kennel Club or another registry if the breed isn't AKC recognized. The breeder should have registered the litter when it was born, at which time he or she received individual registration forms for each of the puppies in the litter. Breeders are responsible for keeping all their paperwork up to date, and they have to record the sale of each puppy. It is then up to you to fill out your pup's registration form and send it in with the required fee to the registering body.

Remember, just because your dog is a registered purebred does not mean his health or worth are guaranteed in any way. You will know the value of your dog by discussing his pedigree with your breeder. If there are no champions or dogs who've earned working titles in your dog's line, then you shouldn't consider breeding him. In fact, your breeder will probably insist you sign a spay/neuter contract. If you want to show your dog, find a breeder who can be your mentor as you enter this exciting new sport.

urged me to get a dog walker. When I was okay with her demands, she was convinced I was responsible enough to take a dog, and I got Exley, an 18-month-old rescue dog.

Nancy was an excellent example of a responsible breeder. As she put it, she wanted to make sure that I was committed to the dog and that I understood the responsibility I was taking on. She didn't want to have to take the dog back—not because she didn't like the dog, or would ever refuse one of her own, but because there were already enough homeless dogs. She wanted to find a perma-nent home for this one. She sent me home with Exley's papers and instructions for care. She also gave me her phone number and asked me to call her if I ran into problems or had questions. When I did in fact call her for advice or with questions, she was always very friendly and of great help.

Not enough breeders are that responsible. There are plenty of breeders who don't ask the tough questions. There are many who don't have any scruples at all. That's why it's important to find a reputable breeder whom you can trust. I was at a point where I could afford Nancy's dogs, but for her, it wasn't just about selling off a puppy or rescue dog. Many breeders are willing to take the time to ask you the right questions. If they don't, you should wonder how much care they take in breeding their dogs.

Pet Shops

Are the dogs you can buy in a pet shop any different than the ones you can buy from a breeder? More times than not, absolutely. As we've discussed, a responsible breeder insures that his or her dogs are bred for a purpose, that they're properly raised and social-ized, and that any health problems have been addressed. He or she takes care to breed two dogs who complement each other in order to produce the best possible dog, most emblematic of the breed standard or ideal. Responsible breeders ask you a lot of questions before they agree to sell you a puppy, and they try to match your personality with one of their puppies.

Many pet shops get their dogs from breeders the media have labeled

Worksheet #4

Questions to Ask a Breeder

1. How long have you been breeding these dogs?
2. Did you breed any dogs other than these? If so, for how long?
3. When's the last time you showed one of your dogs?
4. Are either the sire or the dam finished champions? Can I see their pedigrees?
5. Do either of them have working titles earned in obedience or other performance events?
6. Have the dogs been tested for hip dysplasia, eye problems, heart problems or whatever genetic conditions relate to the breed? (Breeders should be only too happy to show you pedigrees and health certificates. If they're reluctant or say they'll show you when you come to pick up the puppy, don't trust them. These documents should be readily available.)
7. Are either of the parents on the premises, and if so, can I see them? Ask about other siblings, too.
8. Have the puppies had their shots? What shots and when?
9. Is the litter registered? Will I go home with my puppy's registration? (If not, again, suspect trouble.)
10. Can I have the names of references to call?

"puppy mills." These breeders produce dogs with little or no concern about breed standards, temperament, or health problems. As a
result, unsuspecting buyers don't know what they're getting. These
dogs are as purebred as the dogs you get from a breeder, because
purebred only means the mother and father are registered purebreds. These puppies are also as cute as the ones you'll see at a
responsible breeder's, though they may lack the energy or robust
appearance of the responsible breeder's pups.

Pet shops know that puppies are most appealing when they're
six to eight weeks old. That means that to get them to the store by
that age they are usually separated from their mother and littermates
at four to six weeks of age—far too early. These pups miss the nutritional and behavioral benefits of staying in their first family for as
long as they should, and their new families pay the price in health
and behavior problems later in life.

Does this mean good dogs don't come from pet shops? No. I
have friends who bought their dogs at pet stores and have perfectly
fine pets. I also know people who bought their dogs at the mall,
only to find out that the dog has some kind of incurable disease or
malformation. Pet shops are under a lot of pressure from the general
public to sell them healthy puppies. More and more, they either
don't sell puppies or they host adoption days where local shelters
come in so people can get their dogs from the shelter. This is good
PR for the pet shop and good business for the shelter. It also makes
people feel better about the dog they're acquiring.

If you do buy a puppy from a pet store, ask the staff a lot of
questions about its background and whether the store provides any
guarantees of the puppy's health. Take the puppy to a veterinarian
right away for a first physical, and if the vet suspects any problems,
speak with the store staff immediately.

Purebred Rescue

A "rescue" dog is a purebred dog who has been "rescued" from
a former home or from a pound or shelter and is currently homeless. Most AKC breed clubs sponsor purebred rescue groups. When
a dog is dropped off at the shelter or taken into the dog pound, if
that dog is believed to be purebred, that local shelter calls the contact person for the local rescue group. If the rescue coordinator
believes the dog is a purebred of the breed with which he or she is

involved, that dog is taken from the pound and housed in a foster home until the rescue organization can find the dog a home.

Rescue is run generally by breeders who are very concerned about dogs in general. They make no money off this and usually work on a volunteer basis. Much of the cost of fostering is picked up by the family that is sheltering the dog in their house. Each breed has a specific network of these people who have extremely big hearts and only want to see the dogs find a good home.

Do these dogs have something wrong with them? Generally speaking, no. They have been housed by people who could no longer properly care for their animals. Sometimes this is brought about by a death in the family or by difficult circumstances. Rescue coordinators bail out abandoned or unwanted dogs and evaluate them before seeking new homes for them. Many rescue dogs need some stability to help regain their confidence, and foster owners spend a lot of time working with such animals to ensure that they'll adjust to a new home.

They then list the dog with a national or regional network, where the dog will eventually be placed. Generally speaking, all kinds of dogs pass through this scenario. They tend to be a little older than puppies. They can be anywhere from 18 months to 10 years old. They come in all shapes, sizes, and temperaments. The only thing they have in common is that they are all purebreds.

Because they are rescue dogs, they also tend to be cheaper than their puppy counterparts. The rescue associations usually ask you to make some kind of donation to defray the costs of operating the rescue group and the costs of the individual dog. These groups are run by loving individuals who are looking earnestly for the right home for the right dog. You should seriously consider this venue as a means to getting a dog.

Shelters/Pounds

Many local animal shelters are in operation all over the United States. Some dogs are brought there by their current owners, or by the families of those persons. Sometimes the dogs are found on the side of the road and are brought in by a concerned citizen who can't shelter the animal, or they are brought in by the local animal control department.

Many times these dogs are perfectly fine animals who just need a home. In many cases, the animals take a little time to adjust when you first bring them home. Dogs want to be part of a pack. Being moved from pack to pack undermines a dog's self-assurance. As pack position is very important to how a dog sees him or herself, being separated and then situated into a new pack definitely plays games with poor Rover's head. The longer a dog stays with you, the more secure it will become in its surroundings and the more comfortable it will feel with you.

Sometimes the shelters have lots of information on a particular dog, and sometimes they have none. But many of the people who work in shelters are there because they love animals and spend great amounts of time with them. They are often the best judges of how these dogs are and what they like and don't like. They can tell you how they respond to certain things and to other dogs.

In short, if you don't care about purebred vs. mixed breed, there are plenty of dogs that need good homes in these shelters. When you bring them home, they need a little extra loving and space before they can become confident, but they'll make it up to you with love and admiration. In many cases, they're a little older and are already housetrained. Later on, we'll talk about the special needs of rescue and shelter dogs when you first bring them home.

Friends

This is probably one of the least likely—and least desirable—places to get a dog. How much does your friend know about breeding dogs? Maybe he has great fashion sense, knows all the newest, hottest bands, hangs out with cool people, has a great job—but what does he really know about dogs?

Often people have puppies to give away because their dog got pregnant. Sometimes they've bred her to another dog, and sometimes she's found a beau of her own. Although dogs may think they're picky, however, you should know that they don't differentiate by breed. They either like another dog, or they don't.

In many cases, you really don't know what you're getting. And that's when you have to ask yourself a lot of questions. Is

Pound vs. Shelter

- The dog pound is usually an animal control center, where strays have been picked up by the local animal control unit. These operations are usually funded by local government.

- The shelter is usually a local animal care unit that is funded in part by state or local government monies, as well as by donations.

- No-Kill shelters are shelters that don't destroy animals. This is a bit of a misnomer. Many of these No-Kill places just don't accept animals they don't think are adoptable. These dogs are then brought to the local animal control unit for adoption or destruction.

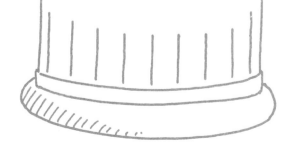

my friend really good to his or her dog? Did they read up on what to do with a pregnant dog? Did they go to their veterinarian and get his or her advice? Do I like my friend's dog? Have I spent enough time with that dog to know whether or not I like it?

Sometimes "friends" come up with dogs when they find a stray and try to find it a good home. This is more common than you think. Make sure to ask as many questions as you can. Try not to be moved by the sad story. You need to find yourself a pet that you can live with for a long time. Although many fine pets have been found this way, make sure to think about it before you bring one home. In short, a real friend won't try to sell you a dog you don't need. Think about the person who's trying to give you the dog, as well as about the dog itself.

Chapter Three

YOUR DOG'S BASIC NEEDS

Bringing Your New Puppy or Dog Home

You've actually picked a dog and the arrival date is near. Now comes one of the most important parts: preparing for your newest little bundle of joy. This is a tougher job than you'd imagine. But it's also fun. The excitement of bringing home your new puppy is wonderful, but don't let some safety precautions elude you in the midst of all the excitement. First, take a look around your home. What do you need to do so that Puppy doesn't destroy all your family's prized possessions, and so he doesn't hurt himself chewing on something that could be harmful? Where will Puppy sleep? What will he eat, and out of what? How will you take him outside? These are the considerations that affect what kind of "equipment" and other supplies you'll need to make sure you and your dog get off to a good start.

The one thing to remember is that whether you're bringing home a new puppy or an older dog, there are still things you'll want to do to protect your house and your dog from any possible disasters.

Puppy-Proofing Your Home

Stage 1

The first thing you want to do with a puppy is limit the amount of space in which he can run around—especially when you're not home. Many people confine the pup to a room or group of manageable rooms in the beginning. Choose a room in which there's a lot of people traffic so your puppy doesn't feel isolated. Pick a room that's fairly easy to clean up, with an easily washable floor surface. Pick a room that's light and airy. The kitchen or washroom are good first choices, whether you're crate-training your puppy or not (and you should be; more on that later!).

There's no way around it—if you're getting a puppy, and you want to limit his space, you need a baby gate. He will not be in his crate all the time, yet he might not be trustworthy enough in his housetraining to have free run of other rooms. Baby gates do a good job of setting up

a solid barrier while allowing the puppy to see into the other room and also smell what's going on in there (very important to a dog). Another nice thing about baby gates is that they're portable and removable. Once Puppy's good in the kitchen and the den, for example, you can put a gate up in front of the stairs or in doorways leading to rooms that are still off limits. Buy the baby gate(s) and save yourself a lot of time and aggravation.

Why do you want to confine your puppy (or new dog)? It's for his benefit and yours. When you're not home, it limits the amount of damage he can do to himself or the house to just one room. Before you leave, if you're not going to be crating Junior, it's easier for you to look around and either move or hide away things that might cause him harm.

Once you've put the baby gates up, you need to look around the room and ask yourself the following question: If you were a dog, what would you chew on? The usual answer: everything. If there are exposed wires, cover them up. The chairs around the kitchen table? If they're wood, put them in the attic for now. Are all bottles and cans out of the way? Are all cleansers and other potentially toxic substances safe inside child-proof cabinets? And don't forget: hide the garbage. Garbage is the dinner of the gourmet dog. Everything wonderful and edible is in the garbage and your puppy knows it. Move it, or come home every day and wonder what condition your house and your dog are going to be in. What can't be moved, especially anything that's made out of wood, spray with a product called bitter apple. Bitter apple usually comes in a spray. It leaves a very bitter taste on things that deters dogs from chewing.

However, you must purposely leave things for your new puppy or dog to chew on. You will find a huge assortment of toys for dogs at your local pet supply store. Choose whatever you like. You'll want a variety of things when you first bring your dog home. You'll soon find out whether he prefers to gnaw on hard rubber, a plush toy, a rope toy, a tennis ball, a chew hoof, or rawhide. Give him these last two in moderation. Too much rawhide is not good for a dog, especially a young pup. Gobs of rawhide have caused some dogs to choke, so it's best to give him that while you're home to supervise.

Toxic Houseplants

Dogs like to chew on houseplants sometimes. An odd habit for a carnivore, but true nonetheless. There are many ordinary house and garden plants that can be toxic to your dog, even in small amounts. The following is a list of plants that could poison your dog. (Plants in italic type are extremely toxic: just a little bit can kill.)

Azalea	Marijuana
Bean plants	Mistletoe
Cactus	Narcissus
Crocus	*Nightshade*
Daffodil	Oleander
Dieffenbachia	Philodendron
Hemlock	Poinsettia
Hydrangea	Potato leaves
Ivy	*Rhododendron*
Lily	

Many of these are outdoor varieties, so you need to watch your dog when you let them outside in your backyard. Others, such as cactus, philodendron, and dieffenbachia, are common house plants. You may want to avoid these plants. You may want to avoid these species if your dog seems to have a need to chew on them. If your dog has ingested any of these, call your vet immediately.

Stage 2

When you're home, give the dog or puppy more space to roam around. Close all the doors to rooms you want to remain off limits. But give him more room than you do when you're not at home. If you have children, close the doors to their rooms, as well as closing the door to the garage, the den, etc. Some houses don't have many doors. Maybe you want to close off the living room or dining room. Buy even more baby gates.

The idea is that the dog should only incrementally increase the amount of space he is able to live in as he gets a little older and starts to understand the rules of the house. Also, the less space you give him, the easier it is to manage him. You'll be able to keep a better eye on him.

Dog-Proofing for an Older Dog

You should proof your house for an older dog in much the same way for a puppy. You're not really sure what a new dog will do in a strange new environment. Better to take precautions. Sometimes they adapt quickly and easily with few problems. Other times, they're unsure of themselves and become nervous. They may resort to old bad habits in order to deal with any anxieties brought about by a change in their living conditions. Have patience. These dogs usually work out with a little love, understanding, and training.

Supplies and Equipment

Whether you've done this before or not, it's important to review the materials you'll need to own a dog. The basic things are obvious—a leash, a collar, an ID tag, a crate, food and water bowls, food, grooming supplies, treats, toys, a bed, and helpful books like this one! However, there are things you need to know about these before you go out and buy supplies or equipment that don't work for you.

Leash

It's best to actually have two leashes. The first one is your all-purpose leash that you'll use for walks around the block and most training sessions. Leashes or leads come in a variety of colors, textures, and styles. There are leather leashes, nylon leashes, and even chain leashes. The best by far (and also the most expensive) is a six-foot-long leather leash. You should have this leash for a long time if you take care of it. Leather is strong, wears well, doesn't stink, and

No Spoiled Dogs

Everyone thinks their own puppy is the cutest. And you know what? They're right. But that "puppy love" causes many smitten owners to overlook behavior they should be correcting until suddenly it's a big problem. This is so with play-biting, possessiveness, jumping up, begging at the table, and other things. I don't want you to be a curmudgeon or such a strict disciplinarian that you don't enjoy your dog, but don't indulge him in things as a puppy (or new dog) that you wouldn't want him to do when he's older.

Here are a few things people later regret:

1. It's cute when your puppy sleeps on the bed. When he's a full-grown 80 pounds and is hogging more than half the bed, it's not so cute anymore. He may also see your bed as his territory and aggressively defend it. Big problem.
2. The famous "Look, he's so happy to see you!" jumping puppy. Cute when he's 12 pounds, obnoxious when he's 60 or 70. And there's nothing sadder than having to barricade your dog when you have company over because you haven't trained him how to properly greet guests. Sad for your dog, of course, and sad for you and your guests.
3. Excessive barking. Again, it may be cute when he's young, but when Fido starts gratuitously barking, it gets annoying real fast.
4. Climbing onto furniture. See Number 1.
5. Feeding from the table. Until the dog is much older, this is absolutely the wrong message to send to your puppy. No one likes a beggar at the dinner table.

If you can relate to any of these problems, take heart in the fact that they're easily solved with training. When your dog understands Sit, Stay, Go Lie Down, Off, and Shush, which should be just a small part of his vocabulary, you can ask him to cooperate with you in these situations instead of banishing him for not acting as you want. You'll both be so much happier!

is comfortable in your hand. Nylon leashes are also strong and come in a huge assortment of colors and patterns. They can even be mono-grammed. Nylon leashes come in handy when you have to walk your dog in the rain and you don't want the leather to get wet. Or if you have to give your dog a bath and use a leash for some restraint. They dry quickly and don't shrink or crack. But they're not comfortable to hold; in fact, some may give you a rope burn if they get jerked out of your hand. Chain leashes are decorative and completely impractical. They're hard to hold, even if it's a look you like. But the choice is yours.

The second leash you'll need to buy is called a training leash. These are usually very long—8 to 10 feet. Many trainers recommend these as part of basic obedience class. Usually you would use it outside. You teach to the dog to stay or come by working at some distance from the dog, letting the leash drag on the ground. If the dog races past you or won't come near enough, you step on the leash and then slowly wind the dog in, praising him as he gets nearer.

Flexi-leads

Flexi-leads are an interesting new twist in the dog-walking world. These operate like the adjustable clotheslines of bygone eras. However, you're holding the contraption, and the dog is at the other end of the line. The idea is that it lets the dog have some freedom to roam, but when he comes nearer to you, the line automatically withdraws and recoils. There is also a button which can stop the flow of the line at any time, so if you need to keep your dog close to you, you can limit the amount of line you let out. These leashes provide people with the opportunity to run their dogs with greater freedom in open spaces where dogs are not allowed off-leash. The only problem they present is a pos-sible burn to those who come too near. If the dog encircles you, or someone you're with, the cord whips around and may cause a burn if it runs across your unprotected skin. You must be alert to any changes of direction or sudden activity on the part of your roaming dog. Overall, though, they're a handy way to have control and let your dog run.

Collars

Like leashes, collars come in a huge variety of materials, styles, and colors. Unlike the leash, however, one size does not fit all; you will need to buy a collar to fit your dog at his current size. Collars should fit snugly but not be too tight. You want something that goes around his neck comfortably and won't slide off the head, but you need to be able to insert two fingers between the collar and the dog's neck. Don't pull on the collar to make the space. It should be slack enough that it happens without creating too much tension.

There are four basic types of collars: *traditional buckle collars; choke chains;* the *pronged collar;* and *electronic collars.* The traditional buckle collar is what I would recommend for the first collar. These collars come in leather or nylon and have the traditional buckle fastener or a clasp fastener. They are adjustable, so your puppy should be able to grow into his buckle collar (though he will definitely grow out of at least one!). You can get a buckle or clasp collar in whatever color or style you want, from a conservative but elegant rolled leather, to black leather with metal spikes, to bright pink, to monogrammed, to decorated with ducks, hearts, or flowers. There are even buckle collars that glow in the dark! Your dog's collar can be a true expression of how you feel about him. Have fun!

The choke chain (now often referred to as a slip collar) is a metal link collar that is primarily used for training. Basically, this is a slip-knotted smooth metal chain that comes in various sizes. The idea is that as the dog pulls harder, the collar "chokes" him, pinching his skin slightly or impairing his breathing. To relieve the tension and breathe easier, he has to stop pulling. Used properly, this is not cruel at all and will save years of wear and tear on your arms and shoulders. Your obedience instructor will demonstrate the correct way to put the collar on and how to use it for maximum efficiency.

This collar should be used only during training and should not be the collar you use all the time. Because the collar has two big rings on either end, it can get caught on things. If your dog catches his collar on something while you're not with him, he could easily choke to death trying to free himself. If you properly train your dog in the beginning, eventually you won't need this collar—though he will always associate it with training, which might help him pay attention to you.

The pronged collar operates like a choke chain in that it tightens around the dog's neck as he pulls harder. But the pronged collar has dulled metal prongs that poke him in the neck as he pulls. Many people use this collar when walking dogs they can no longer control. These collars are especially favored by owners of large, furry dogs, such as German Shepherds, Alaskan Malamutes,

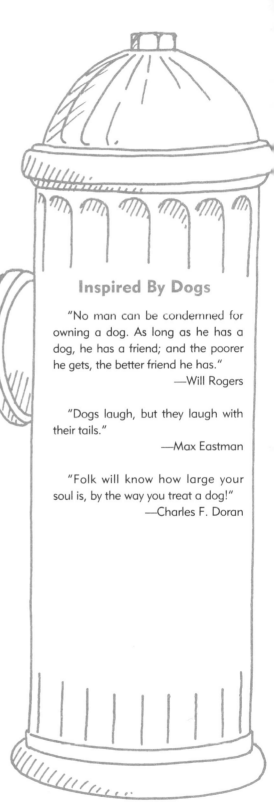

Inspired By Dogs

"No man can be condemned for owning a dog. As long as he has a dog, he has a friend; and the poorer he gets, the better friend he has."
—Will Rogers

"Dogs laugh, but they laugh with their tails."
—Max Eastman

"Folk will know how large your soul is, by the way you treat a dog!"
—Charles F. Doran

and Samoyeds, as sometimes traditional chokers don't always work on these breeds, they have so much fur on their necks. They are also used by people with very strong dogs such as Rottweilers or Saint Bernards. Even if you have one of these breeds, you need some instruction before you start using a prong collar. Speak to a trainer or your breeder about whether it's the collar you need, or just more training classes.

You will also find a number of electronic collars in your pet supply store. There are electronic collars to stop your dog from barking, electronic collars to keep your dog within your property, even electronic collars to be used as training aids by hunters and people who work their dogs at great distances. The most commonly used are the bark collar and the collar that works with an "invisible" electronic fence. All work by "zapping" your dog with a burst of electricity when he barks, or tries to break the barrier of the fence, or you need to get his attention when he's far away from you. All should be used in conjunction with more humane training methods of teaching the dog to shush, mind his property, or respond to a whistle or voice command. They can definitely be abusive in the wrong hands.

Head Halters

These are essentially harnesses that slip over and around a dog's head, like the halters used on horses. The theory is that a dog can be led more easily by the head than by the neck (which is usually a very strong part of a dog's anatomy). These halters are very effective. But they have some drawbacks. First, they look like a muzzle, making poor Spot look like the canine version of Hannibal Lecter. Many people think they are cruel, because they make your dog look more dangerous than others because he's being muzzled. It takes some dogs a while to get used to head halters, too, as they can feel strange at first. But if you have a dog who pulls no matter what, you should try using one.

ID Tags, Tattoos, and Microchips

One of the most important things that your dog could ever have is an ID tag. Here are two true stories. A friend of mine in New York was asked to care for another friend's dog (the friend

International Quarantine Restrictions

The United States has no set quarantine restrictions on pet dogs coming into this country, but does require a valid health certificate showing that the dog is free of rabies and any other infectious diseases. Other countries are far more restrictive; England and Australia, for example, have stiff six-month quarantines on all pets coming into their countries. As the owner, you must pay for the cost of this. Other countries have varying rules; write to the U.S. State Department and request information regarding the country that you are going to.

had to go on a three-day business trip on short notice). Sure, no problem. However, the accommodating friend could not find the collar with the identifying tags on it, and used another collar he found even though it didn't have tags. He took the dog out for a walk. At one point, there was some excitement, and the leash came free from my friend's hand. The dog ran off and was lost. It was four days until he found the dog. The dog was eventually turned into the animal control center by a concerned citizen. My friend had to take four days off from work so that he could scour the animal shelters and animal control centers, frantically looking for the missing pooch. Meanwhile, the owner came home to a near nervous breakdown. The dog was eventually found, but at a huge cost in emotional drama and at the cost of a friendship.

Another time we had a friend whose dog was in a state park, and he took off after some deer. This was a well-trained dog with obedience training, but it disregarded its owner when the smell of venison beckoned. It was late in the day, so the owners were soon looking for the dog in the dark. They were out there for some hours before they found the dog, and only then because they were just behind the car that accidentally hit the dog (fortunately, the dog wasn't hurt). But the family was in a panic the entire time realizing the dog was wearing the collar without tags.

Surely, some of these people could have handled their situations better. But sometimes things happen that seem to be beyond our control. We take things for granted. Make sure you get ID tags that are engraved with your last name and phone number.

With dognapping becoming more and more prevalent, other ID methods have gained in popularity. Another way to permanently ID your dog is to put a tattoo on him. Many people tattoo their dogs with the animal's AKC or CKC registration number. Other people use their Social Security number. The tattoos are applied on the inside of the back leg and they only work if they're registered with the organization that does the tattooing. Local dog clubs sponsor tattoo clinics and charge minimal amounts for the procedure and the service. It is painless.

Another thing gaining in popularity is the microchip—a grain of rice-sized capsule that contains a chip computer-coded with a number. These tiny microchips are injected between your dog's shoulder blades into the muscle mass there where it won't migrate

to another part of the body. The injection looks worse than it is—it doesn't hurt your dog at all. These chips are permanent for the life of the dog, and are easily scanned. Ask your veterinarian about getting a microchip for your dog.

Food and Water Bowls

There is one simple rule with dog bowls: Make sure you buy bowls with wide and heavy bases that are hard to tip over. Especially with puppies, bowls can become playthings. You want to avoid letting this happen. With smaller dogs, obviously, you don't want to have too small a bowl. With larger dogs, make sure the bowl is not just bigger, but also a little heavier. Another consideration when buying bowls is what they're made of. You'll find stainless steel, ceramic and plastic bowls, all in a variety of shapes and sizes. Stainless steel is the best because it's so easy to clean. You need two bowls: one for water, one for food.

Toys

All you have to do is go to pet and toy superstores and spend five minutes in each to know that there are almost as many toys for pets as there are for children. And you will have fun choosing from among them. Some of our personal favorites are things like Kongs, tennis balls, Nylabone Frisbees, and plush toys that squeak. When buying plush for a dog, make sure it's manufactured to take the beating that a dog will inflict on it. Kongs are cone-shaped rubber pieces that are seemingly indestructible, and dogs love them. Frisbees are a lot of fun, too. But most Frisbees, while they feel pretty strong to you and me, are made out of a plastic that just can't take the pounding that a dog's teeth can dish out. That's why the Nylabone Frisbee is the best. Your dog can play Frisbee with you all day long and not puncture it. It also has a little bone-shaped handle on the top, which makes it easier for your dog to pick it up. And of course, you'll want tennis balls for fetch. Tennis balls are especially good because they float in water.

Toys you don't want to buy include those that are meant for children, including action figures, plush animals, any plastic object with a liquid center, footballs, basketballs, soccer balls, and kickballs (they will puncture and destroy these four), baseballs (they'll rip the hide cover off and then who knows what'll happen to all the insides), and anything made of glass or balls of twine.

As stated earlier, a lot of toys for dogs are edible, such as chew hooves and rawhide. These should only be given while you're there to supervise your dog, since cases of choking on the softened rawhide have been reported.

All about Crates

Once upon a time, using a crate was considered a cruel way to train a dog. Today there are still those who believe crates look a little too cagelike. However, the crate is one of the most popular of training tools, and rightfully so. Using a crate gives the owner a way to control his dog. And with a crate, the dog gets his own private "room" in the house. Let's consider some things. First, the dog is a den animal by nature. He likes a closed space which offers him protection and, when he wants, isolation.

Proper crate training starts with the right crate, correctly appointed. You want to buy a crate that will be big enough for your adult dog to stand up and turn around in. There are two main types of crates: wire and plastic. The wire crates fold down and can be carried. The plastic crates are typically referred to as airline crates because they're the ones that are used to transport animals on airlines. The wire crates are open and airy so your dog can see, hear, and sniff everything that's going on around him. Airline crates have only a front opening and some air holes for ventilation; they are much more denlike. One way that owners can make a wire crate more protected is by draping sheets or, in cold weather, blankets over the top of the crate. This shuts out light and drafts.

You might consider having more than one crate for your dog if you want a permanent crate for him in the kitchen as well as one to serve as his bed upstairs with you. Again, the choice is yours.

Whichever kind you choose, if you have a puppy and you've wisely bought a crate that will fit him when he's full grown, he is going to have a lot of room in it. This is not good, because he will be able to eat and sleep in one end and eliminate in the other, which defeats all your housetraining. You want to create a divider to put in the crate that will cut the space down to about half. As your puppy grows, you can move the divider until he doesn't need it any-

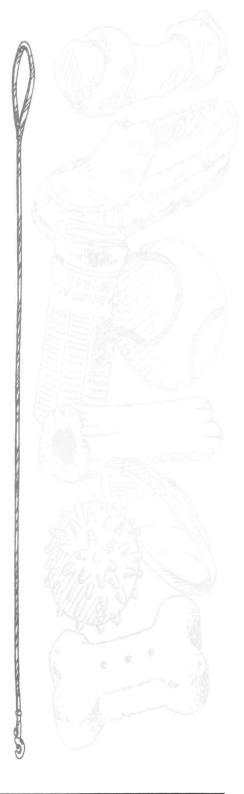

more. You can use anything from stiff cardboard to plywood as a divider. Just make sure your puppy can't grab an end to chew on and devour it.

Once you've selected a type of crate, you want to create the perfect den inside it. The best thing to do while housetraining your pup is to line the crate with a thick layer of newspapers. This way if he spills food or water or has an accident, it's no big deal—you just throw away the soiled papers. Give your puppy a warm comfy bed by folding up an old towel or blanket for him to sleep on and putting it in the back of the crate. Help your puppy associate the crate with good things by feeding him in his crate. The first time you want him to go in, put his food dish just past the opening and let him eat from it. After you've taken him out after his meal and played with him, toss a toy or treat into the crate so he scampers in after it. Close the door behind him, tell him what a good doggy he is, and leave him. He will probably cry, but you have to be strong. He will soon learn that good things happen when he's behaving himself in the crate.

A word to bargain shoppers: Crate prices vary greatly. You can often pick up crates cheaply from friends, in the classifieds, or at tag sales, as many dogs outgrow their crates when they get older. Read more about crate training in the training section.

Beds

No, not yours! His! Let's get this first thing right out in the open: Your puppy should not sleep on your bed with you. I know you want to comfort him and have him near you, but it's not a good idea for several reasons. When a dog sleeps on your bed, you're confusing him. Sleeping in your bed (or one of your kids' beds) with you tells him that he's an equal member of the pack, and that he therefore has as much say about things as you do. This certainly doesn't mean you should banish poor Puppy to the basement to "keep him in his place." But a cozy dog bed or crate placed in the bedroom with you or in one of the kids' rooms will be comfortable for your dog, and better for you to maintain the hierarchy. You need to be the Top Dog in your puppy's or new dog's eyes, especially in the beginning.

There are a number of well-made dog beds available these days, so you won't have to look long or spend a lot to find one that suits your tastes and Puppy's needs. Like collars, beds come in a huge assortment. They're filled with different materials, covered with different fabrics, designed for arthritic dogs, big dogs, tiny dogs, spoiled dogs. This is another area where you can have fun making yourself and Puppy happy. Beds are better than folded blankets or a carpet remnant. Remnants can't be cleaned as thoroughly, and folded blankets may end up being a play toy and will require your constant folding. The only recommendation about doggy beds is that the bed you choose should have an outer shell that can be removed. Many have zippers. Unzip that shell and toss it into the washing machine whenever it starts to look dirty or to stink.

Dog House

Usually these are made out of wood or high-impact plastics. These tend to be made for dogs who are outside dogs. If you're going to keep your dog outside, then you want to make sure the dog house is dry and has some sort of bed. People who keep active sporting and herding breeds still consider this an acceptable way to keep a dog, although experts today tell us that dogs want to be a part of the family unit and suffer psychological damage if they spend too much time alone. But what did you get a dog for if you're going to relegate him to life in a dog house away from his new family? The only justification of a dog house is if you plan on leaving your dog outside and exposed to the elements for any part of the day. In this case, a dog house will provide shade and shelter. Just be sure you keep it clean and comfortable for your dog and that your dog isn't being overexposed to heat, cold, or storms.

Feeding Your Dog

There are so many dog foods on the market today—how can you know whether you're feeding your dog right? Chances are, as long as you're feeding a brand-name dog food that's specific for your dog's stage of life and activity level, you are probably in good hands. Many years ago, this may have not been the case. There were a handful of manufacturers that dominated the industry—Kal Kan, Alpo, and Purina were among the giants.

Using a Doggy Door

For owners who desire their dogs to have access to the outdoors, a small doggy dog built into the back door of the home can be useful. Once you have installed it according to the manufacturer's directions, you may want to try this procedure:

1. At first, keep the doggy door propped in the open position, and lure the dog through several times with a favorite treat.

2. Once the dog is regularly going through, begin to gradually close the door, a bit each day, until after a week or so the door has been completely closed. If you do this gradually enough, the dog will learn that it can push through the door with its head to gain access to the outside.

The only disadvantage of having a doggy door is that it does not discriminate between dogs; the neighbor's dog will learn to use it as readily as your own. You may even find that other dogs, raccoons, or squirrels figure it out!

They manufactured safe dog food. It wasn't exactly exciting, but then again, no one was going to die eating it.

Over the years, things have changed in many of the same ways that our foods have changed. Foods were made to be more palatable, to look nicer, to smell better, and most importantly, to provide the proper nutrients. Gourmet foods appeared on the shelves, and then "scientifically engineered" foods. Today pet food is a billion-dollar industry, close to breakfast cereals and sodas in profitability. As the pet food market has grown and changed, even the old standbys have regrouped and repackaged to produce the quality that consumers demand.

Today, manufacturers spend millions on research and development in order to find some edge in this very competitive market-place. Capitalism has benefited our canine friends, as they now have a healthier, better-tasting and wider variety of foods than they've ever had before.

All this is interesting, but it doesn't help you choose a food, does it?

Follow the Breeder

A safe starter food for those first days and weeks you have your puppy or new dog is the very food he was eating in his previous home (the breeder's). Your puppy's breeder has experience in this area, so it's safe to follow his or her lead when it comes to what to feed your pup. In fact, your breeder will probably send you home with very specific feeding instructions for the first year or so of your puppy's life. There, decision made.

The dog or puppy you'll be bringing home is bound to be nervous already. Since dogs sometimes have adverse reactions to sudden changes in diet, it's best to try to keep some kind of continuity going. This will reassure your dog and should ensure that you won't have to be dealing with any gastrointestinal upsets—not pleasant on your dog's first day in your home!

Make Changes Gradually

If you are going to change dog foods, do it gradually. If you are feeding two cups in the morning, replace half a cup with the new food and mix it with a cup and a half of the old food. Work up to giving him one cup of old food and one cup of new food, do that for several days, and then make the switch completely. Again, the idea is to keep mental continuity as well as physical continuity. A sudden change in diet may elicit adverse reactions, either emotionally or physically. Make this kind of transition as painless as possible.

What Dog Food Contains

This is as simple as shopping for yourself. To find out what's in the food you buy, look at the ingredient list. You're looking for some basic factors here: proteins, carbohydrates, vitamins, minerals, fats, and preservatives. Ingredients are listed in descending order by weight—that is, how much of the ingredient is actually in the product. Therefore, if chicken is right up there at the top, you can be sure you're buying a protein-rich food.

Proteins are present in all kinds of meat and meat by-products, such as chicken, lamb, beef, or chicken meal. These are the best sources of protein for your dog. Many foods use vegetable proteins such as soy. These are harder for your dog to digest, so although you will invariably find them in his food, make sure they aren't a sizable source of that food's ingredients.

Rice, corn, or some other grain should also be among the top four ingredients. That's because carbohydrates, in small quantities, are good for dogs, just as they are for people. However, if there is too much carbohydrate in a dog's diet, you could risk bloat at the worst (inflating of the stomach), or a busy day following Rover on the sidewalks. Wheat and soy can sometimes trigger an allergic reaction in dogs. That's why so many formulas use rice as their starch. Be wary of this.

When it comes to dog food, fat (in moderation) is good! Fat is what keeps the skin supple and the coat shiny. Too little fat, and your dog will end up with a dry, brittle coat and dry skin; too much fat, and you'll end up with an obese, "well-greased" dog. As in all things, moderation and individual consideration are key.

So don't let those pan drippings go to waste, but don't feed a whole dish of them, either. You can drizzle a meal here and there with pan drippings. Your dog will love you for it. Be careful,

Madison Avenue Meets a Dog's Life

Many people know the famous story of Marlboro cigarettes. A long time ago they were a lady's cigarette, and they didn't sell well. Then a bunch of Madison Avenue advertising execs got to gather and recast the entire image of the brand. And thus was the world's bestselling cigarette born. But most people don't know that there's a similar story in the dog food industry.

Kal Kan for years was one of the top dog food brands in America. Back then not too many people really cared what was in dog food. With the onslaught of heightened competition between the major manufacturers, and the new high-end foods coming out, Kal Kan was losing major market share. What's a dog food manufacturer to do?

The execs came up with a plan. They made the food more nutritious and recast the food as an upscale brand—and thus Pedigree was born. Today, Pedigree is one of the best-selling dog foods in America.

though: fat goes bad easily. I've heard of plenty of dog people who've given their dogs rancid fat. The best thing to do is assume that the food you're feeding contains the right balance of fat and other nutrients. Only if you detect a problem in your dog's skin or coat should you consider regular supplements, and even then discuss them with your veterinarian first.

Dogs need vitamins and minerals to keep their bodies functioning, just as we do. A lack of iron means not enough hemoglobin to pick up red blood cells in the lungs, which means a less energetic dog. A lack of vitamin E can result in brittle skin. Vitamin C has been called a wonder vitamin for its curative powers. If you think you should supplement on top of the premium brand you're already feeding, consult your veterinarian first.

Preservatives are of course important in ensuring the quality of the dog food over time. Manufacturers use these ingredients to try and maintain freshness, taste, and texture. However, you want to make sure that many of the preservatives are listed toward the bottom of the ingredient list. Just like you, your dog doesn't need that many preservatives.

It's important to look at the order in which the ingredients appear. Make sure that the higher-quality ingredients are at the top of the list. You really want two proteins (neither of which are vegetable-based) before you get to the carbohydrates. Any kind of chicken, beef, or lamb, or any kind of meal from those meats, is a good bet. Any additives should appear toward the bottom. Some additives can cause an allergic response.

It's not possible to discuss the full range of ingredients and their significance in this book; however, be assured that canine nutrition is a hot topic, and you can find detailed information about it from many sources, including magazines, books, breeders, veterinarians, and on the Internet.

Types of Food

Dry or Wet?

Pet foods come in three standard forms: kibble (dry food), canned (wet food), and semi-moist (burger-type foods). If each claims to be nutritionally complete, do you feed one instead of another or combine them? Your breeder is a good source of advice on this topic.

He or she will have developed a feeding plan that works for the breed. But it doesn't mean you have to stick with it. Many owners feed their dogs a mix of kibble and wet food that's approximately three-quarters dry and one-quarter wet. Both these foods are formulated to provide your dog with the same types and mixtures of proteins, fats, carbohydrates, vitamins, and minerals. While dry food contains the same thing canned food does, it's different because all the water (and often blood) has been taken out of it.

I have talked to many breeders and dog experts, and most feed their dogs commercial, name-brand dry dog foods and supplement those foods occasionally with canned food. There's no denying that canned food adds great flavor to a meal, and a little added meat, which dogs love. The dry food is good not only for its nutritive value, but because it's hard and crunchy. This causes your dog to chew more, and eating the kibble helps clean his teeth by scraping off bits of accumulated plaque or tartar. Wet food, like our soft foods, can accumulate along the gum line and between teeth, contributing to poor oral health. Another consideration, as mentioned earlier, is that mixing in food may adversely affect the dog's digestion. Be careful, and monitor your dog's reactions to any new additions to his regular diet. If your dog does have a sensitive digestive system, then keep him on one type of food (the one which causes him the least trouble) most of the time.

If you feed primarily dry food, you need to keep freshness in mind. The one thing you don't want to do with dry food is store the stuff for long periods of time. The vitamins, which we talked about earlier, are fragile and may break down very quickly sitting in your basement or pantry. Store the food in a cool, dry place, and make sure it's in an airtight container. The idea is to keep the food as fresh as possible for as long as possible. The longer it sits around, the more the beneficial nutrients break down. Even food with plenty of preservatives will go stale if you decide to warehouse vast quantities of it.

Factoring in Your Dog's Age and Activity Level

Part of the difference between the dog foods available today and those that were sold even ten years ago is that scientists now understand that bodies need different nutrients at different ages, and depending on how active the bodies are. A growing puppy or a nursing bitch have much greater nutritional needs than a senior citizen dog whose routine consists of getting up to go to the bathroom, then napping some more. This is another way feeding your dog properly is made easier: Feed a puppy a puppy formula, an allergic dog a hypoallergenic formula, a working dog a protein-rich formula, and so on. Read on.

Puppy Food

Puppy foods are specially formulated to help develop strong bones and good muscle mass. If you read the ingredient panel, you'll see that puppy foods tend to offer more protein and vitamins than normal dog foods and are formulated for excellent health at this very important developmental stage.

If it's so good for him, shouldn't you just keep feeding it to him even after he's grown up? No! It's like being a human. You drink lots of milk when you're growing up, to help develop properly. But as you get older, milk become less important, and too much milk, when you're older, can lead to minor health problems. When your dog is old enough, you should switch him to a food more appropriate for his next life stage, which is typically a maintenance diet.

Maintenance Diet

This is the stage that includes the largest percentage of the dog population; you can think of a maintenance diet as just regular dog food, more or less. In this category, though, there are a multitude of choices. There are high-protein formulas, natural formulas, lamb and rice, chicken and rice, beef, liver, etc. This should be an easy category from which to choose a food, but it's actually not. Each manufacturer claims to have the balance of nutrients that will keep your dog in tiptop shape. The truth is, every dog is an individual, as is every dog owner. Jane might think she's helping Fido by mixing cooked carrots and chicken into his dinner every night, while Joe just pours the food from the bag to the bowl. Who's right and who's wrong? A veterinarian would look at the dogs to find out. Is Jane's dog the picture of good health, slim and alert? Is Joe's dog looking good for the

Chiropractic Services for Your Dog

Many chiropractors now offer services for dogs, cats, horses, and other pets. Why not? If it works for you, it can work for them. Misaligned vertebrae, herniated discs, and pinched nerves can occur in all dogs, particularly acrobatic ones and ones that spend great amounts of time outdoors. Many chiropractors specialize in animals, receiving degrees in veterinary medicine as well as chiropractic. Ask your vet his or her feelings on the matter; he or she should be able to give you a referral. Otherwise, call a chiropractor and ask if he or she works with animals.

kind of breed he is? If both dogs are healthy all over, both are eating well. If you think you need more detailed advice on what to feed or the condition of your dog, consult with your veterinarian.

Lite Formula

Uh-oh, Rover's had too many snacks! Does your dog look like a barrel with four legs? Does it look like Fido suddenly went from happily bounding up the stairs to trudging breathlessly while his stomach drags over the top of every step? Then you should consider switching to a lite formula dog food to get Rover back into good shape.

Lite foods are developed to deliver the same amount of vitamins, minerals, and proteins as other dog foods, but with reduced calories. They tend to contain more fiber, which helps your dog feel full after a meal. Follow the directions and don't overindulge your dog with treats. Remember, while you can be reckless with your own health, you shouldn't be reckless with someone else's, especially your dog's!

Even if your dog's not obese, you may find switching to a lite formula is better for him. Dogs that are in middle age (four to seven or eight years old) but that don't exercise too frequently may be ideal candidates for a lite diet. After all, they don't need the protein and calories their more active friends do, but they still enjoy eating and want their regular healthy meals. Discuss making such a change with your veterinarian first.

Hypoallergenic Diet

Prescription diets are available from your veterinarian. Many of these foods are available from large pet superstores or feed warehouses, if not from your veterinarian. These foods will explain what they contain and what allergies or illnesses they are meant to deal with. Never attempt to put your dog on any kind of restrictive diet without first consulting your veterinarian.

Senior Formulas

When does your dog become a senior? That's a good question that's sometimes difficult to answer. It ranges from breed to breed and dog to dog. Dogs that are eight years old and older at least begin to qualify. But some dogs don't even reach that age, and are considered senior before then. Some dogs race past ten as if they're

still five or six years old. If you are making proper maintenance veterinarian visits, you might want to discuss with your vet whether it's time to put old Fido on a senior formula or not.

Of course, aging is the loss of vigor and ability to perform feats once thought normal during the adult years. Seniors can't run or walk as fast. They sleep even more. Their systems begin to deteriorate just as ours do. Senior dogs need a formula that allows them as much energy as possible without making them heavier and slower. Don't be embarrassed to ask your veterinarian if your old friend may benefit from a senior formula. Hey, you might see her come to new life when she's getting what she needs from her food directly.

When Do I Feed My Dog?

As always, there are no hard and fast rules about how many times a day a dog should be fed. The idea is to maintain a desired body weight—not too heavy, not too thin. It's the amount of food they're eating that remains the most important thing. Other indicators of a happy and healthy dog are the brightness of the eyes, the shininess of the coat, and the activity level of the dog.

Dogs by nature are worse than humans. Many of them would eat to the point of bursting. I've certainly known my share of humans who would do that, too. But dogs do like to eat, in general, and many experts believe that twice a day is correct. It's fun for them as well as a good way for them not to fill up on one meal.

Some experts would argue that instead of making both meals of equal size, you should vary the size between the two feeding times—say, morning and evening. These experts argue that you should feed them the larger meal in the morning. It will give them more time to digest it, and maybe burn it off. Others argue that, especially if you're gone all day, you may want to load your dog up in the morning, too; that way he might be a little sleepier and better behaved while you're off at work.

How Much to Feed?

How often you feed your dog is one thing. How much you feed your dog is another!

Puppies Are Special Eaters

Puppies get to eat more often than adults because of their special nutritional needs.

- Four times a day in little amounts. Usually this is ages 1 to 6 months.
- Three times a day from 6 to 11 months.
- Twice a day thereafter. (I recommend two daily feedings because dogs are so food-driven that mealtime is a highlight of their day. Why not give it to them twice if you can? Also, if your dog becomes ill overnight or during the day, feeding time is the best time to notice that. Some sick dogs will only let on they don't feel well by refusing food.)

Some dogs by sheer weight require smaller amounts. You wouldn't feed a Shih-Tzu the same as you would a retriever. You really should feed a dog what he or she can eat in 10 or 12 minutes' time. Then you might want to feed him that twice a day. Any more than that is probably not necessary. Some dog foods include feeding instructions on the backs of their packages. You might want to look at this as a guideline when you begin. You'll soon learn if you're feeding too much: your dog will lose his waistline and look more portly all around. If this happens, you should immediately cut down on his rations.

What if your dog doesn't finish the food in his bowl? Too bad. Give him 10 to 15 minutes to eat up, and if he hasn't finished everything, take it away and feed him nothing until his next scheduled meal. This forces picky eaters to eat when you feed them. If your dog doesn't finish this time, then if he's not sick, he'll probably finish his food next time. If he shows no interest in the food and seems sluggish or ill in any other way, call the veterinarian.

Treats

From organic cookies cut in fun shapes to beefy chewsticks and beyond, dog treats come in every size, shape, color, and flavor imaginable. There are the recent additions of animal parts (ears, noses, feet, etc.) to the treat bin, and dogs love these; there are also still the ever-popular Milk Bones. The idea is that these treats make dogs' lives fun and extra tasty. However, the word on treats is *moderation*!

Unlike you, your dog cannot feed himself. So, if he develops weight problems due to overeating, especially with things like treats, only you are to blame. Let's be honest—the urge is incredibly strong to give lots of treats to our dogs, especially puppies. However, weight gain is a problem for dogs just as it is for humans and may cause all kinds of illnesses. Treats are not as nutritionally balanced as they are tasty.

One way to reconcile the amount of treats you like to give with how much you should feed your dog is to incorporate regular treats in with the overall amount of food your dog gets in a day. In other words, take out a half-cup of kibble if you know

Is Your Dog Fat?

A good way to test if your dog's too fat is to do the "rib check" test. Standing over your dog with your thumbs lined up along his backbone and your hands reaching over his rib cage, can you feel his ribs below a layer of skin and fur? Looking down on your dog, can you discern a noticeable indent where the ribs end and his back tapers to his tail? Looking at your dog from the side, does the area just behind his ribs rise and tuck in? If you can feel his ribs and detect these indents, your dog is in good shape. If he looks and feels like a sausage, he is one! Talk to your veterinarian about safely putting him on a diet.

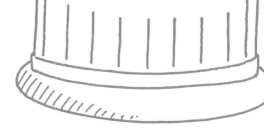

Free Feeding vs. Timed Feeding

Free feeding is when you leave the dog's food available for him to eat all day and the dog eats at his or her leisure. Timed feeding is giving the dog specific amounts of food at regular time periods (breakfast and dinner). Many dog experts agree that free feeding is not a good way to feed any dog for several reasons.

1. When you feed your dog for only 10 minutes twice a day, you are encouraging your dog to think of you as the alpha dog. In the wild, a dog eats according to his station, and the alpha dog establishes that rotation. You establish and keep your place as alpha when you establish the eating time.

2. When a dog eats, he is telling you a lot about himself. Maybe he doesn't like the food. Maybe the food is no good. Maybe the dog isn't feeling well. If one of our dogs ever walked away from his or her dish, the first thing we'd do is take that dog to the vet, if we hadn't already noticed something strange.

3. Free feeding encourages picky eating. Some dogs learn that if they don't eat what's there, if they wait long enough, you'll break down and make them something homemade. Don't do it! Don't worry—they'll eat the next time.

your dog's going to get your leftover Chinese food and a biscuit every time he does his business.

Treats are especially useful during training of any kind, whether it's the simple sit/stay or something more difficult, such as house-training. Treats are a wonderful way to get your dog's attention and encourage good behavior, as well as just letting your dog know he makes you happy.

Water

No discussion of what to feed a dog is complete without mentioning the importance of adequate water. This is a nutrient as important to dogs as it is to other living things. It may be even more important in some cases, because dogs do not sweat. The dog tries to cool off his body by staying out of the sun, sleeping in a cool dry place. He also pants a lot to try to regulate his body temperature. But to cool off or stay hydrated, a dog needs water. This does the job better than anything.

It's important to leave out a clean bowl of water at all times for your puppy or adult. Never regulate the water supply. Dogs can't tell you when they're thirsty, so it's vital that you leave water for them at all times. That way, when they're thirsty, they'll drink.

Another thing—don't let your dog drink out of the toilet. This is not a substitute for a water bowl. I've known few dogs who have died from it, but there are all kinds of bacteria in there. And while your dog has very strong enzymes that might break down lots of other organisms that our bodies can't, it's still not a good idea, no matter how funny or harmless it may seem.

Grooming Your Dog

Grooming your dog is very important. Why? Because the more time you spend taking care of your dog, the happier, healthier, and (you hope) longer his life will be. Does Rover like getting a bath? Not always. Does Spot like getting his toenails clipped? Not likely. But both things are preferable to having stinky, matted coats that are infested with fleas or toenails so long they curl under and pierce the foot pads! These are extremes of lack of grooming, but things like this happen. Not to your dog, though.

The things that we'll cover include brushing, bathing, the importance of toenail clipping, and ear and eye care. These are grooming essentials for all dogs, even if your dog has very short hair. Grooming is not just about making Fido look pretty (do you think he cares how pretty he looks?)—it's about health maintenance. Why do you brush or wash your own hair? Because eventually, if you don't, it feels oily and dirty and unkempt. Washing your dog's skin and coat, keeping his eyes and ears clean and free from infection, and all parts of preventive health care will be discussed in Part 7.

A well-groomed dog will be happier, and you'll be happier because not only will your dog be cleaner—your vet bills will be smaller. With an overall grooming routine, you'll be defeating problems before they arise.

Surprisingly, most dogs are very resistant to baths, ear cleaning, and toenail clipping. They sulk through it at best and can actively protest at worst, causing you to throw down the nail clippers in complete frustration. To prevent this, approach grooming from a positive perspective. With a firm but kind hold on your dog, keep a happy tone in your voice. Barking the word "*no!*" all through one of these sessions is something akin to a nightmare if you consider the experience from his point of view. Have a little heart, be patient and firm, and you will go a long way to having a better-behaved and more cooperative dog.

Brushing

Why do you suppose many dogs stand by you all day long and let you pet them, but then won't let you brush them for a few minutes? Because maybe you're doing it wrong! More often than not the average owner is using the wrong comb or brush, especially in the beginning. Remember—a puppy has sensitive skin, and a spiky brush or hard comb wielded by an overenthusiastic owner can hurt! So be gentle and use a brush that's appropriate for your breed's coat type.

Brushing is a great thing to do. It helps keep the coat in good shape, which also promotes better skin care. Brushing also exposes things like burrs or mats in the coat so you can get them out right away, and will alert you immediately to the presence of fleas.

Brushing is also a way to work with your dog and examine his coat and skin more closely. If there are inconsistencies or infections or rashes, you'll see them a lot more quickly and be able to counteract them much more effectively if you treat your dog to regular brushing. In many cases, brushing is the time when many owners find out about things much more seriously wrong with their dogs, such as tumors (usually in older dogs) or melanomas.

Puppies

If you're going to start with your puppy, then begin with a strategy. With your puppy on a short (but not tight) lead, brush or comb him in long, even strokes, working from the base of the neck toward the tail. Stroke down from the top of the front shoulders toward the feet. Stroke from the bottom of the jaw to the deepest part of the chest. Brush the hairs on his belly (softly!) and on and around his back legs. Don't forget to brush his tail. During these sessions, you want to be making as many happy, cooing noises as possible. You're teaching your puppy to enjoy and welcome being brushed. If you enjoy it, chances are he will, too.

Adults

The same philosophy applies to brushing adults as to brushing puppies: be firm, be gentle, enjoy it, and make it enjoyable. Use the right equipment, and cover all parts of the body.

You may want to include a flea comb in your arsenal of brushes. These are metal combs with very closely spaced prongs. Groomers and owners use these combs to go through a dog's coat. The prongs are so close together that they snare fleas in between them. When you come upon fleas, catch them in the comb, then dip the comb in some rubbing alcohol to stun and remove the fleas. When you're finished, be sure to put a tight-fitting lid on the jar of alcohol, or flush it down the toilet to be sure you're disposing of the fleas. If your dog has fleas, you need to consult the health section of this book and start a flea program immediately. Chances are your dog, house, and yard will need to be treated to remove them completely.

Baths

Dogs react differently to water in different situations. Take the beach, for example. Exley, our German Shorthaired Pointer, loves the beach, racing up and down it when we go, excited as

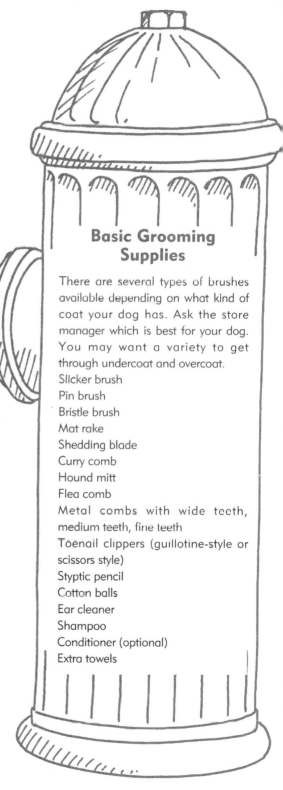

Basic Grooming Supplies

There are several types of brushes available depending on what kind of coat your dog has. Ask the store manager which is best for your dog. You may want a variety to get through undercoat and overcoat.

Slicker brush
Pin brush
Bristle brush
Mat rake
Shedding blade
Curry comb
Hound mitt
Flea comb
Metal combs with wide teeth, medium teeth, fine teeth
Toenail clippers (guillotine-style or scissors style)
Styptic pencil
Cotton balls
Ear cleaner
Shampoo
Conditioner (optional)
Extra towels

Dealing with Matted Hair

Matted fur is one of the greatest enemies of longhaired dogs. Imagine having a big wad of bubble gum stuck in your hair—that's the way dogs feel about mats. They are uncomfortable and unpleasant. Because they trap moisture in and under them, they can damage skin and cause infections. In some cases, you can detangle the mats yourself. Sometimes pouring a little vegetable oil on the spot will help you work a stubborn burr out of longer hair, and you can try a commercial detangler for use on human hair. It's not as easy as it sounds. Trying to work a big mat is a difficult and painstaking job, with few rewards. More often than not, mats need to be cut off. Remember, the dog won't look worse than he does with the mat. He'll be more comfortable, and in the end, the hair will grow back.

can be. Throw a ball into the ocean for him? No problem. Exley dives in at top speed, puts his head into the wave, comes up for air, finds the ball, and brings it back to land. Of course, he wants you to throw the ball again, and again, and again. Our German Shepherd Chelsea got hit by a wave once, and she refused to go near the water again. Soaking wet, she walked around the beach as far from the water as possible, with her tail between her legs. Eventually, she came up to the water's edge to try and wrestle the ball from Exley. That was it. Near a pond or pool they invariably act the same.

Switch scenes. We are now in the backyard at bath time. Chelsea is not thrilled, but she will not retreat or withdraw from the water, even when it's sprayed on her from the hose. Exley, on the other hand, has to be dragged toward the dreaded buckets, and all during the bath he sulks, even trying to pull away if he sees a chance. Completely different reactions to water in completely different situations. Go figure.

Bathing your dog may not be one of the most pleasant experiences, but it doesn't have to be that bad if you once again employ patience, perseverance, and firm kindness. Before you wash your dog, it's usually a good idea to brush him, especially during the shedding season. First put cotton balls in your dog's ears to keep too much water from getting in them. Then wet down the dog with warm water. Start with a big gob of shampoo on your hands and start at the base of the neck, working your way along the body toward the tail. There are many excellent dog shampoos available on the market that are formulated for different coat types and different skin conditions and even to help ward off ticks and fleas. Just be sure you read the instructions carefully—some of these are not suitable for puppies. There are plenty of shampoos that are, so don't let that stop you from exposing Junior to bath time.

Continuing with the washing, as you work your way down the dog's body, rub in a circular motion. Don't be too rough. Make sure to work the shampoo into the dog's coat and skin under the chest and over his hindquarters thoroughly. Make sure you get the tail. Be sure to wet his head before applying a *small* amount of shampoo that you have rubbed between your hands.

Cautiously shampoo his head and ears, being careful not to get soap in his eyes, which will sting. Sometimes it's safer to just give your dog's face a sponge bath without shampoo.

Rinse your dog with lots and lots of clean warm water. I know many people who, after bathing their dog in the tub, turn on the shower to rinse him off. A shower massage unit works well because you can take it down from its perch in the tub and basically hose down your dog in the tub. When you're done rinsing, let your dog shake himself (close the shower curtain if he's in the tub!). Believe me, you'll towel him again and again and not be able to dry him as well as when you let him shake once in an enclosed area.

After the bath and a good shake, you have to dry off your dog so he doesn't catch a chill. If he'll stand for it, you can do what the pros do and use a hair dryer on your dog. This will fluff his flowing tresses and give him that just-primped look. Show dogs are so used to the bath and drying routine that they fall asleep while their owners carefully blow-dry and brush their fur into place. During post-bath brushing, much hair that hasn't actually come off (and lots does) with the water may have been loosened. A quick combing will make the coat that much nicer and keep that much fur from collecting in the corners of your house. When we bathe our dogs, we also take the time to wash the covers of their beds on the same day. Who wants a nice clean dog to go and lie down on something dirty?

Clipping Toenails

For the longest time, our dogs' toenails were cut by professionals. That's how my parents dealt with this, so it's what I thought one did. When I got my first dog, however, I decided I was going to clip his toenails. I did the first and second claws correctly. The third one I cut to the quick and blood went squirting everywhere like a bad comedy skit. My poor dog started howling and pulling away. In the end my kitchen looked like a Quentin Tarantino set. I swore I would never do it again. Eventually I relented. I watched friends who also had dogs and watched them cut their dogs' nails. I watched and learned. Some of us have that opportunity, and some of us don't. If you do, take advantage of it.

Why do we cut our dog's toenails? Because if we didn't, the nails would grow so long that eventually they would start to curl. When the dog steps down on his foot, the nails are pushed up at the base

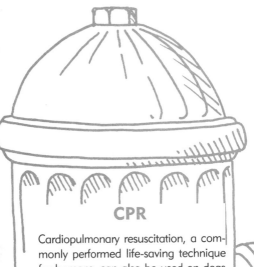

CPR

Cardiopulmonary resuscitation, a commonly performed life-saving technique for humans, can also be used on dogs (and cats), though it is rarely needed. There could come a time when, because of shock, choking, or drowning, your dog must rely on you to perform CPR. Signs that CPR is needed include no pulse or heartbeat, unconsciousness, or cessation of breathing. CPR should begin no longer than a few minutes after heart or breathing functions cease, or else permanent brain damage and death can result.

If your dog has stopped breathing:

1. Place it on its side, open its mouth, pull the tongue out, and check for any foreign objects that might be stuck in there.
2. Check for mucus or blood buildup, then close the dog's mouth and place your mouth over its muzzle, completely covering the nose.
3. Blow easily into its nose and watch to see if the dog's chest is expanding. Repeat this twelve times per minute for as long as necessary.

(Continued)

because the nails are too long. The dog actually walks as if he's lame. This is a tragic condition, and one that's so easily avoided.

When clipping nails, you have to be patient with your dog, and you have to be careful. The idea is never to get too aggressive about cutting the toenails. You just want to clip the end off, no matter how long the nails are. Even if they still look long after cutting off just the tips, don't worry. Ten days later you can get right back at it. That's because as you cut the toenails, the quick recedes. The quick is the inner, fleshy part of the nail, where blood flows and there are nerve cells. For dogs with white nails, you can see the quick (it's the dark shading about half way up the nail). With black nails, you really can't guess where it starts in the nail. Best to be conservative.

What do you do when you have cut the quick? Well, there are different types of clotting agents that are available at the pet supply store. If you really don't have any of that, corn starch is usually pretty good. It also acts as a clotting agent. Try putting direct pressure on the wound, with a clean cloth. Make sure there's plenty of the agent or corn starch before you apply the direct pressure. The wound usually stops bleeding in a few minutes. If you just nicked the quick, the scary episode will be over quickly. However, if you do real damage, you might want to rush your dog to the vet immediately.

So, how do you go about cutting your dog's nails? Well first, you need to get the dog used to having his feet handled. Many dogs don't like this. Reassure him by asking him to lie down on his side, then pet each one of his paws, gently. Say nice things to the dog. Give him treats for his good behavior. Do this several times. Then, on the appointed day, have him lie down on his side. Reward him. Then take one paw at a time and start to clip. Remember, don't cut too far down. Just the tips. What I do is to leave a cookie just beyond Exley's reach, near his head. He pays more attention to it than he does to my clipping.

Ear and Eye Care
Cleaning Ears

The first thing you need to know is that dogs with floppy ears tend to need more attention than dogs with cropped or short ears. Why? Because it gets hot and ugly underneath the ear flap. Circulation of air isn't good in there, and the warm, moist conditions are perfect breeding grounds for bacteria and ear mites. Signs of ear problems are the three following traits:

1. Shaking head constantly.
2. Scratching ears often.
3. Stinky ears: you can smell them from here!

If your dog is showing (or emitting) any of those signs, then it's time to clean those ears. As with everything else, there's a right way and a wrong way to do this. The wrong way is to pry into the delicate ear canal with a cotton swab. The right way is to go to your nearest pet store and find a good ear cleaning solution. Then go home, load up a cotton ball with some solution, and start gently swabbing the inner folds of the ear. Don't go too deep into the ear. Just swab between the crevices of what's called the outer ear canal. It might take three or four cotton balls before you're able to clean his ears out completely.

After you've cleaned the outer ears, squirt a small amount of the solution into the ears, hold the ear flap against the side of your dog's head and rub the ear around a bit to work the solution in. Swab off one more time. Read the directions to properly apply your particular brand. Afterwards, you and your dog will be much happier, and you'll avoid costly veterinarian bills from having to deal with ear infections. A note of caution: If the ear looks really red or raw and your dog is pawing at your hand in pain while you're trying to clean his ears, call the veterinarian. He's got a severe infection.

It's important to note that dogs who suffer problem ears tend to be repeat offenders. In other words, if your dog has had ear problems once, they are more likely to recur. Keeping your dog's ears clean will keep recurrences to a minimum.

Cleaning Eyes

The most important thing about the eyes is that they are the windows to your dog's soul—and his health. Your dog's eyes should always appear alert and clear (unless he's very old). In

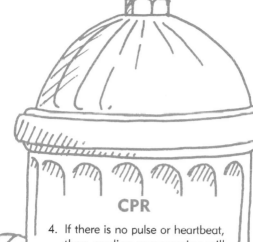

CPR

4. If there is no pulse or heartbeat, then cardiac compression will have to be combined with artificial respiration if the dog is to survive. It will be helpful to have a friend perform the compressions while you continue artificial respiration, but you can perform both if needed. In between each breath (given every five seconds), place the middle three fingers of your favored hand over the dog's heart, at about the fifth rib, and press with medium pressure, then release. The ribs should compress about 1 inch. Compress the chest five times between breaths.

5. Continue compressions and artificial respiration until you get to the vet, or until the dog begins breathing on its own again. Use your best judgment as to when you should stop administering CPR; if the dog does not respond within twenty minutes, and there is no hope of getting help from a vet, it might be best to stop.

terms of hygiene, it's always important to wipe away the crust that builds up in the corners of your dog's eyes. While you might not think it bothers them, it does indeed. Left unchecked, it often is the source of irritation, or worse, may instigate an infection. Make sure to wipe your dog's eyes whenever possible.

Some breeds have large, protruding eyes that are especially prone to getting dirt and dust in them, and to risking abrasion and infection. These include Boston Terriers, Chihuahuas, Bulldogs, Cocker Spaniels, and others. Some breeds, such as Bloodhounds, have droopy eyes. These dogs, too, need extra-special eye care. Regardless of your breed, checking the eyes should be part of your dog's near-daily grooming ritual.

Professional Dog Groomers

Especially if you own a longhaired breed or a breed that needs a particular look, such as a Schnauzer, a Poodle, a Shih Tzu, or a terrier, you may want to use the services of a professional groomer for your dog at least twice a year. Professional groomers are very experienced and will make sure all the proper things are done to your dog. They are expert at clipping nails, cleaning his ears and eyes, and bathing and trimming the coat to near perfection. You may not recognize your dog after a day at the groomer's! There is no shame in leaving your dog with a groomer. You can't possibly know the many trade secrets they've learned from their years of experience and network of mentors and friends. Try them—you'll like them.

Housebreaking

The first thing every new owner should know before bringing a dog into the house is how to teach him where to relieve himself. The good news is that all dogs can be housebroken. The bad news is that a dog rarely becomes housebroken by just being let out several times a day. This comprehensive housebreaking plan requires dedication—but it's simple and foolproof:

- Crate your dog when you can't watch him so he won't relieve himself (if you prefer, use another type of space, as long as it accomplishes the same goal)
- Supervise (umbilical cord or shadow) your dog when he is out of his crate
- Feed him a high-quality diet at scheduled times (no treats, people food, or edible toys such as pig's ears)
- Teach him to eliminate on command
- Clean up his accidents immediately (remove debris or moisture, then treat with neutralizer and cleaner)
- Never correct him after the fact
- Keep a log of his habits (when and where he pooped or peed, and when and how much he ate and drank)

Crating

Until a dog is perfectly trained, he needs a safe place in which he can do nothing wrong. So when you can't keep your eyes glued to your dog and monitor his every move, confine him to a place where inappropriate behavior—soiling, stealing, shredding, chewing or scratching—isn't

an option. I suggest crating because it eliminates the risk that he'll damage woodwork, flooring, wall coverings, or cabinetry.

Assuming you ultimately want your dog to enjoy freedom in the house, crating is almost a rearing necessity. Crating is widely accepted by behaviorists, dog trainers, veterinarians, and knowledgeable dog owners as a humane means of confinement. Provided your dog is properly introduced as specified below, you should feel as comfortable about crating him in your absence as you would securing a toddler in a highchair at mealtime.

Whether the enclosure is a room, hallway, kennel, or crate, it should be:

- The right size. It should be large enough that the dog can stand without his shoulders touching the ceiling of the crate, but if he soils the area, it's probably too large for him.
- Safe. Homemade enclosures may save you money, but you would feel awful if he poked himself in the eye, stabbed or hanged himself, or swallowed wood splinters or material such as wallpaper or blankets because you ignored potential dangers. Make sure there are no protrusions or sharp edges, and no ingestible components.
- Dogproof. If he is prone to chewing, scratching, or jumping up, prevent access to any woodwork, linoleum, furniture, counters, garbage, or windows so your home doesn't become a victim of your puppy's destructiveness during his training period.

Crating Introduction

Allow your dog to dine in his new crate. Place him and his food inside and sit with your back blocking the doorway of the crate. Read a book until he's finished eating, then take him out. For his next meal, prop the crate door and sit at the opening with your dog and his food. Place a few pieces of kibble inside at a time so he is walking in and out to eat. If your crate has a metal pan, place a mat on it to provide good traction and reduce the noise caused by the dog's movement. To encourage your dog to go in more readily, arrange a barrier on both sides of the crate so he is channeled inside.

Next, teach your dog to enter and exit enclosures on command. Put his paws right in front of the opening. With one hand on his collar and the other pointing into the crate, command "Bed." Pull him in by the collar as you place your hand under his tail and behind his rear legs to prevent him from backing away. If necessary, lift him in. Immediately invite him out with the "Chin-touch Okay" and try five more quick repetitions.

Practice several repetitions of this routine three times or more every day so he goes to bed on command—without being enclosed. If you shut him in and leave him every time he is put in the enclosure, he may develop a bad association with crating. But when he learns to go in the crate on command as a result of frequent practice, he is more likely to also accept being enclosed.

Read the Labels

Always check the label of a toxic product for instructions regarding the proper action to take in case of ingestion by a human or an animal. Antidotes as well as symptoms may be listed, as well as whether to induce vomiting or to simply dilute the poison by administering fluids.

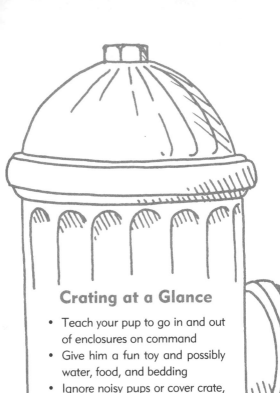

If you reserve his favorite toy for the times he spends in the crate, he may actually look forward to crating as an opportunity to play with it. Leave food and water out of the crate; dogs don't need it in there and most will dump or scatter it instead of eating or drinking. Create a peaceful environment by covering the crate with a sheet or, if his tendency is to pull it in, surround the crate with a couple of stiff panels for a more enclosed, denlike atmosphere. Avoid leaving a TV or radio on because your puppy may become a victim of unsettling and noisy programming and advertisements. Replace that cacophony with white noise; the gentle whir of a fan puts dogs at ease.

Sometimes a dog will bark, yodel, whine, or howl when crated. Unless he is trying to tell you he has to go potty, ignore any noise he might make. Most dogs will quiet down if you act oblivious. If yours doesn't and you or your family members are losing sleep or sanity, startle him into being quiet. Try throwing an empty soda can containing a few pennies at his covered crate, clap your hands sharply twice, or anoint him with the spray of a water pistol between the eyes. You can also create an earthquake by attaching the leash to his crate and giving it a jerk as he barks. If he's keeping you awake at night, move the crate close to your bedroom door. This way you won't have to leave your bed to administer a correction. If you're using a leash jerk, attach the handle to your bedpost for easy access. Once he's learned to sleep quietly through the night, gradually move the crate back to the original location.

Umbilical Cording

A crate-trained dog is not house-trained. Your dog is likely to attempt naughty behaviors when loose, and therefore he needs plenty of supervised exploration to learn the house rules. If your dog is out of his crate, keep your eyes glued on him or, better still, umbilical cord him so when you can't follow him, he'll follow you. This gives you the opportunity to cut short misbehaviors before they become habits.

Tie his leash to your belt on your left side. Give him only enough slack to keep him at your side without your legs becoming entangled. If he attempts to jump up, chew, bark, or relieve himself without your approval, you'll be able to stop him instantly by jerking the lead. You'll be able to train your dog as you tinker, work, or relax at home.

Crating at a Glance

- Teach your pup to go in and out of enclosures on command
- Give him a fun toy and possibly water, food, and bedding
- Ignore noisy pups or cover crate, or use startling correction (water pistol, shaker can, hand clap, or leash jerk)

Umbilical cording is a fantastically simple technique and an important training tool, which every able-bodied household member should use. You can even umbilical cord two dogs at once. Or when one pet is trained and the other isn't, you can cord the untrained dog while the giving the reliable one his freedom.

Schedules

Most dogs leave their litter to enter their new home at about two months of age. At this age, the pups eat a lot and drink a lot. They have limited ability to control their elimination and no idea that it might be important. Feeding and potty times should be adjusted to help the puppy reach his potential in the housebreaking department as quickly as possible.

Diet and Feeding

Feed specific amounts of high-quality puppy food at specific times. If your dog eats on a schedule, he's more likely to potty at regular, predictable times. Pups should be fed three times a day up to three or four months of age, and after that can be fed twice daily for the rest of their lives. If your schedule requires you to be gone for six or more hours at a time, feedings can be disproportionate. Consider feeding a larger portion when you will be home for a few hours and will therefore be able to give him the opportunity to relieve himself.

Feed a high-quality diet. Buy a dry kibble made of nutritious, easily digestible ingredients, minimal fillers, and no food coloring (these will stain your carpet if the dog has an accident—not only will you be miffed at your dog, you'll be angry with the dog food company and have a lasting memory of the event). You may pay a little more, but your dog will eat a bit less and therefore eliminate less. You will find these foods at better pet shops, or your veterinarian may sell them. Ask your breeder or veterinarian to recommend a good diet.

Look for signs that the food you've chosen agrees with your dog. He should maintain the proper weight and muscle tone, have a healthy sheen to his coat, and display plenty of energy. Gas, loose stools, constipation, itchy skin, bald patches, or listlessness indicate a problem that may be diet-related. Investigate possible solutions by consulting with your veterinarian. When switching food, do so gradually over a period of at least five days. To maintain the firmness of his stools, begin with a 20–80 ratio of new to familiar foods, and switch the ratios 10–20% daily.

Dogs experiencing difficulty with housebreaking will achieve greater control sooner if they're fed a single, totally consistent diet. Therefore, avoid giving your dog treats, people food, or edible toys such as pig's ears, rawhides, or cowhoofs. Additionally, dogs who are not nutritionally indulged are less likely to become overweight or aggressively possessive when food is near.

Flood Control

With pups who urinate frequently, you might try restricting water. But before doing so, tell your veterinarian about your plans. He or she might want to perform some diagnostic tests beforehand to rule out bladder or urinary tract problems. In severe cases where, despite a clean bill of health, the pup still continually urinates, offer water only before taking him out to relieve himself. With pups who just can't seem to hold it throughout the night, withhold water for three hours before going to bed.

Don't necessarily put food and water in the crate with your dog when you leave. He will be more likely to have to soil if you do. Besides, most pups will dump the bowls and swim in the food and water, rather than eating and drinking.

Elimination on Command

Understand how much *your* puppy needs to go potty and teach him to do it on command. When active rather than resting, you will notice a significant increase in the frequency of elimination. At two to four months of age, most pups need to relieve themselves after waking up, eating, playing, sleeping, and drinking—perhaps as often as every 30 to 45 minutes, depending on the type and amount of activity. At four months, the dog may be developed like an adult internally, but expect him to behave like a puppy. Most adult dogs can gradually and comfortably adapt to three to five outings per day.

Teach your dog to eliminate on command. This lesson is handy both when he is too distracted and won't potty or when he's on a surface that he's inclined not to potty on—for example, a kennel run, wet grass, or where other dogs have been. Others will go potty only if they're in a particular area or taken for a walk. By teaching your dog to eliminate on command, you can get him to go where you want and when you want, and simplify the housebreaking process. Here's how to do it.

Leash your dog and take him to the potty area. When he begins the sniffing and circling ritual which immediately precedes elimination, start chanting a phrase like "Potty, Hurry Up." What you say is unimportant, but it should sound melodic and should always be the same phrase. Use the same words for defecation and urination. After a week of chanting while your dog is relieving himself, begin the chant as soon as you enter the potty area.

Schedule Guidelines

6–14 weeks
Feed: 3 times a day
Water: Free access except withhold water while crated and about two hours before bed
Potty breaks: Every 4–6 hours if crated after urination and defecation; every hour (give or take 30 minutes) if the pup is out of the crate exploring

3–4 months
Feed: 2–3 times a day
Water: Same, except if necessary to help develop control, withhold water for hours at a time. Always allow your dog ample opportunity to drink at least five times a day (perhaps give water every time he goes out to ensure adequate hydration)
Potty breaks: Every 4–8 hours if crated after urination and defecation; every 45 minutes to 3 hours if out of the crate and active

4–6 months
Feed: Twice a day
Water: Same
Potty breaks: Every 6–9 hours if crated after urination and defecation; every 1–4 hours if out of the crate and active

6 months and up
Feed: Twice a day
Water: Free access (unless limiting is necessary)
Potty breaks: 3–5 times a day

"He forgets to relieve himself when he is outdoors—but he remembers as soon as he's back in the house."

Leashing your dog during potty breaks will enable you to keep your dog moving and sniffing within the appropriate area, and thus speed the process of elimination. If you sense your dog is about to become distracted from his duty of looking for a potty spot, use a light, quick jerk on the leash as you slowly move about the area yourself.

"He takes forever to go potty."

Only give your dog a few minutes to potty. If you give him twenty minutes, he is likely to demand thirty next time. After a couple of minutes, put him back in his crate long enough to make him thankful for the next potty opportunity you give him.

Have your dog earn playtime by pottying first and playing afterward. Potty breaks will be much less time-consuming if your dog learns to associate the initial act of walking outdoors with the act of going potty, not playing.

And finally, avoid praising or rewarding with food, since anticipating those things may actually distract him from his primary goal. Besides, the sensation of going potty is a reward in itself.

"I know he needs to relieve himself, but sometimes he won't have a bowel movement."

If your dog won't go potty but you know he should, run him a couple of blocks to stimulate his metabolism. If that doesn't work, try the popular trick of dog show exhibitors: Take a whole paper match stick and put just the flint end into the dog's rectum. If your dog has a tail, hold and lift its base while you insert the flint portion of the match stick. If your dog has a nub instead of a tail, you'll hold and lift more skin than tail.

Then take him to the potty area and if he needs to poop, he probably will. After a couple of experiences with the matchstick and your chant, your dog is likely to have made the association between your chant and going potty.

"My adolescent dog rarely has accidents, but I take him out constantly. How can I safely cut back on his outings and ensure that his housebreaking won't regress?"

Many owners make the mistake of continually taking a dog out before he really needs to go. Although they do so hoping he won't soil the house, they are actually preventing him from developing the capacity to hold it. Since housebreaking is a matter of teaching the dog to control his bladder and bowels until he has access to the outdoors, taking the dog out too frequently slows the housebreaking process. When you think he doesn't need to go out but he does, try umbilical cording or crating him for a half-hour before taking a walk.

How to Handle Messes

No matter how careful you are, occasionally inappropriate elimination happens. If your dog has an accident:

- Never correct the dog after the fact. Do scold yourself by saying "How could I have let that happen?"
- Startle him by tossing something at him or picking him up in midstream and carrying him outside to stop him in the act.
- Clean up messes immediately. Remove debris and blot up any moisture, then use a cleaning solution, and finally treat the soiled area with an odor neutralizer.

Keep a Diary

Write down the amounts and times you feed your dog, and any unusual consistency of his stool. If you later encounter a training or health problem, your notes may make the solution apparent.

Also, make note of when you are taking your dog out and what he is doing. Document any accidents so you are alert to the potentially problematic times and can make needed adjustments. Take inventory of when your dog isn't going because, at least 90 percent of the time, he should go potty when you take him out.

A truly housebroken dog is repulsed by the notion of going in the house. Every consecutive hour your dog spends wandering the house, sniffing and exploring, without an accident brings you closer to this ideal, but anytime he uses the house as a toilet, previous good behavior is usually canceled out.

"How long does the housebreaking process take?"

Plan on a year or more to complete the housebreaking process. Although your dog may be flawless for days, weeks, or months, under certain conditions any dog can backslide.

Can I Make a Living in an Animal-Related Career?

There are a number of career choices you can make that either directly or indirectly involve animals. Some examples are:

Animal Control Officer
Animal Rights Activist
Breeder
Groomer
Pet Products Designer
Pet Psychologist
Pet Sitter
Pet Store Salesperson
Shelter Employee
Trainer
Veterinarian
Zoo Employee

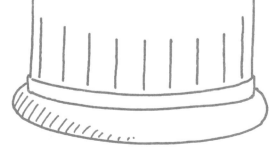

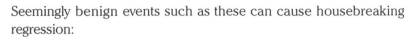

Seemingly benign events such as these can cause housebreaking regression:

- Changes in diet can disrupt normal elimination patterns.
- Weather changes (too hot, cold or wet, or noisy thunderstorms) can make outings unproductive potty times.
- New environments (vacation homes, new house, or friend's house) may be treated as an extension of his potty area rather than his living quarters.
- Some medications (like allergy medications) and certain conditions (like hormone changes associated with estrus) can cause more frequent elimination.

Paper Training

Owning a small dog offers lots of advantages. One of these is that if you don't want to have to walk him outdoors, you can teach him to eliminate on papers indoors. To start, get full-sized newspapers (not tabloids) and a16-square-foot wire-mesh exercise pen, available from dog supply catalogs such as RC Steele (1-800-872-3773) or by special order from a pet shop. Place the pen on an easy-to-clean floor and line the bottom with newspapers opened flat out. For one week, keep your dog in the fully papered pen anytime you aren't supervising or exercising. Then, put a bed in the pen and gradually reduce the papered portion to one full-sized newspaper, overlapping five sheets to ensure proper absorption. Once is he is pottying on the paper, open up the pen within a small room or hall. When he consistently soils on the paper, gradually give him access to the house, room by room, when you are able to supervise him. Shuttle him over to the papers if he attempts to go elsewhere. If he begins missing paper to any degree, follow the confinement and umbilical cording procedure described for outdoor training, except take the dog to the paper, rather than the outdoors, to eliminate.

Once trained, some paper-trained dogs only go on their papers; others prefer the outdoors but will use papers if necessary. You can paper-train a previously outdoor-trained dog and vice versa, but you'll avoid extra work by deciding what you want up front.

Potty Training

Until your dog is perfectly potty trained, remember:

1. A dog who can hold it for long periods while he's in his cage or at night is not necessarily well on his way to being housebroken. Don't judge his capacity and trustworthiness by his behavior while crated. Metabolism slows down with inactivity, so even a totally untrained dog may not soil for up to twelve hours when he's caged. Dogs aren't trained until they understand that it's okay to move about, explore, and go potty outdoors, but they must "hold it" as they move about and explore indoors.

2. Dogs enjoy playing, observing, and investigating and often forget about going potty when they're left alone outdoors. Don't let your dog out without supervision and assume that he went. Even if your dog has just spent a lot of time outdoors, he may mess soon after he comes back inside.

3. Dogs often indicate when they want to go outdoors and play, instead of when they need to potty. Don't rely on or encourage him to tell you he wants to go out. Many dogs will indicate frequently and always eliminate when taken to the potty area. Their bladder and bowel capacity and control will be underdeveloped. So, if your dog is used to going out on demand to go potty, he may have to relieve himself immediately whether you're available or not.

Don't encourage indication. Instead, train your puppy to control his elimination with supervision, a proper diet, and a reasonable "potty break" schedule. Once he's housebroken, you could encourage him to bark, paw, or ring a bell by bumping it with his nose before letting him out. But housebroken dogs don't need to be taught how or when to indicate. If the need arises, they'll get your attention or hold it if you aren't available.

Puppy Kindergarten

Puppies have so much potential, curiosity, and intelligence. That's why puppy training begins the moment your dog comes into your house—whether you want it to or not. Soiling, biting, jumping, barking, and running are natural behaviors; as a new puppy parent, it is up to you to show him where and when those behaviors are appropriate and, more importantly, where they are inappropriate. Begin teaching and socializing your puppy as early as eight weeks of age if he is properly vaccinated and his good health is confirmed by your veterinarian. Although the techniques in this chapter are best suited for puppies two to four months of age, you'll find the information valuable when training older dogs, too.

Socialization

Congratulations on this great new addition to your family. Now, make sure you show him off. Not for your sake, but for his. This eminently important process is called socialization. When the socialization of puppies is neglected, they never reach their potential. They're less adaptable, harder to live with, and, in my observations, less happy. A dog who's received frequent and early socialization thrives on environment changes, interactions, and training procedures. He is also more likely to tolerate situations he's accidentally, and unfortunately, exposed to—such as kisses from a pushy visitor or a Big Wheel riding over his tail.

Usually, the socialization process consists of providing a safe environment for your dog to explore. Concentrate on four areas: socializing your dog to people, places, things, and other animals. In unpredictable or potentially unsafe situations, keep your dog leashed. That lets you prevent a wobbly youngster from trying to pick him up, and you can keep him off the sidewalk as a skateboard zips by.

Socialize him to people, making sure he gets plenty of experiences with both genders and a variety of races and ages. Go to the park, a parade, the beach, outside a shopping center, or to an airport if you're bold enough to pretend you belong there. Occasionally, leave your puppy in the care of a trustworthy, level-

Dog Equipment

Equipment such as crates, Bitter Apple spray and cream, doggy seatbelts, Nylabones, Kong toys, and sterilized bones are referred to in the following chapters. These common items are available through pet stores, mail-order, and, in many cases, discount department stores.

headed friend for a minute, an hour, or a day. Your objective is to teach the pup to be self-assured in your absence; therefore, don't say good-bye or hello to the puppy. Treat the situation as a nonevent so your puppy is less likely to experience separation anxiety.

Think about items people carry and equipment they use. Expose your dog to wheelchairs, canes, bicycles, lawn mowers, Big Wheels, and roller skates.

Take your puppy as many places as possible so he becomes a savvy traveler who is accustomed to elevators, stairways, manholes, and grates. Acclimate him to walking on a variety of surfaces such as gravel, wire, sand, cobblestone, linoleum, and brick. Because some dogs prefer to eliminate only in their own backyard, teach him to eliminate on command (see page 122) in different areas, so weekend trips and the like won't be a problem. If you want to foster enjoyment of the water and your dog isn't a natural pond puppy, walk him on-leash on the shoreline. Once he is at ease with that, venture into the water. Gently tighten the leash as you go, forcing him to swim a couple of feet before you let him return to the shoreline. Never throw any dog into the water.

Let him get to know other animals—dogs, cats, chickens, horses, goats, birds, guinea pigs, and lizards. Often, upon meeting a new species, a puppy is startled, then curious, and finally some become bold or aggressive. For his own protection and for the protection of the other animal, always keep him leashed so you can control his distance and stop unwanted behaviors by enforcing obedience commands.

Whatever you are socializing your puppy to—animals, objects, or people—approach in a relaxed manner and avoid any situation that would intimidate the average puppy, such as a group of grade schoolers rushing at him. Be prepared for three reactions: walking up to check it out and sniff, apprehensive barking with hackles raised, or running away. No matter his response, remain silent. In the first, and by the way, best, scenario, he is thinking rationally and investigating his environment. Don't draw attention to yourself by talking, praising or petting. Allow him to explore uninterrupted. This good boy is entertaining himself and being educated at the same time. If your puppy lacks confidence or displays fear, don't console him, because this will reinforce his fear. Use the leash to prevent

him from running away. If he is still slightly uncomfortable, drop some tasty bits of food (such as slivers of hot dogs) on the ground. Most puppies will relax after a nibble or two because the uncomfortable situation has been positively associated with food.

If loud noises frighten your puppy, desensitize him by allowing him to create racket. Offer him a big metal spoon with a little peanut butter on it. Give him an empty ½ gallon or gallon milk jug with the cap removed and a bit of squeeze cheese in the rim to bat around. It won't be long before he is creating hubbub and loving it. Of course, if the clamoring drives you nuts, feel free to limit his playtime with these items. Also socialize your puppy to walking on leash, riding in the car, and being examined and groomed.

Leash Breaking for Puppies

Put a buckle-type collar and lightweight leash on your puppy. For 10 to 30 minutes, 3 times a day for a week, watch him drag it around the house or yard. Better still, attach the lead prior to playtime with another dog or a favorite toy. He'll step on it, scratch his neck, refuse to move, or maybe even scream, all of which you should ignore. Since many dogs like to chew the lead, you may need to thoroughly spray it before each session with a chewing deterrent such as bitter apple.

When he is comfortable about dragging the leash, pick up the handle and coax him to walk on your left side by carrying and squeezing an interesting squeaky toy. If he really fights you, attach the leash handle to a doorknob and let him struggle with that while you drink a cup of coffee. Watch him out of the corner of your eye to confirm that his antics aren't endangering him. Repeat the procedure for five or ten minutes at a time until he is relaxed before attempting to walk with the leash in hand again.

"My puppy pulls ahead and sometimes tries to walk behind me and then on the wrong side. How can I teach him to walk at my left side?"

Practice "sneakaways" on a six-foot leash. Put your right hand with your thumb through the loop and the excess slack in your right hand so the leash is draped across your left thigh. Then walk with your puppy on your left side. If he attempts to forge ahead, pivot 180 degrees to the right and walk briskly in the opposite direction.

Remember, he can't pull you if you refuse to follow. If he lags behind, keep your left hand off the leash and continue walking ahead so your thigh will pull into the leash. This will prevent him from walking on the wrong side and encourage him to remain at your left side.

Car Riding

As soon as your puppy is large enough, teach him to enter and exit the car on command. Practice this by leashing him, walking him up to the car, and commanding him to go in as you give him a boost. Invite him out of the car by calling "come" as you gently pull the leash. Practice several of these, several times a day, until he goes in and out on command. Even before your puppy is ready for that lesson, decide where you'd like him to ride. Crating is the safest option. If it isn't the most convenient, try a doggy seatbelt, which is available at many pet shops or by mail order. Don't feed your puppy for hours prior to riding if he has any tendency toward carsickness. It is also a good idea to keep the air temperature inside the car comfortably cool (if you roll down a window, choose one that your puppy cannot stick his head out of). Additionally, you'll reduce the chance of motion sickness by avoiding bumpy roads and abrupt stops or turns.

Grooming and Examinations

This section addresses training your dog to accept grooming and examinations. As to the specific grooming procedures, techniques, and products to use, talk to an expert such as a breeder, handler, or groomer. The manufacturers of Oster clippers offer detailed booklets and videos on many breeds. These are available from Oster retailers. You can also refer to an all-breed grooming book such as *Stone Guide to Dog Grooming*.

Begin by acclimating your pup to handling of all areas of his head. Look in his eyes, ears, and mouth, and check out his feet (feel the toes, pads, and nails) and body (run your hands along his legs, underbelly, chest, and tail). Touch his gum line, his teeth (don't forget the molars), and inside his ears. Hold his collar with one hand so you can jerk it to settle a feisty pup. Open his mouth as you would do if you were giving a pill—gently grasp the

Puppy Hygiene Checklist

Ear canal: Be alert to infections, which are characterized by odor, discharge, redness, swelling, itching, or irritation and require prompt veterinary attention.

Teeth: Check that your pup is losing baby teeth as his adult teeth come in. Brush teeth regularly—this is the only way to avoid tartar buildup.

Brushing: Tools for:
Smooth coats—washcloth, mitt, or rubber groomer
Shedding coats—Slicker brush or shedding blade
Tangling coats—Slicker brush followed by comb to check your work

Bathing: Use dog shampoo and simplify the job by using a utility tub with a hose attachment.

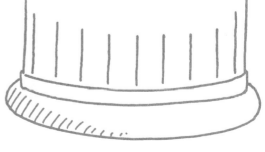

Puppy Classes vs. Home-Schooling

Puppy classes are a great way to socialize your dog, learn about puppy development, and acquire training skills. If the curriculum covers training and problem prevention, you will automatically learn about adolescent stages and your puppy will gain valuable socialization in this controlled environment.

If you prefer less structure, other classes offer off-leash playtime. This environment can diminish the confidence of submissive puppies and increase displays of dominance in bold puppies. Classes that forego off-leash playtime and instead teach obstacle courses are a better bet, since they instill trust and foster a working relationship between puppies and owners.

Find out who offers puppy classes in your area by looking in the Yellow Pages and asking your veterinarian, local humane society, breeder, friends, neighbors, and co-workers. Then observe and compare programs before making your decision and enrolling. If there are no worthwhile puppy classes in your area, you'll need to socialize and train your puppy on your own. Reading and putting into practice the things in this chapter should give you most of the information you need. If you have special concerns, contact a private dog trainer and behavior consultant in your area.

upper jaw with one hand and the lower jaw with the other, fingers behind the canine (fang) teeth. Try all these things when he is standing on the floor and also when he is on a table or other small elevated surface such as the top of a washing machine. If possible, tie a leash to an overhead pipe or ceiling hook so that the snaps hangs down just low enough to attach it to his collar to create a noose-like arrangement. And just like a professional groomer, never leave your dog unattended when noosed.

Additionally, teach your puppy to accept being rolled on his side and examined or groomed. Start by practicing the "settle position." Kneel on the ground at his side and reach around him as if you were giving a bear hug. Clasp his legs on the opposite side and gently roll him by moving his legs under his body and toward you. Then, with your hand holding the rear leg, slide his bottom between your knees and straddle him. Place your hands, palms down, on his chest with your thumbs facing one another below his armpits to prevent him from wriggling away. Remain still and calm. When he relaxes, release him by saying "Okay" as you loosen your hold. Practice this procedure on seven- to eighteen-week-old pups.

Control Mouthing, Biting, and Chewing

Here's the lowdown on the things your should be giving your pup to provide for his needs and reduce the chance of him putting his teeth around the wrong things.

Proper Toys

To avoid problems, give your dog only toys such as Nylabones, sterilized bones (from a pet shop, not a grocery store), rubber Kongs, or squeaky toys and balls of the proper size and durability for your puppy. These are solid, chewable items. Encourage your dog to chew on them by smearing a tiny bit of liver sausage, peanut butter, or Cheez Whiz on it or, better still, inside, if the item has a hole.

Be aware that certain items can increase problems with inappropriate chewing, soiling, or guarding behavior. Avoid giving your puppy personal items to chew on, such as slippers, socks, gloves, or towels. If your puppy is attracted to the family's stuffed toys, don't allow him soft dog toys that are made of fleece or

Picking Up, Holding, and Carrying

The easiest way to pick up your puppy without risking injury is to reach under his chest (brisket) between his front legs with one hand and place the fingers of your other hand between his two rear legs, keeping your thumb under his tail. As you straighten your knees to stand, smoothly bring him into your chest so he is leaning into you. Puppies can get wiggly when you least expect it, so make certain his weight is fully supported by your hands, fingers, and forearms. Young children and awkward people shouldn't pick up the puppy. Instead, they should either get down to his level or let him sit on their lap, if he is small and calm enough. Many dogs do not like to be carried, but all should learn to tolerate being picked up and held briefly.

stuffed. If he's attracted to rugs or tassels, don't provide him with rope- or raglike toys.

Edible products such as rawhide, pig's ears and cowhoofs increase your puppy's thirst and can upset his stomach and even get lodged in the intestines—a medical emergency. And some puppies get defensive and possessive around edible items. If your puppy is having house-soiling problems or gets tense in the presence of these edible items, get rid of them. Of course, if you want to give them and they keep your puppy busy without causing side effects, consult your breeder or veterinarian.

Mouthing, Snapping, and Nipping

During teething when pups are from three to six months mouthing is common. Natural though it may be, you must stop mouthing of flesh and valuables regardless of when it occurs, so that it doesn't become habitual.

Here are some tips:

- Keep your puppy leashed any time mouthing may occur (especially in the house), provide him with plenty of exercise, and encourage play with proper toys such as Nylabones and Kongs. Flavor the items by dipping them in broth for a special treat.
- Offer your puppy wash rags that you've wetted, wrung out, and frozen. Chewing on these relieves the discomfort of teething. Replace with a fresh one when it begins to thaw.

Correct mouthing by either:

- Screeching "ouch!," jerking the leash, and eliciting play with the proper toy,
- Using bitter apple spray on pup's lip line while gripping collar with free hand.

Correct chasing or nipping of children by never allowing unsupervised contact. Always intervene to curtail disrespectful, inappropriate actions from puppy or child. Attach a leash to your pup that will allow you to jerk it as the child says "ouch."

Playing Too Rough

Avoid rough play such as pushing and pulling, tug of war, and growling. Instead, get down on all fours, swing your hair, and pounce, or play retrieving games, chase, and hide and seek.

Socializing Your Puppy

Perhaps your veterinarian advised you against exposing your puppy while his immune system is developing, but you fear the risks of neglecting his socialization during this critical period. Though you may not be able to walk him around the big city, you can start a socialization program at home.

- Desensitize him to noises by letting him play with an empty plastic half-gallon or gallon milk jug or big metal spoon.
- Accustom him to walking on a variety of surfaces such as bubble wrap, big plastic bags, and chickenwire. Put a treat in the middle so he gets rewarded for his bravery.

(Continued)

If games get too rough or out of control, stop jumping and biting by saying "Ouch" as you abruptly leave the game. If you choose to resume play, do so only after leashing the pup. That way you can jerk the leash to stop the bad behavior and immediately continue your game.

"How do I know if I'm playing too rough with my puppy?"

Never work him into a frenzy; learn how to make games fun and low-key. You should be able to stop the game at any time and walk away or roll your puppy into the "settle position." Never use games to frighten your puppy or hurt him. If he ever hurts you during play, make sure he knows you don't approve by using the techniques listed under "Controlling Biting and Mouthing."

"My puppy won't stop biting and jumping when I say "ouch" or jerk the leash. Is there any other way to stop him?"

Issue a stronger correction by spraying bitter apple on his lip line as he is biting. Make sure to hold his collar with your free hand as you spray to ensure proper aim. Also, only engage in play when the puppy is leashed and you have the bitter apple bottle in your pocket. Consider giving and enforcing "sit," "down," "come," or other commands to redirect his energy, or try rolling him into the settle position (described on page 133) until he regains his calm disposition.

Other Dogs

Rough play among dogs is usually harmless amusement for humans and canines. If they're generally friendly and tolerant of one another, dogs or puppies rarely inflict injury. They will get noisy and animated: growling, barking, squealing, tumbling, and dragging one another by convenient body parts (such as ears and limbs) is common. Break up the game only if one of the dogs is being endangered, or if the play occurs in a formal living room or while people desire quiet. Don't raise your voice to break them up. Instead, leash one or both dogs and give a subdued command to stop, accompanied by a jerk of sufficient strength to ensure that they follow your request.

Socializing Your Puppy

- If his experiences with meeting new people will be limited, metamorphose using costumes. Wear hats, masks, and capes, walk with a cane, or limp, skip, and hop.
- Handle him as described in the grooming and examination section (page 133).
- Take him for car rides with permission from your veterinarian.

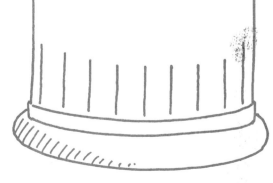

Chewing on Stuff

In addition to providing young, curious puppies with proper toys and exercise, it is best to puppy-proof your house by keeping intriguing items out of reach—eyeglasses, remote controls, laundry, plants, and dried flowers. Allow him to drag a leash or tie it to your belt to umbilical cord (see page 120) so you can correct with a leash jerk or bitter apple spray if he begins exploring the wrong thing, then play with appropriate toy. If he is off-leash, distract him from inappropriate chewing with a sharp clap of your hands as you say "Hey!", followed by praise and play with an appropriate toy. Smear bitter apple cream on tempting woodwork. Confine your puppy in a safe place when you can't supervise him (see "Crating," page 118), and teach the shopping exercise.

Shopping Exercise

Teach the difference between his toys and taboo items. Choose a word to mean "get that out of your mouth" (use the same word whether he has a finger, a slipper, or a dead rabbit). Place a number of personal items and paper items on the floor and allow your pup to explore. As he picks up a taboo item, command "drop it" as you jerk the leash, moving away from the item toward one of his toys. Get him to play with the correct item.

"Oh, no! I'm having a bad-dog day."

If he doesn't drop the taboo item as you jerk his lead and move away, spray your finger with bitter apple and slide your finger along his gum line as you command "drop it." If he still doesn't drop it, spray bitter apple directly against his lip line.

Even Good Puppies Behave Like Puppies

Claire had attended my puppy class with her eight-week-old chocolate Lab, Moose. Months later I ran into her at a conference. She bragged about his behavior, which made me proud. Then she announced that she'd been leaving Moose loose in the house, which made me worried. Upon seeing the shocked look on my face she tried to reassure me that she regularly checked on him, which she was just leaving to do.

A few hours later I saw Claire again. Devastated, she said that Moose had demolished a recliner during her absence that morning. Ironically, I was relieved. The only reason a seven-month-old Lab would be trustworthy is if he was listless because of some illness. Claire may consider giving him freedom after he is one year old, but for now, she vows to crate her very normal seven-month-old puppy.

If you prefer not to learn first-hand about the dangers of giving too much freedom too soon, puppy-proof your house by keeping it tidy, keeping doors closed and personal items out of reach and, as a preventative measure, smearing bitter apple cream on tempting woodwork and electrical cords. Confine your puppy in safe place when you can't supervise him. Finally, keep him leashed and correct while in the act of chewing, then encourage him to play with an appropriate toy.

Jumping Up

Some puppies have no desire to jump up. They're content to let you bend down to pet them. Others jump up either because they are very bold and sociable or because they've been rewarded for doing so with petting and attention. If you prefer your dog not to jump up, remain quiet and walk away from him, shuffle into him, or stand on his leash so it tightens just as he begins jumping. The last technique is particularly useful if people are unintentionally being too exuberant and allowing the puppy to jump up.

Jumping on counters and furniture is the result of giving your puppy too much unsupervised freedom too soon. Distract your untrained puppy every time he considers looking at the counter or hopping on the furniture: toss a shaker can at him, clap your hands sharply, or jerk his leash even before he misbehaves.

Many owners of small dogs—myself included—don't mind jumping up. Still, it is important to teach the "off" command as described in "Basic Commands," page 169, so the behavior can be stopped when necessary.

Digging

Avoid leaving your puppy unsupervised in any area that has digging potential. If he attempts to dig, use a leash jerk or sharp noise to distract him, followed by praise and the offering of an acceptable toy.

Problem Prevention

Giving a puppy or untrained dog freedom in your house can be deadly. Natural curiosity and boredom could make them

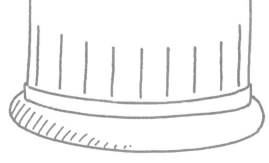

Proper Toys

- Wet, twisted, frozen wash rags to relieve the discomfort of teething. Replace with another when it begins to thaw.
- Nylabones, sterilized bones (from pet shop, not grocery), rubber Kongs
- Avoid giving personal items, soft toys, or edible products

chew electrical cords, ingest toxic substances, or destroy valuables. When dogs are given freedom too soon, those that don't accidentally execute themselves often become homeless because of damage the owner is angry about but could have and should have prevented. Dogs are opportunists. This doesn't mean they are bad; it just means we're foolish if we walk out of the room, leaving goodies on the coffee table, and truly believe our dogs would never even think about touching them.

If you don't know where your puppy is, he is probably into something he shouldn't be. Save your valuables, your sanity, and your puppy by watching his every move, umbilical cording him, or confining him to a safe, destruction-proof area.

Some people unintentionally teach bad behavior. Read over the following most common mistakes and identify guilty parties if you like.

- Impassioned hellos promote hyper-excited greetings.
- Feeding your pup while you're cooking, eating, or snacking encourages begging, possessiveness, or an upset stomach.
- Putting strong-smelling items in the waste basket or leaving any trash can easily accessible invites garbage raiding (remember, a dog's sense of smell is much keener than ours).
- Not securing clothing, children's toys, and linens encourages stealing.
- Repeating commands teaches the puppy to ignore them.
- Lack of exercise and meaningful activity forces the puppy to look for outlets—such as digging and barking—to relieve his boredom.

Overview of Problem-Solving Strategies

1. Prevent problems from occurring:
   - Confine your dog
   - If it's tempting, get it out of his reach—paper, garbage, personal belongings, and paraphernalia such as remote controls and eyeglasses
   - Close off areas with problem-making potential: shut the kids' bedroom doors so he can't confiscate their toys, for instance, or block off the living room so he can't see or hear the mail carrier's approach

2. Distract your dog or channel his energy into work:
   - Encourage him to play with a toy to curtail attempts to chew woodwork or dig in the garden
   - While massaging the feet of a sensitive or ticklish dog, ask a helper to offer tidbits
   - Stop barking, jumping up, or nipping by giving obedience commands in rapid-fire succession
3. Correct every attempt to misbehave:
   - If your dog tries to jump on guests, stand on his leash
   - If your dog tries to grab the leash, spray bitter apple on it
   - If your dog barks at you for attention while you read the paper, anoint him with a water pistol between his eyes
4. Accept the undesirable behavior and stop complaining about it:
   - Do the same thing as always
   - Expect the same result
   - Adopt a laissez faire attitude ("It's all right if he's on the furniture, barks, dumps garbage, etc.")

Simple Commands

You can begin teaching commands and tricks when your puppy reaches eight weeks of age. Since puppies are sometimes too distracted to be interested in food, the following method explains how to use your hands and the leash to enforce your commands. The added advantage is that your puppy will learn to accept handling and restraint and therefore behave better for the veterinarian.

There are some general rules for teaching sit, down, and come commands: Use a buckle-type collar; give commands only when you can enforce them and never repeat them; praise your puppy before releasing him from duty with the "chin-touch okay" (step forward as you gently touch his under jaw and say "Okay" as an invitation to move). When your puppy is sixteen weeks, begin training as outlined in the next section, "Basic Training."

Sit

To teach the "sit" command, put your dog on your left side, hold his collar with your right hand, and put your left hand on his loin just in front of his hip bones and behind his rib cage. Command "Sit" as you pull upward on the collar and push down-

ward on the loin. Praise him, then release him with the "chin touch okay."

Down

To teach "down," follow the same procedure as described for "sit," except as you command "Down," pull downward on the collar as you use the palm of your left hand to push down on his shoulders or neck. When he lowers his body to the ground, pet his tummy. If he rolls on his side or back, continue praising, then release him with the "chin-touch okay." If your dog braces and won't lower his front end to the ground, lift the paw that is bearing most of his weight as you push downward on his shoulder blades. If his fanny stays up as his front end lowers, simply keep your palm on his shoulder blades until he relaxes his rear legs and lies down so you can give him a tummy rub.

Come

Leash your pup and wait for him to get distracted. Call "(Puppy's name), come" and reel in lead as you back up and say "Good, good, gooood!" Kneel down to celebrate his arrival and release with the "chin-touch okay."

Pass the Puppy

Get your family to join the program by leashing the pup when at least one other member is present. Have one person hold the leash while the other holds the pup. When the person holding the leash handle calls "Buddy, come," the other lets go so the pup can be reeled in as the trainer of the moment backs up. Then that person holds the pup and passes the lead to the next person. This exercise can be practiced daily for up to 15 minutes; if you all habitually use the same, consistent training techniques, the puppy will learn to respond to everyone in the family.

"Who should work with the puppy?"

Since dogs thrive on consistency, ideally one person should be the trainer. But if the puppy is a family pet, he can adapt to a multiple-trainer system and feel a special connection to everyone who works with him. If family members aren't committed to learning the proper skills, agreeing on rules, and working with the puppy, the person with the most interest should take responsibility.

Basic Training

Proper Equipment

The most important pieces of equipment for basic training are a well-fitted collar, a 6-foot leather leash, and a 15-foot longe line. Additionally, when working toward off-leash control, you'll need a tab (a short nylon rope) and a 50-foot light line. All are described in some detail below.

Collars

When you begin training, use the collar your dog wears around the house. It should be well made and properly fitted. If it's not, or if he doesn't wear a collar, start with a snugly fit buckle-type collar, flat or rolled. Consider switching to a slip collar, a prong collar, or a head halter if you've used the procedures recommended in this book but, because of his size or strength, would like an extra measure of control.

Slip chain collars: When using this type of collar, take advantage of the quick slide-and-release action of a slip chain with flat, small links. It should be only ½ to 2 inches larger than the thickest part of your dog's skull. Although collars this small can be difficult to slide on and off, snug collars deliver timelier corrections. This type also stays in place better when properly positioned—high on the neck, just behind the ears, with the rings just under the dog's right ear.

So the slip collar will loosen after corrections, make sure the active ring (the one the leash attaches to) comes across the top of the right side of your dog's neck.

Nylon slip collars: Neither round nor flat nylon slip collars offer the slide-and-release action of a chain, but they do deliver stronger corrections than buckle collars. As with any collar, the nylon slip should only be tightened momentarily while correcting; constant tension means the dog isn't being told when he's doing well and when he's doing poorly.

Prong collars: Strong or easily distractible dogs may benefit by use of a prong or pinch collar. The prongs come in four sizes—micro, small, medium, and large. The length is adjustable by removing or adding prongs. Since many brands of these col-

Proper Flea Collar Use

Most flea collars can lose part or all of their effectiveness when wet. Remove them when bathing the dog or when the dog goes out in the rain. Also, don't use a flea collar in combination with powders or topical flea sprays, as their combined strength may be toxic to the dog, resulting in rashes and the loss of fur.

lars will fall off without warning, when you're working in open areas, consider fitting your dog with a buckle or slip collar in addition to the prong, and attach your leash to both.

Some people think prong collars look like instruments of torture. If you're turned off by the appearance of the prong collar, look for another tool to aid you. But if you are both apprehensive and curious about this collar, it's actually a very humane tool when properly used. Ironically, some harsh trainers abhor them and some soft trainers embrace them. Cruelty or kindness isn't linked to whether a dog wears a prong collar, but rather to the way it is used. If you want to use one, have an experienced trainer show you how to properly fit and work with it.

"How do I stop my dog from backing out of his collar?"

Your first line of defense against your dog backing out and escaping is using the right collar—for instance, if you work him on a buckle collar, use a sturdy one that won't fall off. Even then, there are no guarantees if the dog has developed this dangerous and naughty habit. Try using the double-collar trick. Have him wear both a buckle collar and a slip chain and snap your leash to both collars. When he backs out of the buckle collar, the slip chain will tighten. This not only prevents his escape, it also teaches him to go with the flow instead of fighting you.

If the collar used for training is different from the one your dog usually wears, he probably won't obey well when he isn't wearing his training collar. Treat him like an untrained dog and be prepared to enforce all your commands, so he'll behave regardless of which collar he's wearing.

Leashes and Lines

Leash: To teach commands and mannerly walking and to umbilical cord your dog, use a 6-foot leather leash. Use a ¼-inch width for dogs up to 15 pounds; use a ½-inch width for dogs 16–45 pounds; use a ¾-inch width for dogs 46–75 pounds; and use a 1-inch width for dogs over 76 pounds.

Longe line: Many exercises, including sneakaway and advanced distance stays, are done on a 15-foot nylon cord called a longe line. Since many pet stores don't carry them, just

How to Acclimate Your Dog to the Flea Collar

If you decide to use a flea collar on your dog, you should begin slowly. At first, put it on the dog for only a minute or so, then remove it. While the collar is on, reward the dog with a treat and play with him. Gradually lengthen the time the dog wears the collar, so that after a week the dog is completely accustomed to it. Some dogs find these collars irritating. If you don't follow this acclimation procedure, your dog may object to the presence of the collar and attempt to remove it, perhaps hurting himself in the process.

go to a hardware store and buy a swivel snap and 15 feet of nylon cord—¼-inch diameter for a medium-sized dog, and ⅛-inch smaller or larger for small or large dogs, respectively. Tie the snap on one end and make a loop for your thumb on the other.

Tab: The tab is a piece of ¼-inch diameter nylon rope, approximately 18 inches long. If your dog is tiny or giant, adjust the length and width. Tie the ends of the rope together, then slip the unknotted end through the ring of the collar and, finally, thread the knot through the loop. The knot will keep your hand from slipping off the tab as you give a jerk to enforce commands. But when you're not holding it, it will be dangling on your dog's chest, which means he may be thinking about mouthing it—in which case, you can't use it. So if he takes it in his mouth, tell him "Drop it." If necessary, enforce your command by saturating the tab with a chewing deterrent spray or giving your dog a cuff under the jaw.

Lightline and glove: The lightline is a 50-foot nylon cord. Use parachute cord for large dogs, Venetian blind cord for medium or small dogs, and nylon twine for tiny breeds. The lightline is tied to the tab and used as you make the transition to off-lead work.

When you're working with the tab and lightline, wear a form-fitted gardening glove to ensure a better grip and to prevent rope burn.

Other Equipment

You may already own some of the following items and wonder how they fit into your training program.

Head halters: A head halter can control a dog's head and nose far more effectively than other collars. It can deter sniffing and partially control eye contact. One strap rests behind the ears and another fits around the muzzle. If your dog's trachea or esophagus is sensitive when pressure is applied, the head halter won't irritate the condition, but it will give you great control. And you can easily stop a large dog from lunging or pulling by turning his head toward you, even if you aren't strong.

Harnesses: Avoid harnesses for basic obedience training. They're designed to allow unrestricted pulling for sledding, drafting, and tracking dogs. The head lowers and they mush forward—a stance that's not conducive to learning the tasks in this book.

The only exception to this advice is the use of a "no-pull" harness. This device is handy if you need a temporary shortcut to keep your

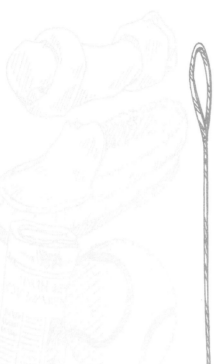

dog from pulling on his leash because he lacks proper training or you're unable to correct the behavior using the guidelines in this book.

Retractable Leads

Features: These popular leads come in lengths from 8 to 32 feet. You can let the dog venture away and explore without getting his legs entangled, thanks to a constant, slight amount of tension. The buttons on the easy-to-grip plastic handle allow you to lock it at a length as short as 4 inches for some models, or as long as the total length or any length in between. Sounds great, but unknowingly owners are teaching sloppy behavior. Allowing a dog to dart and criss-cross the handler's path puts him in danger and tells him that he's in charge.

Proper Usage: To make your dog adapt to your pace and stay by your side, lock the lead in the shortest position. The plastic handle allows you to give a stronger jerk than the leash allows, which is especially useful if space is limited or footing is bad. When you arrive at his potty area or meet up with a canine playmate, unlock the lead and give your permission, then let the dog pull out the length.

Things to avoid: Retractable leads aren't an all-purpose training tool; because of the narrowness of the cord and the weight of the handle, it's not an appropriate replacement for the longe line when you're practicing the key exercises described later in this book. Retractable leashes make it easy for handlers to allow pulling and casting out, and therefore they can undo much of the control and attention you're trying to establish through basic training.

Using Treats to Train

Most trainers want their dogs to obey out of love rather than because they were beaten or bribed. But since most dogs love tasty treats, food has long been used as a training aid. There are basically three ways to use food: (1) as a lure to get the dog to perform a task, (2) as a reward for completing an already learned task, or (3) as reinforcement for behaviors offered by the dog (click and treat training).

Most people use treats and body English as a lure because it is the fastest way to entice the dog to perform a task. But be aware: there is a huge gap between following a lure and obeying a command. To bridge that gap, learn how to enforce your commands with your hands and leash. This will also prove invaluable if your dog isn't interested in the treat because he's full or distracted.

If you would prefer not to use treats, don't. Though using treats can enliven a dog's response to an already learned command, I have never found it necessary to use food to teach a task. In fact, I've preferred to stay away from it so I can see when the dog is actually learning commands rather than just performing actions.

Clicker and Treat Training

Clickers are often used for training service and trick dogs. Simply put, when the dog does something desirable, he is given a signal (usually a distinct sound) that the behavior is right, offered a food reward and, eventually, taught to do it on command, possibly without the food. This method has long been used to train a variety of species, including cats, birds, and monkeys. Many trainers use the click of a tin cricket to signify the appropriateness of a behavior. For instance, if the objective is to teach a dog to sneeze, the trainer would wait for him to do that, click the tin cricket and offer a treat or other reward. Because of the power of association, soon the dog reacts to the sound of the clicker with as much delight as to the treat. Therefore, if the dog is working far away or retrieving and can't be given a treat, the clicker communicates that he is doing a great job. Of course, many people do the same thing with the word "Good!" instead of the clicker. With animals who are unresponsive to verbal praise—such as rodents and farm animals—the clicker is an invaluable training tool, but a variety of methods are equally successful when teaching basic dog obedience.

Patience

Dog training is an adventure of sorts: never predictable, sometimes elating, and sometimes tedious. Be optimistic about your dog's potential, but expect his progress occasionally to be slow or nonexistent. Don't, however, abandon your original goals and settle for meager results: Shoddy, half-learned obedience can cause

annoying problems or allow them to fester. Many owners give up on training but later decide to give it another try—this time approaching it with far greater determination and achieving far better results. Whether this is your first time around or your last-ditch effort, recognize that a degree of frustration is part of the learning process. If frustration or doubt strike, keep training. You may be five seconds from a learning breakthrough. Don't let your frustration or impatience win!

Finally, learning anything new—including how to train your dog—is challenging, so show yourself compassion. I've been training dogs for twenty-two years. I don't want to make mistakes when training, but sometimes I do. If I attempt to train, I may make a mistake. But if I never try, I'll never have the dog I really want. Decide what kind of behavior you want and pursue it with patience and kindness.

Basic Skills: Sneakaways

Use the sneakaway as the foundation for teaching commands and solving problems, and to teach your dog to walk nicely on lead. This mesmerizing exercise teaches your dog to be controlled and attentive despite distractions. Even without specifically addressing problem behaviors, you may find they magically disappear as your dog learns his sneakaway lessons. At the very least, you'll find sneakaways improve his general trainability and therefore greatly reduce your workload.

Walking Sneakaways

To begin the sneakaway, put your dog on the longe line (the 15-foot nylon cord described under "Equipment"). Then take your dog to an obstruction-free area at least 50 feet square. Put your thumb through the loop of the line and your other hand under it. Plant both hands on your midsection to avoid moving them and jerking your dog. He may get jerked during this exercise, but it won't be because of your hand movement.

As you stroll with your dog, watch him closely but inconspicuously. If he becomes distracted or unaware of you, immediately turn and walk briskly in the opposite direction. The line will tighten abruptly if he isn't following as you move away.

The sneakaway is simple; When your dog goes north, you go south. When he is thinking of things in the west, you head east.

After an hour of practice—split up any way you like over the next two days—your dog should be keeping his legs tangle-free, be aware of your movements, and be willing to be near you.

"My dog is throwing a temper tantrum and doing everything besides following me. Is this normal?"

Occasionally, even after an hour of practice, a dog may refuse to budge. Others may throw their paws over the longe line and shake their heads furiously or bite the line. With both types, you may be tempted to stop momentarily, coax, carry your dog, or quit. Resist the temptation; those actions just encourage the behavior and add to your dog's confusion. Instead, create an umbilical cord for him by tying his leash to your belt. For two days, make him walk by your side as you perform your daily activities around the house and yard. After a few hours of umbilical cording, staying near you should be second nature. Now practice sneakaways again, using a slip chain or prong collar. If you do so for a total of three hours over the course of a week, he is likely to be following happily.

"What should I do when my dog gets hopelessly entangled?"

As a result of panic or feigned helplessness, a rare dog may jump, spin, and severely entangle himself in the line. Ignore his self-created dilemma and refuse to rescue him. After two or three days you will never see the behavior again.

"My dog does a sneak attack. How can I stop him?"

Your vivacious dog is probably body-slamming or nipping at you for amusement. To stop the behaviors, silently reel in the line quickly and smoothly; grip the back of his neck, listing his front feet slightly off the ground, and press the bitter apple bottle nozzle against the corner of his lip and spray. Or simply substitute a cuff under the jaw for the spritz of bitter apple.

Running Sneakaways

In step 2, instead of walking away, pivot and run when your dog's attention wanders from you. Once he's begun running after you, stop dead. Also, take inventory of your dog's personality, desires, and fascinations. These may include noises, smells, certain activities, food, toys, different areas, or other animals and people. From now on we'll refer to those as distractions. Each time you practice, run a little faster as you sneak away and use more challenging and irresistible distractions.

"My dog follows and watches me constantly."

Good. If your dog is aware of your intentions, stand still or amble. Though you pretend to be entirely relaxed, mentally be ready to sneak away fast if your dog gets bored and turns his attention elsewhere.

Leash Walking

Begin step 3 once your dog is content to be near you no matter what distractions are around. This step teaches him to walk on a loose leash at your left side. Attach the 6-foot leash to his collar and put your right thumb in the handle. Enclose your fingers around the straps of the handle below. Hold the midsection of the leash with the right hand, too, so your left hand is free. The leash should have just enough slack to touch the middle of your left thigh when your right hand is at your hip—unless you are really tall and your dog is short, or vice versa; the taller the handler and shorter the dog, the lower on your leg the leash will hang.

"How can I stop my dog from pulling ahead?"

When your dog forges ahead, open and close your hand to release the slack, then grip the handle as you pivot and run away. Do this when his shoulder is only inches ahead of your leg, rather than waiting until he is tugging at the end of the leash or lunging frantically ahead. When your dog is running after you, pick up the slack in the leash again and stop dead.

"When I sneak away, instead of returning to my side, my dog dashes ahead again."

If your dog runs right past you, pivot once again and sneak away before he bolts ahead. If your dog is a charger, watch his body English closely so it becomes easy to anticipate when to do multiple, direction-changing sneakaways.

"How do I stop my dog from lagging and crossing behind?"

If your dog attempts to lag, reduce the slack by tightening the leash a bit—about 1 to 5 inches—as you briskly walk forward. The dog may bump into the back of your legs for the next few steps, but that, along with the fact the leash tightens against your left thigh with every step, will encourage him to return to your left side. Remember to keep your left hand off the leash so nothing interferes with your thigh pulling into the leash.

"Can I stop my dog from sniffing the ground and ambling when we walk?"

Yes. If your dog is off in scent-land or continues to lag, "puddle jump" with your left leg so he will be jerked back to your left side. As you walk, take a large step with your right foot and instead of taking a normal step with your left, take a leap as if you were clearing a little puddle with your left leg leading. The smaller and more gentle the dog, the less distance you'll need to cover in your jump.

"What is so special about the sneakaway? Can't I just jerk the leash with my hand to teach my dog to walk nicely?"

Sneakaways teach your dog to watch you in anticipation of your speedy departure. As a bonus, your dog will enjoy the sneakaway if he likes running with you. Being astute observers of human behavior, it's easy for him to avoid the correction by "catching you" before the line tightens. So sneakaways not only teach your dog to walk nicely—he'll also watch you, have fun, and never be the victim of an unjust correction.

Sneakaways teach your dog that when he is attached to a line that you're holding, he is expected to control himself even though he isn't under command. This lesson in self-control is the foundation that makes everything else in dog training—problem solving, command training, and off-lead control—easy.

Prove Your Stuff

Take your dog to a new, distraction-filled area. Put him on his longe line, holding just the handle, and take a walk. If his interest begins wandering, sneak away fast. Continue taking him

Key Points to Sneakaways

Remember these key points when practicing sneakaways:

- Keep your hands steady so you don't use arm movements to jerk your dog.
- Don't allow your dog to hear you move or stop, or see you with his peripheral vision. Avoid tricks like scuffing your feet, or inching, bowing or arcing away; instead, always sneak directly away, with conviction, so your dog will learn to pay attention to you rather than your tricks.
- Move at a constant rate until your dog is following you, then stop dead.

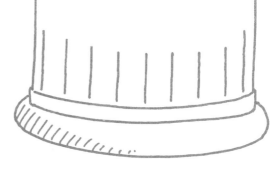

More Key Points to Sneakaways

- Be silent. If your dog is doing so well you feel inclined to praise him, you may be ready to skip ahead to "Commands."
- Use momentum to your advantage by heading away from dog while there is still generous slack in the line. Calculate your departure so you'll be able to take two running steps *before* the line tightens.
- If your dog is doing brilliantly, avoiding jerks no matter how cleverly you attempt to sneak away, start teaching tasks and commands.

to new areas several times a week for 20-minute walks until he's willing to walk on a loose lead, aware of your movements for the entire walk.

Commands

"How long will it take to train my dog?"

Everyone's idea of what constitutes a trained dog varies. If your definition includes having the ability to control your dog around distractions and obey heel, sit, down, stay, and come commands, the answer depends on how quickly you can learn basic dog training skills. If you are willing to devote 20 or 25 minutes of daily practice for 10 weeks, both you and your dog are likely to achieve excellent results. Plan your training agenda, being sure to note the number of repetitions and specific ways to practice each exercise. Some days you may feel you're getting nowhere, but the cumulative effect of this strategy never fails to develop a proficient team. Especially if you've trained other dogs, keep in mind that dogs, like people, have different aptitudes. For people it may be language, not science, and for dogs it may be stays, not recalls. Some dogs respond to formal training the way some people respond to book learning: easily and naturally. Formal training is recommended for all dogs and is most beneficial for those confounded by it. Dogs do learn how to learn, so that after ten weeks, it becomes difficult to separate the naturals from the initially confused or resistant.

Breed-Specific Training

Just like people, all dogs should be evaluated based on their individual temperaments and characteristics. No breed has a patent on problems or virtues. Therefore, stereotyping breeds does more harm than good. You may have been told that Shelties bark, Huskies run away, and Golden Retrievers are great family dogs. I've known many Shelties that were naturally quiet, Huskies that were trained to obey off-lead, and Goldens that were nasty because of improper handling. Nothing absolves you from the responsibility of working with your dog, regardless of its breed's good or bad reputation. You should heed warnings to be extra conscientious because of certain breed tendencies—

teaching a sporting dog to listen to you even in heavily scented fields rather than following his nose, for instance; being on the lookout for aggressive tendencies toward other dogs in terrier breeds and stopping it before it starts; or socializing herding breeds a lot, especially when they are four to six months old, so they don't become skittish.

Praise

With some dogs, a word of praise goes a long way. Others appear unaffected by it. Gracious dog trainers use lots of praise at the right time in the right way to acknowledge and congratulate specific actions, concentration, and worthy intent. Experiment with a variety of ploys to find what delights your dog no matter what his mood. I've found quiet, interesting sounds, combined with scampering movement, gentle pushes, and vigorous, light brief scratching with my nails usually elicit a good response. Whatever you use, your dog's reaction is the most important indicator that you are on track. Does your type of praise make his eyes bright and get that tail wagging? If he's bored by your technique, working to find out what he likes will improve every part of your relationship.

Never praise your dog if he does his work in a distracted or preoccupied manner; he may think you are praising his inattention. Instead, do sneakaways to help him realign his priorities.

Teach Any Command Using Twelve Ingredients:

1. Decide what you'd like your dog to do.
2. Decide what clear visual or auditory signal you will use to initiate the desired action.
3. Give verbal commands using the right tonality, inflection, and volume (don't plead, mumble, or shout).
4. Preface verbal commands with the dog's name. The name and command should sound like one word ("Buster heel," rather than "Buster . . . heel"). Just one exception: Don't use his name in conjunction with the "Stay" command, since hearing his name implies he should be attentive and ready to go.
5. Say the command only once.

Sneakaway Summary

Goal: To maintain control, attention, and a slack lead around any distraction, as a foundation for all other training.

How to practice: Hold 15-foot nylon longe line with right thumb through loop and all the slack dragging.

Days 1 and 2: Walk silently and quickly away from your dog when he is inattentive or attempts to wander more than 5 feet from you.

Days 3 and 4: Same as first two days, but (1) run away when he is inattentive or wanders; (2) use distractions; (3) stop dead when line goes slack.

Days 5 and 6: Same as 3 and 4, but (1) run as fast as you can; (2) use more tempting distractions; (3) train in different locations.

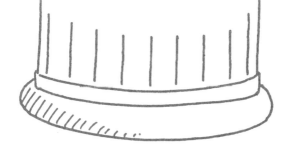

6. Make an association: While teaching, give the command as you make the dog do the action (for example, say "Sit" as you pull up on the collar and push down on the dog's rear).

7. Give commands only when you can enforce them—otherwise, you risk teaching disobedience.

8. Decide on reinforcement: How are you going to show the dog what to do? Unlike the other eleven steps, this will change depending on your dog's stage in training.

9. Show your appreciation with precisely timed praise.

10. End every command by releasing with the "chin-touch okay."

11. Test your dog's understanding by working him around distractions before progressing to the next level.

12. Don't take obedience for granted. Dogs forget, get lazy, become distracted, and inevitably fail to respond to familiar commands. Especially if he rarely makes a mistake, correct him so he understands the rules haven't changed and neither should his behavior.

Chin-Touch Okay

Just as important as the cue you use to start an action is the one you will give to end it. Release your dog from duty with a word like "okay" or "all done." Pair this word with an outward stroke under the dog's chin. Dogs who rely on a physical and verbal release cue are less inclined to "break" their commands. For the first three weeks, step forward when you deliver the "chin touch okay" to make the dog move from his previous command on cue.

Recommended Warm-up For Lessons

- Running sneakaways: Practice until the dog is following you attentively regardless of distractions.
- Leash length sneakaways: Hold leash by placing your right thumb through loop of leash. Put slack in right hand, too. Remove left hand from leash and walk with dog at your left side.
- **How to practice:** Drop slack and run to correct forging. Walk briskly ahead to correct lagging and crossing behind.

Stationary Commands: Sit Stay

Sit stay at a glance:

1. Sit command (three steps)
   Pull up/push down
   Jerk up/push down
   Two-handed upward jerk
2. Sit stay (one step away)
3. Leash length sit stay

Step 1: Sit Command

Teach the "sit" command by putting your dog at your left side, holding his collar with your right hand, and putting your left hand on his loin just in front of his hip bones and behind his rib cage. Command "Sit" as you pull upward on his collar and push downward on his loin.

Talk, pet and praise, but don't let dog move. When necessary, reposition him by pushing him back into the sit as you tighten up on the collar. After a few seconds, release with a "chin touch okay."

"My dog is so stiff I can't push him into the sit, no matter how hard I try."

If he is rigid and won't budge, then move him forward and walk him into the sit.

"My dog squirms or nips any time I restrain him."

Some dogs will turn their heads to mouth or bite you or roll over on their backs. Keep a firm grip on the collar and firmness in your wrist as you pull him up into the sit. Once he is facing forward with his front paws on the ground, loosen your grip.

After three days with no sign of resistance, command "Sit" and wait for a response. To reinforce your command, push downward on the loin and give a quick upward jerk on the lead. Release with the "chin-touch okay."

Finally, eliminate the push and just use a sharp, split second jerk-and-release action. If after two jerks he doesn't sit, use a jerk-and-push combination. Emphasize the jerk and use the most minimal push possible. Release with the "chin-touch okay."

Using Distractions in Dog Training

Priorities change when a dog becomes distracted. He might never think of disobeying—unless food is being prepared, leaves are blowing around, people are laughing, and talking or cats, rabbits, or birds are present. Prevent distractions from rendering all your obedience training useless by making fascinating temptations a part of every training session. Do sneakaways to get control, and then give commands to teach listening skills. His dignity will grow in proportion to his obedience, so he'll be more relaxed in those social settings even when he's not been commanded.

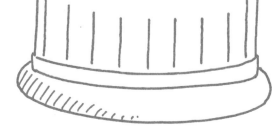

"I've been working on the sit command daily for weeks, but my dog still needs to be pushed into the sit."

Many dogs find it rewarding to be touched, whether you are petting them or pushing them into the sit. Therefore, to teach a reliable "sit" on command without a push, jerk to provide an incentive.

Prove Your Stuff

Sit your dog on a strange-feeling surface—plastic bubble wrap, gravel, or a wire grate. Place him in the sit if he refuses, then try a more normal surface such as wet blacktop, slippery linoleum, or sand. Then command him to "sit" on something really comfortable, such as a thick rug, plush carpeting, or a pillow. Several times a day practice the sit on the most difficult surfaces first, then medium, and finally easy. Consider the command mastered when he willingly obeys the first "sit" command on the strangest surface.

Step 2: Sit Stay One Step Away

Before you begin: Your dog should "sit" on command and wait to be released with a "chin touch okay."

How to practice: Hold leash taut over dog's head. Command "Stay," step in front of him, and act busy while producing distractions. Act busy, use many distractions, return to praise frequently and, finally, release with "chin touch okay." Moving the head and wagging the tail is acceptable, but you should correct scooting forward, rotating, and attempts to stand with an upward jerk. If one jerk doesn't stop it, the jerk was too slow or light. If two stronger, faster jerks don't work, use a jerk-and-push combination. Some dogs respond well to two or three light jerks given in quick succession.

"My dog likes to lie down when I tell him to stay."

If your dog tries to lie down, tighten the leash enough to prevent him from lowering comfortably into the down position and give him praise as he realizes he doesn't have enough slack to lie down. Loosen the lead and prepare to repeat this sequence many times during the next week of training if your dog is one who is inclined to recline.

You may be wondering why you should care about lying down on the sit stay if you're not working toward obedience or field competition. The answer is simple: You need your dog to sit, not lie down, so you can look in his mouth, administer medication or car ointment, or wipe dirt off his paws. Say what you mean and mean what you say to avoid confusion in all areas of training.

Step 3: Leash-Length Sit Stay

How to practice: Command "Stay" and walk out to the end of the leash, holding its handle. Use distractions such as stepping side to side, bending down, pulling forward lightly on the leash, or dropping food or toys in front of your dog. This teaches him that no matter what your preoccupation or what activities surround him, he stays put. Frequently tell him he is "good." Stop movement immediately by (1) sliding your free hand down almost to the snap of the leash as you step into your dog, (2) quickly maneuvering your dog back into place without saying a word, (3) jerking upward, and then (4)moving back to the end of the leash.

Prove Your Stuff

Enforce sit stays while you (1) address a postcard, (2) read the headlines, (3) pop in a video, (4) empty the garbage, (5) download a computer file, (6) tie your shoes, (7) wrap a gift, (8) get stuck on hold, (9) weed a flowerbed. When you no longer need to allow spare time for corrections, your dog has mastered the sit stay.

Stationary Commands: Down Stay

1. Down command (four steps)
   Down with push
   Down with push and jerk
   Down with two-handed jerk
   Machine gun down
2. Down stay
   Correction
   Progression

Step 1: Lie Down with Push

Goal: To introduce your dog to the "down" command.

How to Give a Proper Leash Jerk

1. Grip the leash about 4 to 8 inches from the snap so you have optimal control of the timing, direction, and strength of the jerk.

2. Maintain a belly of slack in the leash before and after the jerk so it's free of tautness and tension and only tightens for the split-second jerk. The leash moves like a piston from point A (slack) to point B (tight) to point A (slack).

3. Place both hands on the leash so none of the leash is exposed between them. Whether training a giant breed or a tiny toy who needs only a featherweight correction, a two-handed jerk ensures you'll have better control of the speed and power of your jerk.

How to practice: Place your thumb and index finger behind your dog's shoulder blades and on either side of his backbone. Command "Down" as you push. Practice by scratching his tummy, and then release him with a "chin touch okay."

"My dog is so strong I can't push him down."

If your dog braces, use your right hand to pull his head down to the ground as you push. Another option is to push as usual with the fingers of the left hand as you use your right hand to lift the front paw that is bearing most of his weight. If you still simply can't get him down, discontinue work on the down and concentrate on perfecting the sit stay around distractions; rare is the dog who resists the down after becoming completely cooperative on the sit.

Step 2: Lie Down with Jerk and Push Combination

Goal: To teach your dog to lie down without the two-finger push.

How to practice: Enforce "down" by simultaneously using a two-finger push and a quick jerk. Jerk diagonally toward your dog's right rear foot by holding the leash close to the snap while you stand facing the dog's right side.

Step 3: Jerk Only Correction

How to practice: Enforce "down" by using a two-handed jerk without the push. If two jerks don't work, combine a firm jerk with a very light two-finger push.

Step 4: Machine Gun Down

Goal: Teach your dog to "down" without a hand signal or touch by practicing thirty downs a day in quick succession.

How to practice: Practice rapid-fire downs by commanding "Down," giving praise, and releasing with a "chin-touch okay." Repeat the sequence for one minute, three times per training session. You should be doing ten to seventeen downs per minute for optimal results.

"How long does it take to teach the 'down' command?"

Exceptional dogs may learn the verbal "down" command in a week. With an average of twenty repetitions per day, most dogs will "down" 50 percent of the time after one month.

But getting certain dogs into the "down" can look like a scene from All-Star Wrestling. It's better to deal with these shenanigans in your house than at the veterinarian's office, where similar protests will be common if you haven't done this homework to abolish tantrums.

"My dog behaves like a contortionist when I practice the 'down,' and her silliness prevents me from making progress."

Many dogs try to weasel out of the "down" with their paws and mouth. Though they aren't actively threatening, the owner may be advised to wear a sweatshirt, pants, and gloves so flailing nails and teeth can't scratch the skin. Three ten-minute sessions practicing down, release, down, release, over and over usually teaches compliance. Have one hand on the collar pulling downward and the other on the pressure point behind the shoulder blades.

"I'm afraid my dog will bite me when I practice the 'down.'"

Menacing protests call for more practice with sneakaways and the sit. Teach an instant response around any distraction with a gentle "sit" command and preface "down" practice with leash-length sneakaways in a highly distracting environment. When the dog is giving his attention to you instead of the temptations, he is likely to cooperate on the "down" as well. Also, instead of drilling down after down, only do two or three at a time. Practice another exercise, do a couple of "downs," and repeat the pattern so that during each session, you practice twenty or thirty "downs."

Prove Your Stuff

- Eliminate body English by putting your hands in your pockets and evaluating yourself in front of a mirror. Your mouth is the only part of your anatomy that should move when commanding "Down."
- Whisper the "Down" command.
- Turn your back and look over your shoulder at your dog to give the command.

Basic Guidelines for "Stays"

- Just before leaving your dog, use a hand signal along with your "stay" command. To signal, flash the palm of your free hand, fingers down toward his eyes.
- Use distractions—people, places, movement, food, toys—to test him and confirm he's learning.
- Be acutely attentive. Move in to correct the instant your dog begins leaving the "stay" position; otherwise, he'll wonder what the correction was for.
- Correct silently. If your dog didn't listen the first time, repeating yourself will only cause further confusion or disobedience. Let your hands and leash alone amend his error.
- Adjust the strength of your correction to your dog's size, level of training, why he moved, and how excited or distracted he is. If an appropriate correction is ineffective, it should be strengthened.
- Leave instantly after the jerk.
- Finish all "stays" by walking to the dog's right side, giving praise, then using the "chin touch okay" release.

- Stand in the shower (without running the water), sit in your car, and lie on a bed, stairs, or sofa. See if your command still has authority.

Down Stays

Usage: Tell your dog to lie down and stay for grooming and examinations, during meals, or as guests arrive, or just to calm your dog.

Before you begin: Your dog should do a leash-length "sit stay" around distraction and should "down" on command.

How to practice: "Down" your dog and command "Stay." Examine his ears, eyes, teeth, and paws. Use the jerk alone or the combination jerk and two-finger push to correct movements such as crawling, rolling, or ascension. Praise him frequently when he cooperates, and return to his right side to praise and then release him with the "chin touch okay."

"My dog stays in place but doesn't pay attention to me."

Although there is no need for the dog to stare at you while he is in the down stay, you should correct grass munching, sniffing, or licking himself by grabbing the back of his neck and giving a gentle closed-fist cuff under his jaw.

Progression

Follow the same progression described for "sit stay":

1. One step in front
2. Leash length

Stationary Commands: Stand Stay

Step 1: Stand

Goal: To teach your dog to stand from a sitting position and not to move until he's released.

How to practice: Begin with your dog sitting. Hold the collar so the knuckles of your right hand rest against the dog's chest. Run your left hand along either side of the dog's body, to the front of the rear leg along the stifle (knee), as you command "Stand." Push backward gently on the dog's stifle and forward on the collar if the dog doesn't stand on his own. Say "Good dog" as he begins to stand. Take your hand off the stifle and start petting him. Continue holding the collar and praising him until you release him with a gentle push to the side and "Okay."

"Help! I'm having a bad-dog day."

If your dog is submissive, fidgety, or sensitive about handling, don't despair. Put a leash or piece of rope under the girth of the submissive dog who thinks he should sit when you hover over him. Simply command "Stand" as you lift the rope. Loosen the tension when he stands, but prepare to tighten it again if he doesn't stay standing. For a fidgety or sensitive dog, heel him along a wall, command "Stand" as you pull forward on the leash, and touch his stifles with a yardstick to prevent unnecessary movement.

Step 2: Stand Stay

Before you begin: Your dog should stand without resistance and remains in place for thirty seconds until released. The dog should also know the sit-stay.

Goal: Your dog will stay standing while you circle and examine him.

How to practice: Stand your dog, command "Stay," and begin circling your dog. Keep one hand on the collar and use the other to stroke his head, feet and body. If your dog tries to move his feet, stop him by using a horizontal jerk opposite the movement. Accompany the jerk with a light touch on his stifle with your free hand so he cannot sit as you correct him. Release him with a push to the side as you command "Okay." Gradually increase the duration of the stand, beginning with ten seconds and working up to a minute or two. Most dogs will do a one-minute stand stay after two weeks of practice.

"How quickly will my dog learn the stand stay?"

Exceptional dogs will do a one-minute stand stay for examination in the first session. Most dogs will require about two to ten weeks of daily practice to achieve the same result. This should consist of sitting for thorough examinations by strangers, as well as separate practice with brief stand stays. Eventually they

will understand that "Stand, stay" means to keep their feet still until they're released.

"My dog tries to sit or lie down when I correct him for moving on the stand stay."

When practicing the stand, give all leash corrections in a horizontal direction while you're standing by the dog. Never jerk upward, downward or from a distance because, in dog language, an upward jerk means sit, a downward jerk means down, and a jerk from a distance means come forward.

Moving Commands: Heeling

Heeling (Three Steps)
1. Position and procedure
2. Automatic sit
3. Perfecting heel position with turns

Like the skill and art of dancing, the benefits of heeling stretch well beyond the exercise itself. Dancing is a wonderful form of recreation on the dance floor, but the posture, alignment, controlled energy, balance, and poise practiced in dance movements spill over into everyday tasks.

The heel command teaches the dog to walk at your left side, regardless of your pace or direction, and to sit when you stop. Gone are the days of him pulling ahead or dragging behind, weaving from side to side, or getting underfoot during walks. As the dog learns to heel and you learn how to teach him to move precisely, a deeper learning takes place for both of you. To remain in position, the dog's awareness, watchfulness, and willingness must grow. Since you need to watch your dog very intently during the process, you'll develop a sense of what the dog is going to do before he does it—otherwise known as reading your dog. Trust and respect develop as you and your canine partner master the art of heeling. This newly formed bond will help you channel the dog's energy more efficiently, no matter what the task, challenge, or obstacle.

Step 1: Heeling
Goal: Teach your dog to maintain heel position, on your left side, with his shoulder aligned with yours, and his body 3 inches from your leg. The position is the same whether you're moving for-

ward, turning, or stationary. When you stop, your dog should sit automatically.

Before you begin: Practice sneakaways (steps 1–3) for at least one week, until your dog is attentive to you despite distractions.

How to practice: Hold the leash in your right hand with your right thumb through the loop and four fingers holding the slack just as you did during leash-length sneakaways. Command "(Dog's name), heel" as you begin walking. Prepare to stop by grabbing the collar with your right hand and using your left to place his rear end into a sitting position so his right front foot is alongside your left ankle.

"How can I get my dog to stop when I stop?"

As you walk along preparing to halt, control your dog's position using the fold-over maneuver. Grab the leash with your left hand and hold it taut over dog's head, then use your right to grip the braiding or stitching of the leash just above the snap. Next, take your left hand off the leash and use it to place dog in a sit in perfect heel position as you halt.

"When I'm heeling my dog, he doesn't stay at my side."

If your dog forges ahead, do a leash-length sneakaway. Drop the slack of the leash, grip the handle, hold your hands at your waistline, and run away. As the dog returns to your side, return to the original leash grip, holding the slack, as you continue walking.

"My dog walks behind me instead of in heel position."

If your dog lags behind, say "Good dog!" as you spring ahead by taking a puddle jump with your left leg first. As you do this your left thigh will pull the leash, and your dog, back to heel position. The jump ahead will also prevent the dog from crossing behind to the right side.

Step 2: Automatic Sit During Heeling

Before you begin: Your dog should sit 80 percent of the time on command, as you stop, without needing to be touched or told.

How to practice: Warm up by:

1. Commanding "Heel."
2. Preparing to halt by gathering the leash in both hands.
3. Giving a light upward jerk as your finish your last step. After two or three halts and good attention from your dog, halt and gather the leash. Jerk only if the dog doesn't stop in heel position and sit immediately.

Step 3: Perfecting Heel Position with Turns

Goal: Stop tendencies to heel too far from or too close to you, and to correct slight forging and sniffing of the ground by using sharp left and right turns.

How to practice: Use the "Jackie Gleason left turn" to stop slight forging, crowding, and sniffing of the ground: Turn 90 degrees to the left, then step perpendicularly into your dog so your left foot and leg slide or step behind his front legs. Shuffle into him until he becomes attentive and moves back to the left side. Practice slowing your pace abruptly, then turn left immediately if your dog's shoulder is even an inch ahead of yours.

If your dog attempts to cross in front of you to the right side, tighten the leash with your left hand as you continue to step into him.

To stop wideness, sniffing or lagging, use the puddle jump following a right turn. Pivot 90 degrees to your right on your left foot, take a large step in your new direction with the right foot, and leap forward with your left leg as if you were jumping over a puddle. As you jump the puddle you should feel the leash against your left thigh, pulling the dog forward. Steady your leash by holding your right hand against your right hip as you leap.

"My dog still lags and sniffs when I jump ahead."

Jump and praise simultaneously to motivate your dog. Hold the leash in your right hand so the slack will remain in front of your thighs as you jump.

Moving Commands: Recall (Come)

1. Reel
2. Jerk
3. In pursuit with leash
4. Distance
5. In pursuit with light line

Step 1: Reel

How to practice: Leash your dog and take him for a walk. If he begins sniffing something, gazing around, or meandering off, call "Buddy, come!" Immediately back up quickly as you reel the leash, praising enthusiastically. Kneel down when your dog arrives, using verbal praise only. Release with a "chin touch okay" and continue practicing the sequence.

"My dog comes toward me, but keeps her distance."

Some dogs will come but stay out of reach or dart right past you. Some owners, without realizing it, encourage the dog to cut his approach and stay farther away by attempting to cradle, caress or hug the dog. Petting the dog as he arrives can create or worsen these recall problems because extending your arms makes it appear you are protecting the space in front of you. Instead, use verbal praise to acknowledge, encourage, and congratulate the dog's arrival and keep your hands to yourself.

Step 2: Jerk

How to practice: After twenty step 1 recalls, your dog is probably running toward you faster than you can reel. Now see if he'll leave distractions when you stand still and call "Come." If he doesn't respond promptly, use a piston-type horizontal jerk toward you as you praise and back up. If he does respond to your command, praise and back up. When your dog responds to your command around strong distractions 80 percent of the time, proceed to step 4.

Step 3: In Pursuit Recalls on Leash

Goal: Teach your dog to stop and come when called, even if he's running away or you're following him.

How to practice: Three times this week, create a situation that would cause your dog to forget his training and pull toward a distraction. For example, ask a fellow dog owner to accompany you on a walk. Instruct him to walk his dog about 10 feet ahead of you. Your dog is likely to want to catch up to them. As you are walking directly behind your dog, call "(Dog's name), come." Jerk the leash, back up and praise if your dog doesn't respond to your command. If he does

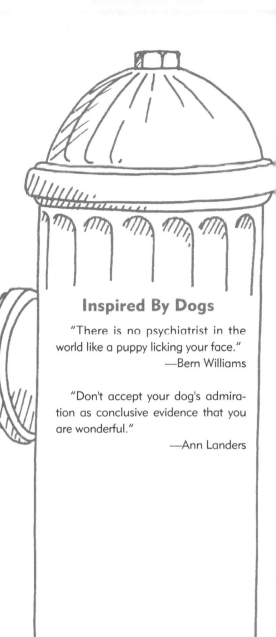

Inspired By Dogs

"There is no psychiatrist in the world like a puppy licking your face."
—Bern Williams

"Don't accept your dog's admiration as conclusive evidence that you are wonderful."

—Ann Landers

respond, praise and crouch down, then release with a "chin touch okay."

"My dog stops when I call him, but he doesn't come to me."

Don't stop following until either the dog starts coming back or you jerk the leash to make him come.

Step 4: Come at a Distance

"Wrap, Run, and Praise" (wear a glove when using line).

Before you begin: On leash, your dog should come on the first command, on a loose lead, around any distraction.

How to practice: Attach a long, lightweight line to your dog's tab. When he's distracted, position yourself over the line and call him. Praise him during the entire recall, from the time he begins taking his first step toward you until you release him with a "chin touch okay." As he arrives, squat down and release with the "chin touch okay." If the dog ignores your command, correct him by grabbing the line and using "wrap, run, and praise"—wrap the line around your hand twice just above where your thumb attaches to your hand, make a fist around the line, and anchor your hand on your waist as you run away from your dog, praising all the way. Release with the "chin touch okay" when he arrives by you.

"I get all tangled up reeling in the line."

After you feel the line jerk, drop it, face your dog, and crouch down with your hands behind your back as you keep praising.

Step 5: In Pursuit "Come" on the Light Line

Goal: Teach your dog to stop his pursuit and come back if you call, regardless of how far away he is.

How to practice: Go to an area where your dog would like to venture out and explore. Wear a glove and have your dog drag the light line. Do the "wrap, run, and praise" with a slight variation: As he is moving toward a destination or following a scent, pick up the line, wrap it around your hand, anchor your hand to your waist, and start running. Time your command so the leash tightens to jerk him a split second after he hears the command.

"I practice the "Come" command by telling my dog to sit and stay, then walking away and calling him to come.

He does so well in class, but poorly at home and when playing."

The training situation (in which your dog is poised and totally controlled in stay, intently watching you walk away) in no way resembles real life (in which a dog gobbling rabbit droppings is entranced by the activity and oblivious to you). Raise your dog's understanding by practicing the following exercise.

Out of the Blue Recalls

Goal: Whether his last recall was a minute ago or a week ago, he will reliably obey the "come" command.

Before you begin: Perfect sneakaways around distractions and "in-pursuit recalls" (steps 3 and 5)

How to practice: Twice weekly for thirty minutes, take your dog to a new location, one he will eagerly explore and continually investigate. Try parks, fields, a friend's yard, or anywhere you can enforce your command properly. Attach a very long 50- to 200-foot light line to his collar and allow him to roam. Put on your gloves and every five minutes or so, when he least expects it and is running away, call and "wrap, run, and praise."

Exercises and Usage

Obedience isn't supposed to be treasured like a fine crystal vase you admire and display but don't use. Anything you teach your dog should be used constantly and consistently. Wear and tear may not look good on crystal, but the more you utilize obedience, the more positively ingrained in your dog it becomes.

Of course, you'll be using the "heel" command on walks and the "come" command anytime you need your dog nearby, and you probably can think of all sorts of times to use "sit," "down," and "stay" commands. Additionally, consider using your obedience commands for all these purposes:

Sit stay: Use to stop or prevent jumping up, fidgeting for grooming, begging.

Sit: Use before and during petting to control shyness, apprehension, or enthusiasm. Also use it if he begins to pester people, kids, or other animals, before feeding, when you're putting on a collar or attaching a leash, and at street curbs.

Stay: Use during mealtimes to keep him away from the table.

Rapid-fire obedience commands: If your dog has any tendency toward aggression when you approach him, make him come to you and execute a few commands for you. Also use rapid-fire commands if he has something you want him to relinquish, or an object he might get possessive over, to accomplish your objective without reaching for him or the object. Your lifestyle will determine how and when you use obedience commands. For instance, I live in a studio apartment in a complex of condominiums, hotel rooms, and long-term rentals. Additionally, the building houses two popular restaurants, a salon, a tailor, and a realtor. Daily we pass guests, residents, patrons, and dogs during our outings. BJ accompanies me—or perhaps I should say I accompany her—off leash. I tell her to sit in the elevator and when I get the mail, do laundry, and chat with friends. She is trained to walk near me, passing on the same side of any obstacle, whether alive or inanimate. She is not to go through doors opened by anyone other than me. She is curb trained so I don't have to worry about her going into the street if she's with me while I'm loading or unloading my vehicle with gear. Even if I have to go where dogs aren't allowed, I can take BJ (who weighs only nine pounds) along in a "Doggy Duds" over-the-shoulder bag. Regardless of one's living arrangement and lifestyle, a well-behaved dog is much more likely to enjoy a great variety of activities with his owner.

Household Obedience

Maybe your dog obeys fine in the backyard and at class or in the park, but won't listen in the house. That is your cue to leave the leash dragging from his collar in the house so you can stop misbehavior and enforce commands. If he does well until the leash comes off, try this intermediate step: Replace the leash with a tab and a 5- to 10-foot piece of light line, and then follow this training routine.

Goal: Perfect obedience commands and teach him not to run away from impending corrections.

Before you begin: Your dog should have a good understanding of basic on-leash commands.

How to practice: Attach 5 feet of light line to your dog's tab and give him commands periodically. Tell him to sit in odd places where he is allowed but has never been expected to obey—on the stair landing, or a sofa, or in the bathtub, for instance. Give commands while you wash dishes, fold laundry, wrap a gift, open mail, put on your jacket, or attach a collar and leash (have an additional collar and leash attached so you can enforce). When he is interested in what other household members are doing, or who is in the yard, at the door, or pulling into the driveway or garage, give commands. In all these situations "sit" is practical, but also utilize "down," "come," "front," "stay," and "heel" for variety. Enforce by jerking the tab as you would a leash—jerk the tab up if you want him to sit, downward for "down," and forward for "come," "front," or "heel."

If he tries to run down the hall or under the dinner table or around the couch, calmly walk down the line until you reach the tab.

Other Commands

Wait
Off
Quiet
Drop it

Wait (Five Steps)

1. Wait at door
2. Wait at door with distractions
3. Cross through
4. Out of sight

The "stay" command means freeze in the sit, down, or stand position, and therefore is very restrictive. The "wait" command, though, allows your dog to move about, but only within certain areas. You can use it to keep your dog in the car or out of the kitchen. The only thing "wait" has in common with "stay" is that both last until the next direction is given, twenty seconds or twenty minutes later.

Step 1: Wait at Door

Teach the "Wait" command at doorways first. Choose a light-weight door and estimate how wide your dog's front end is. Open the door 2 inches more than that as you command "Wait." Stand there with your hand on the knob of the partially open door, ready to bump the dog's nose with it should he

Basic Guidelines for "Come"

- Don't put your authority at risk by calling "Come" when your dog may not obey and you know you can't enforce.
- Standardize your voice, always using the same enthusiastic tone which suggests urgency, to say "Buddy, come!"
- Appeal to your dog's chase instinct and help ensure a faster recall by moving away after calling "Come."
- Use verbal praise only, because petting may repel him.
- Praise enthusiastically while he approaches. If you wait until he arrives, your lack of commitment will reduce his commitment to the process, too.
- Squat to acknowledge his final approach and arrival.
- Make him come all the way to you. If you suspect the dog isn't going to make a direct approach, move opposite from the dog's line of movement so he gets jerked toward you.
- To reward a good response, release immediately with a "chin touch okay." Periodically delay the release as your dog's recall becomes faster and more reliable.

attempt to pass through the opening. Be sure never to shut the door while correcting. Instead, leave the door open with your hand on the door handle, ready to stop attempted departures with an abrupt and silent bump of the door. If necessary, butt him with a quick movement that makes it appear the door is snapping at him every time he tries to peer or charge out. Leash your dog so that, if your attempts to deter him fail and he successfully skips across the border, you can step on the leash and prevent his escape.

Step 2: Wait with Distractions

Practice at familiar and unfamiliar doors as a helper tries to coerce your dog to leave. Your helper can talk to the dog and drop food, but your helper shouldn't call your dog. As your helper remains on the opposite side of the door, engage in lively conversation to teach your dog that even when you are preoccupied, the "wait" command is enforced. When that lesson has been learned, you'll no longer need the leash.

"Does it matter which direction the door opens or what type of door it is?"

The procedure is the same whether the door opens in or out. Practice with lightweight doors until you feel confident that the timing and strength of the tap is appropriate to deter your dog. Then apply the technique at heavy or sliding doors.

"How can I stop my dog from barreling through the door?"

If your dog waits but bounds through the door when released, mowing down anything in his path and dragging the unfortunate master gripping his leash, say "Sit" following your "chin touch okay." Insist he stop dead by using a two-handed upward jerk if necessary. Practice the pattern of "wait, okay, sit, come inside" until he is responding on a slack leash. After inviting him through a main door, command "Sit" immediately following his exit. When he does it on a slack lead the first time through, start doing the same pattern with the leash dragging. If he obeys with the leash dragging, let him drag the light line, and finally try it off-lead. He should now usually proceed through doorways in a mannerly fashion, but surprise him with that "sit" command a couple of times a week to keep him sharp.

Off (Get Down)

Teach your dog the "off" command if you want him to stop jumping on people, furniture, or counters. To enforce the "off" command:

1. Quickly bump him in the chest with your knee.
2. Jerk the leash opposite the direction of his jump.
3. Slide your toe sideways under his rear feet to take him off-balance.
4. Tap his nostrils quickly and lightly with your open palm. If your dog jumps on other people or when he isn't close by, always have him leashed so you can deliver timely corrections. Say "Off" a split second before the correction and avoid using the "down" command for jumping up if you say that when you want him to lie down.

Quiet

There are three steps to teaching your dog to be "quiet" on command.

Introductory phase: Teach the "quiet" command by leashing your dog and creating a situation likely to elicit barking—seeing a cat, engaging in ruckus play, being around children, or hearing the doorbell ring. Command "Quiet" when he vocalizes and distract him with a sharp jerk of the leash or a quick spritz of bitter apple against his lip as you hold his cheek to ensure an accurate spray. Praise him when he is quiet.

Correction phase: After a half dozen corrections, issue the command and only correct when necessary. Always have your dog leashed and bitter apple in hand before commanding "quiet."

At a distance: If you're commanding from a distance or when your dog is tied outside, kenneled, or caged, attach a long leash to him so you can deliver a jerk—from any distance—as he hears "Quiet." Though not as timely, you can enforce the "quiet" command by running up to spritz and leaving quickly. Some dogs are so pleased you've come back that they continue barking every time you leave, despite the correction. That's why remote corrections—whether launching a shaker can, spraying water, or jerking—are better.

"All I have to do is show my dog a shaker can or bitter apple and he behaves."

Always keep bitter apple or shaker cans silent and hidden, before and after use, to ensure that they are never used to issue empty threats. Warning him to behave as you expose your ammunition will only teach him to respect the bottle or can. To teach him to respect you, wait until he has disobeyed to demonstrate how you intend to back it up.

"Will bitter apple harm my dog's eyes?"

Yes, it can. Therefore, never spray bitter apple at your dog. Use it as the dog is chewing or barking, and press the bottle against his lip line before you depress the sprayer. The more you have used the bitter apple correction, the tougher it's going to be to spray quickly and accurately. Keep the bitter apple hidden in your hand, ready for use, and before taking the bottle out of hiding grip your dog's collar with your free hand to ensure better aim.

"Should I say 'quiet' every time my dog barks?"

No, in fact, feel free to praise and encourage your dog for appropriate barking, such as when an intruder is near. There is nothing wrong with a dog barking if you can silence him easily when necessary. But it isn't necessary for a dog's well-being that he be allowed to bark, so if you find any and all barking disturbing or unacceptable, correct it.

Drop It

Use the "drop it" command to teach your dog to release objects from his mouth or not to pick something up. Some dogs, and virtually all puppies, like to chew, carry, and mouth anything they can—hands, clothing, the leash, gravel, cigarette butts, landscaping timbers, tissue. Your first reaction may be to pry his jaws open to remove it, but if you do, he'll soon be prowling for another item to grab. Teaching "drop it" will reduce his scavenging tendency.

Accompany the "drop it" command with a sharp jerk of the leash, as you quickly back away and offer to play with an acceptable object. If your dog has something in his mouth and your jerk doesn't cause him to drop it, spray your finger with bitter apple and touch his gum with the sprayed finger as you issue the "drop it" command.

Leave It

If he hasn't yet picked up an item, but he's thinking about it, you can either use the "drop it" command or introduce a new word such as "leave it." In either case, when you notice him eyeballing a taboo item, give your command and a quick jerk of the leash as you back away from the item while praising all the way. This looks very similar to step 2 of the "come" command, but use the "drop It" or "leave it" command before he takes possession.

Social Skills

Overcoming Fear

For your dog's sake, ignore your natural desire to console a fearful dog. Whether his phobia involves inanimate objects such as garbage cans, loud or strange noises, other dogs, children, or places like the veterinarian's office, hallways or stairwells, reassurance only reinforces fear.

His fright will diminish if you insist he concentrate on something else. Give obedience commands in rapid fire sequence for two minutes or until he is relaxed, or at least responding automatically to "sit," "down," "stay," and "come." Then initiate playtime by running, nudging, patting the ground, or talking silly. Continue rapid-fire commands if he seems preoccupied by his fear. Practice first in situations in which he's uncomfortable but not panicked, then gradually progress to greater challenges.

"My dog is frightened of the stairs. How can I teach my dog to go up and down?"

If possible, begin practice on no more than a half a flight of stairs or use a very wide stairway with good traction. Leash your dog, grip the railing, and progress up or down one step at a time, looking straight ahead to convey confidence. Ignore his balking and expect the first step to present the biggest challenge. By holding his leash short and tight you'll prevent him from losing balance if he begins scrambling. Repeat methodically and mechanically for about fifteen minutes or until your dog takes stairs without hesitation. Introduce a puppy by placing him on the bottom stair. Then, either wait for him to gather the courage

Whole Lotta Shaking

Dogs shake and shiver even when they aren't scared or cold. Some dogs, particularly toy breeds, seem to shake for no reason. Others learn, from perhaps one experience, that if they start shaking they have their consoling owner's undivided attention. If the owner coddles him in response to shivering at the veterinarian's office or grooming shop, a dog is likely to do it every time he goes.

So what is the best advice when you notice your dog is shaking? Warm him if he is actually cold, do not touch him if he is scared, and keep your eye on him if you aren't sure but suspect there is no good reason for his quivering. Avoid reinforcing the behavior with affection, sympathy, concern, or attention.

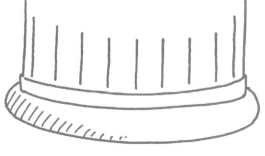

Car Rides

During car rides, contain and secure your dog by:

- Crating
- Purchasing a "doggy seatbelt"
- Installing a pet barrier in your vehicle
- Tying a nonchewable leash to the seat belt fitting, allowing only enough slack for your dog to sit or lie down in place

to jump off, or try coaxing him by sitting on the floor with something he likes. When he's mastered one, place him on the second-to-last stair, progressing one stair at a time until he can do the whole flight. If a puppy will walk down stairs, usually he'll have no problem going up.

Trouble-Free Car Rides

Good car-riding manners ensure safety for both driver and dog. A dog who sticks his head out the window exposes his eyes to injury or, if you swerve or brake abruptly, he may fall out of the car. His movement can obstruct your view and that, along with barking or whining, can distract you. Reduce the chance your dog will develop bad habits like vocalizing and lunging by containing him during car rides. Also, in the unfortunate event you have an accident, he won't be thrown about the car or escape through a broken window and run into traffic. You'll appreciate the additional benefit of a cleaner car with less hair-covered upholstery and nose-printed windows.

Veterinary, Groomer, and Kennel Visits

These experiences are more pleasant if your dog is under control. Test and improve his obedience by using it as you invite him out of the car, walk around the grounds, and into the building. Hand him over to caretakers without fanfare and expect him to remain somewhat composed when he's returned to you. Especially when you venture away from home, treat the outing like a training session rather than a vacation from obedience.

Chapter Five

ADVANCED TRAINING

What's It All About?

Obedience trials test and score the dog's ability to perform specific exercises. The American Kennel Club sanctions the majority of these events, though trials governed by the United Kennel Club, States Kennel Club, and others are quickly gaining popularity. Since the rules are either exactly the same or include only minor variations regardless of which kennel club is governing, little additional training is required to earn more titles. In AKC and most other obedience competitions, dogs work toward titles in three levels, each progressively more difficult. The classes, titles, and general summary of requirements are as follows:

Novice—Companion Dog (CD): On- and off-leash heeling, recall and stand, sit and down stay. Novice is the only class in which the dog is leashed for part of the performance and, when the leash is removed, the handler can guide the dog by the collar while moving from one exercise to the next.

Open—Companion Dog Excellent (CDX): Drop on recall, retrieve on flat, retrieve over high jump, broad jump, and sit and down stay with the handlers out of sight.

Utility—Utility Dog (UD): Hand signals, scent discrimination, moving stand, and directed jumping and retrieving.

Open and Utility are considered the advanced classes. In these, the leash is removed as the team enters the ring and the dog is never touched except to be measured or praised. In order to earn a title in each level the dog must earn three qualifying scores. A perfect score is 200 points, and to qualify a dog must earn 170 points and 50% of the available points for each exercise.

Dogs who earn a UD are eligible to compete for two other obedience titles. The UDX (Utility Dog Excellent) is earned when he qualifies in Open and Utility class at the same show ten times. The OTCh (Obedience Trial Championship) is won after the dog accumulates one hundred points. Points are earned if the dog places first or second in Open or Utility, and the number of points earned is determined by the size of the class. This is the only competitive obedience title, meaning a dog earns points by defeating dogs rather than simply performing exercises in accordance with the rulebook. Special competitions, otherwise known as tournaments, are held for the best of the best. In order to enter, the dog must prove himself at AKC or other kennel club sanctioned events. Top obedience dogs are ranked each year using various systems designed by breed clubs, obedience clubs, and obedience publications such as *Front and Finish*, or *The Dog Trainer's News*. Although these aren't official designations, they're esteemed and sought after.

American Kennel Club competitions are limited to registered and ILP (indefinite listing privilege) dogs, but many other governing bodies allow mixed breeds to compete. All obedience competitions allow spayed and neutered dogs to participate. If you'd like to observe an obedience trial, call local training clubs (listed in the Yellow Pages) or browse dog show superintendents' pages on the Internet. You're likely to find there are events several times each month within easy driving distance.

Dog Training as a Hobby

Obedience trialing is a rewarding endeavor that doesn't require extensive travel or financial resources. Anyone can participate in the sport of dog obedience; desire is far more important than natural talent. Top competitors include people of all ages and physical conditions. Dogs of all breeds and backgrounds (rescued and formerly abused dogs, too) appear in the winner's circle. Most handlers participate for the reward of a better trained dog, the camaraderie with peers, and the thrill of earning an occasional title.

Choosing a Dog Trainer or School

Whether you are looking for professional, in-person guidance, socialization for you or your canine, or all of the above, dog training programs are popular nationwide.

Gather names by looking in the phone book and newspaper, and by asking your veterinarian, humane society, groomer, kennel, friends, neighbors, co-workers, or relatives for recommendations.

Call and ask questions about class curriculum, training philosophy, location, years in business, class size, instructor qualifications, and cost. If you are satisfied with your phone conversation, go watch a class in session. If you are unsure whether you'd like to join this organization, visit other dog training classes.

Many competitors hire private instructors either as their sole means of coaching or to supplement group instruction. In either case, most trialers gather informally with other trainers to practice working their dogs around distractions. Your canine social circle will quickly expand as you go to training classes, seminars, and practice matches.

When selecting a private instructor inquire about techniques, his personal obedience trial experience, and titles earned. Ask, too, about his

experience with your breed, and for client referrals. Finally, good rapport with a private instructor is a must. It will help you stay inspired and motivated to work your dog when the going gets tough.

Whichever route you choose, expect to occasionally be frustrated or mildly skeptical. Give training a chance to work. Periodic confusion is a normal part of the learning process and not a reason to quit.

Advanced Exercises

Perhaps you're not sure if you are interested in obedience competition, but you definitely want to continue training your dog beyond the basics. The following exercises are fun to train, improve control, and will be helpful should you decide to compete. Congratulations on your interest. Let's get started!

Hand Signals, Whistles, and Snap Commands

It's imperative to use clear, concise, and consistent commands. But don't feel obligated to use a customary or standard command like "Heel" if you'd prefer to use a word like "Side" or a foreign word like "Fuss." In fact, perhaps you don't want to use words at all. A snap of your fingers followed by a point to the ground could mean lie down; in fact, that will come in handy when you are brushing your teeth and you want your dog to stop misbehaving. Whistles are commonly used in the field because the sound travels so well. Initially though, the dog must be trained close to the handler to understand the association between behaviors and whistles. Generally, one toot of the whistle means sit and stay, and multiple toots mean come into "Heel" position.

Teaching hand signals is easy. Always give your hand signal in a distinct way so the dog doesn't assume you are just scratching your nose. Obedience trial regulations allow the handler to use a single motion of the entire arm and hand but penalize any body motion. I suggest beginning with the down, sit, stay, heel, and come handsignals. Teaching watchfulness so he doesn't miss your signal may be difficult. Any time your dog's attention wanders, use sneakaways to bring back his focus.

Teaching your dog any task is the same whether you use a standard command or something else: Give the cue (the specific hand signal, whistle, verbal command, etc.) as you show him what you want and give praise.

Rapid-Fire Commands

Teach your dog to obey the commands you practiced in the Basic Training section in fast motion. If you've gotten into the bad habit of waiting for your dog's attention before giving commands, he may be in the habit of not giving you his attention as quickly as he should.

Goal: To improve your dog's reliability and enable him to obey commands given in quick succession.

How to practice: Command "Sit," release with "chin-touch okay," command "Come" and run 20 feet, release, command "Down," release, "Heel" your dog at various speeds and include halts and turns, release, and command "Down." That sequence should take 15–25 seconds. Once you've mastered that, work up to sequences of three to five minutes.

"I have very little time to train my dog."

By practicing rapid-fire commands, you'll become a more efficient and effective trainer and therefore need to train for much shorter periods to see terrific results. Additionally, if your dog doesn't have a high exercise requirement, rapid-fire commands are a great way to expend his energy as you stimulate his mind.

Play During Training

Is your dog still difficult to control when his adrenaline rises and he gets really excited? Develop an on/off switch so he can have a grand old time acting like a dog but instantly obey commands you give. Not only does this allow you to gain control of an energetic dog, it also teaches him to respond to your commands without a warm-up.

How to practice: Use toys, vigorous movement, and intense verbal praise to encourage rambunctious behavior; sneak away any time dog is uninterested in your play. Start giving commands when your dog has become focused on playing or has gone out of control. Tell him "Sit" or "Down," and then move around, praise him, and toss a toy or drop food as a distraction. Use quick, concise, strong corrections whenever necessary. Return, praise, release, and play. Command "Heel" and walk toward the food or toys, around them, over them, back toward them and then halt in front of

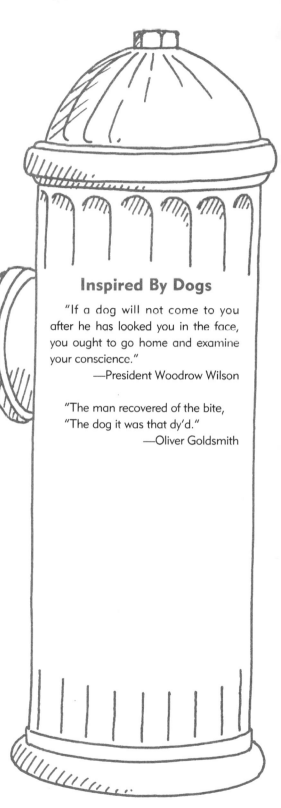

Inspired By Dogs

"If a dog will not come to you after he has looked you in the face, you ought to go home and examine your conscience."

—President Woodrow Wilson

"The man recovered of the bite,
"The dog it was that dy'd."

—Oliver Goldsmith

these distractions, ready to enforce an automatic sit. Pick up a toy and play with good-natured teasing. Tap it on the ground, hide it behind your back, run away with it, then toss it for him. If he shows a lack of interest, scramble to get it and act like you won a prize. Play keep-away and hard-to-get. When he shows interest and resumes playing, give a command, then release him quickly and play with him some more. Then, holding the leash, toss a toy or throw food and call "Come."

Dogs quickly learn that the more promptly they obey, the sooner they get to play, and thus play becomes a reward for obedience—not a bribe. Although better obedience is a great benefit of practicing play during training, you'll also be discovering how to elicit nice play, which is the hallmark of a truly well-bonded relationship.

Distance Sit Stay

Goal: To teach your dog to hold the sit stay, no matter how far away you are. The procedure described below frees your hands and allows you to go further away without the risk of your dog running off.

Before you begin: Your dog should "Stay" with extreme distractions when you're a leash-length away (see Leash Length Sit Stay, page 155).

How to practice: (1) Tie your longe line to a stationary object. (2) Heel your dog to the snap of the longe line, so he sits facing away from where it is tied. (3) Snap the longe line to collar (leaving the leash attached to collar, too), command "Stay," and walk away. Your dog will be jerked by the tied line if he bolts. To stop any undesirable movement, run back and use a two-handed grip on the leash (near the snap) to move dog back to the area, then into "sit" position with a jerk.

Out of Sight Stay

Goal: Your dog will learn to remember your instructions even when you leave his sight.

Before you begin: Perfect the "distance sit stay."

How to practice: Sit your dog behind the corner of a building, command "Stay" and step out of sight while still holding the leash. Throw distractions into his view.

"Oh, no! I'm having a bad-dog day."

If he moves, correct immediately by sliding your hand down the leash toward collar and then giving an upward jerk. After correcting, disappear around the corner as promptly as possible.

Down Stay—at a Distance and Out of Sight

Use the techniques just mentioned to teach the "distance and out of sight down stay," but reinforce by giving a downward jerk as described in the Basic Training section.

Traveling Sit and Down

Teach your dog to "sit" or to "down" when he's running or far away. You'll find this useful if he is playing in the park or about to approach someone or something he shouldn't.

Before you begin: When standing at your side, your dog should obey the "Sit" and "Down" commands around distractions.

How to practice:

Step 1 (pivot sit): Walk forward with your dog on "Okay" release. Command "Sit" as you pivot to face him and jerk up simultaneously. Say "Gooood dog!" as you back away to the end of the leash. Return to your dog and repeat the procedure.

Step 2 (pivot down): When your dog sits on command without the jerk, begin teaching the moving down. Command "Down" as you pivot and jerk downward. Back away to the end of the leash as you give praise. Return to your dog and repeat the procedure.

Step 3 (walking sit and down): When your dog will stop and position himself on command, say "Sit" or "Down" as you look over your shoulder and continue walking. If he doesn't stop dead, run back to him to correct.

Step 4 (running sit and down): When your dog will position himself on your command as you continue walking, give the "Sit" or "Down" command when you are running together.

Troubleshooting tip: If your dog is having difficulty with the down, perfect the "traveling sit" procedure (steps 1, 3, 4, and 5) before attempting "down" again.

Step 5 (out of the blue sit and down): When your dog least expects it, give a "sit" or "down" command. Initially try it as your dog is meandering around the house. When he has mastered that, give "sit" and "down" commands during outings. Try to get him to immediately sit or down on command, regardless of his activity or location.

General Rules:
1. If your dog doesn't stop dead on command:
   Run back to correct him
   Use the same leash correction you use for breaking a sit or down stay
2. Praise him verbally for compliance
3. Return to him and release with a "chin touch okay"

Front

The "front" and "come" commands are both used to make the dog return to you, but the "front" command will require your dog to sit when he arrives. Unlike "come," "front" is a command your dog has never disobeyed. To ensure that no bad habits develop, only share this new command with people who are as willing to enforce it as you are. If an emergency arises, "front" could save your dog's life.

The Steps
1. Reel
2. Jerk
3. In pursuit with leash
4. Distance
5. In pursuit with light line

Step 1: Front
Goal: Teach your dog that "front" means to come briskly and sit facing you with his paws in front of your feet until released with the "chin touch okay." In this position the dog will be close enough for you to easily touch him.

How to practice: Call "Front," then reel in the leash as you back up and praise. As he arrives in front grab his collar with one hand and place his rear end straight with the other. Release with a "chin touch okay." Repeat this exercise at least ten times per day for a week.

After one week, only gentle guidance should be required to sit your dog, and after four weeks, he should sit automatically. When the dog usually sits automatically but forgets if distracted, enforce the position with a jerk up as you use your other hand to control the straightness of the rear.

"I can't get my dog to sit straight because he struggles when I try to place him."

It isn't uncommon for come dogs to vigorously fight your attempts to precisely position them in the sit. Calmly hold his collar and firmly reposition him no matter how much he flails, twists, or attempts to turn. With your hands still on his collar and rear, tell him he is good when he settles down and then release him with the "chin touch okay."

Follow steps 2 through 6 as described for the "come" command (see Basic Training, page 163) but substitute the "front" command and make the dog sit squarely in front of you until you release him with the "chin touch okay."

Off-Leash Commands

The concept of off-leash training is a bit of a misnomer. All teaching is done on leash. Off-leash work only reinforces the good work he does on-leash. If not fully prepared on-leash, the dog's lack of understanding will multiply when the leash comes off.

"How do I know if my dog is really ready for off-leash?"

Try this experiment before attempting off-lead work: With your dog dragging his leash, and your arms folded or in your pockets, give a "sit," "down," or "come" command in a non-threatening tone of voice. That should be easy. Now choose the strongest temptation for your dog—the doorbell, an open field, or the presence of other animals—and try the experiment again. Praise him if he listens, but pick up the leash if he doesn't. If he is now pulling on the leash, sneak away. If he stands by you as you pick up the leash, fold your arms, leave the lead totally slack, and give a single command to "sit." If he obeys, read on. If he doesn't, review sneakaways and basic on-lead commands around distractions before returning to this section.

Steps:
1. Heeling with leash behind back
2. Straitjacket commands
3. Lightline commands
4. Weaning off light line

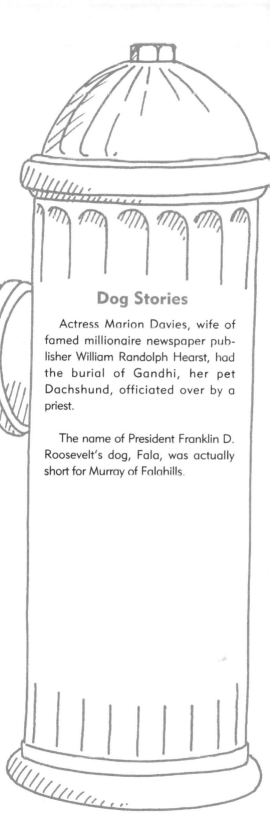

Dog Stories

Actress Marion Davies, wife of famed millionaire newspaper publisher William Randolph Hearst, had the burial of Gandhi, her pet Dachshund, officiated over by a priest.

The name of President Franklin D. Roosevelt's dog, Fala, was actually short for Murray of Falahills.

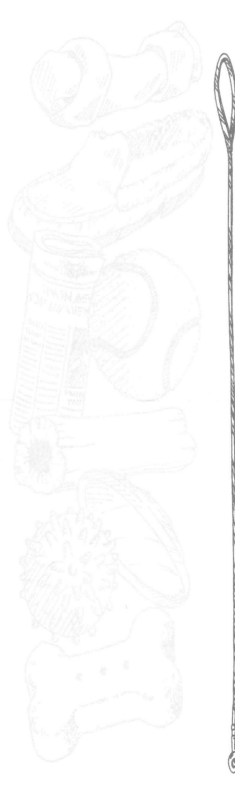

Heeling with Leash Behind Back

Goal: To prepare your dog for off-leash control, teach him to maintain his position regardless of where the leash is.

How to practice: Hold the slack (but not dragging) leash behind your back, in your right hand. Turn left to correct forging. Pat your thigh and gently jump ahead without tightening the leash to encourage the apprehensive or lagging dog. If he continues meandering away from the heel position, grab his leash with your left hand, place it inside your left thigh, and jump ahead while praising.

Straitjacket Commands

When teaching on-lead obedience, some people consciously or unconsciously use excessive body English and gestures, which no longer seem significant when the dog gets further away during off-lead work. Often, we wrongly assume disobedience occurs because the dog is off-leash, but actually he was never taught to obey the command without the additional cues.

How to practice: Attach the leash, fold your arms, or put your hands in your pockets, and give "sit," "down," "stand," "stay," "come," and "front" commands. Use no gestures, just your voice. After all, he'll only hear your voice and the gestures will be wasted if he is running away.

Avoid touching the leash to enforce these "straitjacket" commands. Instead, walk to his collar to make an "off-leash-type correction." Reach for his collar and enforce "sit" with an upward jerk, enforce "down" with a downward jerk, and enforce the recall commands by jerking him forward toward you as you back up.

"How can I correct my dog if he tries to run away?"

Replace the leash with a longer line if he tries to dodge you as you reach for him. This will allow you to walk right up to him by stepping on the line. Be calm and confident. Always practice around distractions, until, in the rare event he disobeys, the dog doesn't dodge you as you reach for his collar to correct him.

Lightline Commands

For this transition phase, you'll need some different equipment—a lightline and a tab (see Basic Training, equipment page 000).

Purpose: You maintain your ability to correct your dog's mistakes as he proves his readiness for off-leash obedience.

Before you begin: Practice the on-leash distraction test, leash-behind-the-back heeling, and straitjacket commands.

How to practice: Tie a long, lightweight line to the tab and let your dog drag it as you practice commands. Only touch the line and tab when correcting. Control your dog with commands. If he disobeys and runs off, step on the line, then walk along it till you can give his collar the appropriate corrective jerk.

Heeling: Confidently command "Heel" as you move out briskly. Encourage a reluctant or lazy dog by patting your leg or puddle jumping as you give praise. Use lots of turns, halts and speed changes to keep him focused. Quickly move in the opposite direction if he leaves the heel position, and praise him as he returns. Perfect 90-degree turns before attempting a 180-degree pivot during heeling. Stop immediately and enforce the automatic "sit," or turn left into your dog to cut him off if he begins forging.

"What can I do if my dog continues to wander or forge ahead?"

If he doesn't respond to encouragement, correct lagging by using the "wrap, run, and praise": Walk to your dog and reach for his tab, then slide your hand from his tab, down the line a couple of feet, and twirl it around your hand. Put your hand on the inner thigh of your left leg and puddle jump or run ahead as you praise. Drop the line and continue heeling after this correction.

"My dog just sits still and won't move when I command 'heel.'"

Practice by calling "Come" and running 20 feet. Squat to praise him and resume heeling practice when, three times in a row, he runs happily by your side. If he won't budge on the "come" command, walk to the tab and give it a horizontal jerk with praise as you run to the destination. If he still won't move, practice calling "Come" and running with line in hand for the remainder of the session.

Sit, Down, Stay, Come, and Front Commands:

Practice these commands, correcting errors by jerking with the tab, the same way you did on the leash.

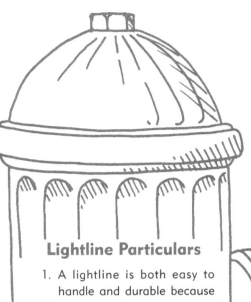

Lightline Particulars

1. A lightline is both easy to handle and durable because it's made of nylon.
2. Choose a test weight that is strong enough to hold your dog in the smallest diameter possible.
3. Make sure it is long enough that you feel confident letting it drag on the ground—long enough that if you need to correct, you will be able to reach it before your dog is out of range. Fifty to 100 feet should be enough for any dog who has had the advised prerequisite training.

- Remember, the only time you touch the lightline is to either step on it or grab it to stop your dog from running away.
- To wean your dog off the line, gradually cut off the length.

Weaning Dog off Lightline

The real meaning of off-lead control lies not in the dog's ability to obey commands, but in your ability to approach him without him running away. No matter how well trained he may be, no dog is ever perfect; he will make occasional mistakes. Before going completely off-line, make certain your dog doesn't run when he sees you approaching. Before you enforce the command, praise him for standing his ground and letting you approach. Attempt this step only when your dog no longer tries to dodge his responsibilities—or you.

Goal: To achieve total off-lead control.

Before you begin: Your dog obeys commands around distractions without needing a reminding correction, and he accepts impending corrections without thinking about running away. After one month of practice with the line dragging, you should feel confident to begin weaning the dog off-line by beginning the cutting process.

How to practice: Every three to seven days cut off 20 percent of the lightline if your dog continues to respond obediently around distractions.

Go

This is an easy one if you've taught your dog to go into his cage on command (see Crating page 118). I use this to tell my dogs to go upstairs, downstairs, into and out of the car, and to their beds. To begin, get treats, a rug or blanket, your crate, and your leashed dog. Place the treats in your pocket and the padding in the crate. Sit your dog 3 feet from the opening of the crate and command "Stay." Place a treat inside the crate, tap on the crate so he focuses on the opening, and command "Go." He'll probably run in and eat his treat. Give praise as soon as his foot touches the pad. After he eats his treat, quickly repeat the same procedure three more times.

Now teach your dog to go to the pad by taking it out of the crate. Repeat the same procedure with one minor change: After you tell him stay and place the treat on the pad, you'll tap your finger on the pad and stand up straight before telling him "Go." Repeat three more times before moving the pad and practicing the same routine in a new location. For your next practice ses-

sion, proceed in an identical fashion, except stand next to your dog when you tell him "Go."

In your third session, repeat the procedure outlined for lesson 1, but omit the treats. When he is on the pad, tell him to sit or down if you like, and praise him. In your fourth session, sit him 3 feet away from the pad and tell him to "Go" without first tapping the area. If he goes without hesitation to the three areas, increase his distance from the target area or start working on new areas.

When the dog is familiar with the "go" command in six areas, reduce the size of the pad or remove it. Dogs can learn to generalize that if you are walking together and say "Go" it means move ahead in a straight line. If you say "Go" and an enclosure is in close proximity, he should walk inside. In close quarters such as a hallway or bathroom, saying "Go" as you point at the doorway means he should exit the area.

If he fails to "go" to the appropriate area on command, refrain from repeating yourself and instead use the leash to guide the dog quickly and pleasantly to the right spot so you can praise.

Retrieving

Many dogs have natural aptitude for retrieving. Others, though—even many of the retrieving breeds—consider this task boring, repulsive, or simply a game in which they grab something and teach you to chase them. Obedience and field trial trainers have comprehensive programs to teach this exercise to future competitors. But if you simply want to have some fun with your well-trained pet, bringing out the natural retriever in your dog is fairly simple.

First, get something your dog wants to play with—a squeaky toy, a soft or stuffed item, a bone, or a ball. Encourage his interest by tapping it on the ground, rubbing it on his body, and hiding it behind your back. When he is interested in the item, toss it out a few feet. If he hesitates to chase or grab it, snatch it up yourself and tease him by tapping it in front of him, hiding it, then tossing it again. You will retrieve more than he will the first few sessions, but your interest in the toy will bring out his competitive spirit and desire to capture it before you do.

Maybe your dog needs no encouragement to chase, but he won't bring the toy back or drop it. Keep a leash or line on him, and as soon as he picks up the item, praise as you run away from

him holding the line in your hand. Since a jerk of the line may cause him to drop the item, adjust the speed of your run so he is pulled toward you.

If your dog locks his jaws and refuses to relinquish his prize, give rapid-fire commands. Deliver your commands and reinforcement so quickly that your dog stops focusing on his vise-grip hold on the toy and starts concentrating on your commands. When your dog drops the toy as soon as you begin rapid-fire commands, it's time to start teaching the "drop it" command. Tell him "Sit," then command "Drop it" and enforce by jerking the leash sideways or blowing in his nose.

Speak

Teaching your dog to speak on command is an excellent way to develop watch-dog intuition. Many dogs don't naturally bark at the door but can be taught to do so. If you practice knocking on the door and asking your dog to speak, most dogs automatically learn to bark when someone's at the door. Also, many clever tricks can be built around the dog's ability to bark on command.

To teach "speak" you must find an object, activity, or situation that causes your dog to bark and praise him lavishly. When it becomes easy to initiate barking, begin giving a command and/or signal, and praise. After a few sessions, your command and signal is likely to trigger barking.

Jumping

Jumping, like retrieving, is great exercise, and you may eventually want to combine the two exercises as they do in obedience trials for the retrieve over the high jump. Or you may simply send your dog through hoops or over fences, barrels, or your outstretched arm or leg. Measure the height from the ground to your dog's elbow: about 5 inches for a Chihuahua and about 24 inches for a Great Dane. Introduce your dog to jumping with four to six items that are no higher than that. A propped up two-by-four, a ladder standing on its side, and a broomstick resting on the rungs of two chairs are examples that might be easily accessible and appropriate for your dog's size. Leash your dog, command "Heel," and walk over the items. Hold the leash just taut enough that he can't avoid the item. Never jerk the leash—that will negate his ability to negotiate the jump in a natural, coordinated fashion. Since the hurdles are very low, he will likely walk over them instead of jump.

This is fine, because your purpose is to allow him to get familiar and comfortable with the objects, not to develop a jumping style. When he steps over without hesitation, position yourself 10 feet from the jump, command "Hup," and run him over and past the hurdle so he can come to a natural stop rather than an abrupt one.

After twenty repetitions, put him on the longe line and sit him 10 feet from the jump. Walk to the other side of it so you are facing him and tap on the top of the jump. When he looks at the jump, command "Hup" and back up so he can clear it. Gradually raise the height of the jumps and repeat the process of running over, then calling over. Next, introduce your dog to portable jumps, too—your arms and legs. Leash your dog, tell him to stay next to a wall, and walk 3 feet away. Get on one knee and put the other leg out in front of you so your heel is on the ground and your toe is touching the wall. Command "Hup" as you pull your dog over your ankle. After a few repetitions sit on the ground, outstretch your arm so your finger-tips touch the wall and command "Hup." Enlist the help of another person to handle your dog's leash as you give the commands. Your helper should pull the lead taut, rather than jerk it, to encourage the dog to jump over your limbs. While you have that helper, get a hula hoop and ask him to hold it just a tiny bit off the ground. Sit your dog three feet away, command "Stay," put his leash through the hoop, and as you say "Hup," gradually back away from the hoop.

As your dog's confidence grows, you may want to gradually raise the height of the obstacles until he's jumping the height of his shoulder. To ensure your dog's safety, remember that higher jumps require good traction and plenty of take-off and landing room.

Quick Fixes for Common Problems

Problem Prevention

Who said dog training was difficult? You can stop bad behavior before it starts by taking these simple precautions.

1. Treat arrivals and departures as nonevents. The easiest way to encourage good behavior around guests is to ignore your dog as you come and go. If play and attention occur the instant someone makes an entrance, your dog will return all that love and affection by jumping, clawing,

or barking, and nobody will to want to be near the overly exuberant beast.

2. Feed nothing but dog food, feed it only in his dish, and place it in a quiet spot.

    Dogs who are never given food from the table, counter, or hand have little incentive to search for food outside of their bowls.

    Dogs who are never fed table scraps will be much more content to eat their own food.

    Let dogs eat in peace at a prescribed time, and food will never become a reason to get defensive.

3. Maintain good housekeeping.
    Keep your cabinets closed.
    Keep clean and dirty clothing secured.
    Immediately remove tasty garbage from the house—every thing from meat, bones, and wrappers to feminine hygiene products and tissues.
    Cover your garbage baskets or put them behind closed doors.
    Keep cat boxes and food out of reach.

4. Prepare for a visit from Oscar Madison. Practice "set-ups" so that your dog will never try to jump, steal, or shred, no matter how tempting the situation. Occasionally open cabinets, leave laundry or a purse on the floor, leave the dishwasher open, place liver sausage on a counter and chips on the coffee table. Then prepare to silently launch a shaker can—a soda can with eight pennies inside—at him.

5. Be generous with praise. Reward your dog with praise each time you ask him to go in, out, up, down, on, or off. Otherwise you may find him entertaining himself by leading you in a chase when you ask him into the house, car, or tub. Although you probably called him for a reason, treat his response to "come" as a separate event. In addition, frequently practice telling him to go in and out of the house, car, or crate even when you aren't going to ride, confine, or leave.

6. Take extra precautions when routines are upset. If your dog is underexercised, your work schedule changes, you're going on vacation, you're fighting with household members, or

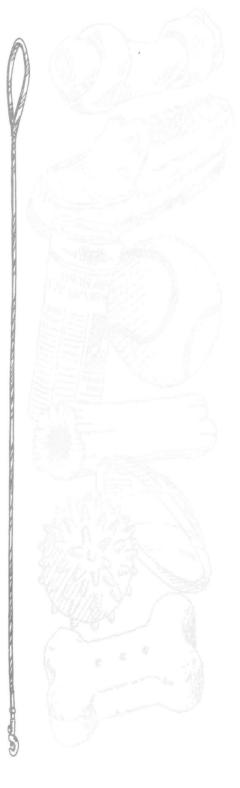

expecting guests, your dog's behavior is likely to change. Expect the worst. Treat him like an untrained dog, taking every precaution to ensure you aren't giving him opportunities to be naughty until things return to normal.

7. Give your dog the right outlets. Provide him with hard things to chew on, fun stuff to play with, adequate exercise, and an understanding of your obedience vocabulary.

   Make certain that his toys agree with his system and don't cause vomiting, gas, or diarrhea, and that they're not dangerous (ask your vet). And don't cause confusion by turning personal items such as shoes, towels, socks, and rags into playthings; it can encourage indiscriminate chewing.

   Play nice games like fetch (don't fight with him, growl or bark at him, pull on him, or play tug of war with him).

   Establish a vigorous exercise program for high-energy and large dogs.

   Train your dog in basic obedience. You'll be able to speak the same language, develop a stronger bond, and replace bad behavior with good.

Recommendations for Preventing and Solving Problems

Aids
Crates, bitter apple spray, doggy seatbelts, and special chewing items will be referred to in the following chapters. These common items are available through pet stores, mail order, and, in many cases, discount department stores.

Steps
Most problems can be resolved with a step-by-step plan. The following steps will be referred to under the headings of several problems.

1. Medical clearance: Confirm there is no medical reason for the problem by consulting your veterinarian.

2. Increase exercise: Provide vigorous aerobic exercise for a minimum of fifteen minutes, at least three times a week. Try jogging your dog on foot or alongside a bike, or having him continuously retrieve or swim. For specific exercise-related ques-

tions, consult your veterinarian and a breeder or another expert who is familiar with your breed and dog.

3. Confine properly: Every dog needs a place where he can do no wrong in your absence. Kennels and crates are best suited for this purpose.

4. Umbilical cording: Tie your dog to your belt with a short leash so his legs won't tangle and neither will yours. Your hands will be free so you can do what needs to be done and train your dog simultaneously.

5. Supervise: Eliminate windows of opportunity by keeping his every movement under surveillance.

6. Obedience training: Enable yourself to stop inappropriate behavior instantly by attaining one-command control around all distractions.

7. Mind exercise: Continually teach him new tasks—tricks, obedience, or specialized work (hunting, herding, etc.). Develop a better relationship by pursuing challenging and stimulating goals.

8. Calm entrances: Though your dog may greet you with enthusiasm, remain emotionally detached and don't return the affection until you've been in the house with him at least fifteen minutes.

9. Set-up: Concoct a situation that would cause your dog to attempt a misbehavior when you are physically and mentally prepared to stop him.

10. Bitter apple spray correction: This correction must only be initiated while your dog is misbehaving. Hold the collar and/or the back of your dog's neck as you press the nozzle of the spray bottle against his lipline, then spritz. Never let your dog see the bottle in your hand unless you are actually correcting.

11. Jerk the leash: Snap the leash quickly in the direction opposite to his misbehavior.

12. Startle correction: Distract your dog as he contemplates or actually begins to misbehave by tossing shaker cans (empty soda cans with eight pennies inside), clapping your hands together sharply, spraying a water pistol between your dog's eyes, or blasting a boat horn.

13 Beanie corrections: Bop your dog on the nose, forehead, or shoulders as he starts to misbehave or thinks about it. Use a beanbag rattle (a paper lunch bag filled with a quarter-cup of dried beans; twist the top of the bag so the beans rattle when you bop your dog).

14. Booby-traps: Set traps that will correct your dog remotely when triggered by his misbehavior—for example, strategically placed mousetraps, shaker cans, or electronic "Scat Mats."

15. Diaper: As your dog learns to control his elimination, keep your house clean by fashioning a diaper for your dog—fasten a towel or bandanna with Velcro, tape, or pins around his waist and tail. Or, use boy's underwear, sticking your dog's tail through the fly. Keep him leashed and supervised until you teach him to ignore it by using a jerk of the leash when he shows the least bit of interest.

Jumping Up on People

When guests or family members enter your house and shower the dog with affection, they teach the dog to jump up and act crazy. Encourage visitors and members of your household to show self-control. Though play, fun, and enthusiasm are an important part of a well-balanced, bonded relationship, they should never be associated with people coming and going. Practice calm arrivals by making it a habit to busy yourself doing other things, oblivious to your dog's prancing, barking, jumping, or panting. Insist that guests and family members do the same. Within two weeks of practicing uneventful arrivals, usually jumping up entirely subsides.

If calm arrivals haven't cured your dog, continue practicing them, but in addition, try these strategies:

• Enforce the "wait" command (see Basic Training). Teach your dog to listen to the "Wait" command no matter how inviting the distraction on the other side of the door. If you have total control when the door

Dog Stories

General George S. Patton had a white Bull Terrier named William the Conqueror, whom he called Willie.

Famed World War I German flying ace Manfred Von Richtofen, known as the Red Baron, was also known to fly with his pet Great Dane, Moritz.

opens, it is easier to maintain control when guests are inside, too.

- Don't give your dog easy targets for jumping. Jumping on a moving target is very difficult, so ask people to shuffle into the dog when he begins to bound. If he tends to jump on those who can't or won't shuffle, snap on a leash and step on it in, so he has only enough slack to begin jumping but will be jerked long before he is able to pounce on someone.
- Use the "off" command (see Commands, page 169)
- Teach the "down stay" (see Basic Training). The "down stay" is incompatible with jumping up and therefore a good prescription. Unfortunately, it's also the most difficult command to enforce with an excited dog, so establish control before attempting the "down stay"; perfect the "wait," then enforce the "off," next correct barking, and finally, focus on the "down stay."

Jumping Up on Furniture

Many people enjoy having their dogs on the furniture. Dogs love it, too: furniture smells like you, it's comfortable, and it usually affords him a better view of what is going on both inside and outside. Once you allow him on furniture, it becomes his domain, so don't expect him to wait politely for the next invitation. If he's sneaking on the furniture despite your consistent disapproval, provide your dog with his own piece of furniture—a very comfortable dog bed (store-bought or homemade). Conversely, make your furniture uninviting by placing plastic coat hangers, chicken wire, or Scat Mats on the cushions.

If you want to stop your dog from getting on the furniture, use a leash jerk or toss a shaker can at him as he makes his move, then tell him to go to his bed (see Advanced Training). If you ordinarily allow him on furniture teach him to get "off" on command (see Basic Training).

Separation Anxiety

Having to leave a dog alone is worrisome if he gets frantically frustrated when he's separated from his owner. Overly dependent dogs commonly respond to separations by continually barking, whining, and howling, destroying their living space, and attempting to escape by chewing, digging, and jumping over fences and out of windows. In addition to causing expensive damage, many dogs injure themselves. When panicked, they are oblivious to the physical discomfort of laryngitis, bloody-raw gums and paws, broken teeth, self-mutilation caused by chewing and licking, and even broken limbs as a result of jumping out of windows.

Avoid both after-the-fact corrections that increase anxiety and consoling tones or gentle petting that embed the neurosis. Instead:

- Exercise vigorously and regularly
- Improve his ability to handle all sources of stress by teaching reliable obedience
- As you come and go, remain relaxed and refrain from addressing your dog
- To directly increase his tolerance of separations, practice the three exercises described in the next section.

Exercises for Separation Anxiety

Random tie outs: Insist that he remain quiet when you leave. Take your dog to indoor and outdoor areas, familiar and unfamiliar, filled with or absent of distractions. Silently tie his leash short to a stationary object and walk away for a few minutes. Sometimes remain in sight and other times walk out of sight. To correct noise making, toss a shaker can, spray him with water or run over to spritz his mouth with bitter apple. Concentrate on the areas that make your dog most uncomfortable. Practice every other day for a half hour until he'll be silent regardless of where you leave him, where you go and how long you're gone.

Out-of-sight sit and down stays (see page 178): At least every other day practice fifteen- to twenty-minute down stays with lots of distractions.

Whirling dervish departures: Dash from room to room grabbing your keys, briefcase, jacket, lunch box, etc. Rush out the door and to your car, then back out of the driveway, motor around the block, pull back in the garage, and saunter into the house. As you put your keys, jacket, and paraphernalia away, completely ignore your dog. After relaxing for a few minutes, repeat the frenzied departure and relaxed arrival over and over for an hour. To thoroughly desensitize your dog to comings and goings, repeat this pattern three times the first week, then once a week for a month.

When at home, make it a habit to periodically confine your dog. Sequester him in a quiet area and place your recently worn sweatshirt or bathrobe on the floor on the other side of the closed door. If your smell permeates his room, he may not even realize it when you finally do leave. Give him his favorite toy only when you confine him. Make the toy more desirable by spitting on your hands and rubbing it up with your scent before every offering. Reduce the agitating sounds of neighbors or delivery people by creating "white" noise with a motorized fan to soothe your dog. This is a better solution than subjecting your dog to TV and radio stations with their unsettling cacophony (bells, whistles, applause, sobbing, screeching, and laughter). Then, when you do actually leave, follow the same routine.

Since separation problems can periodically return despite these precautions, reinstate these recommendations as needed.

Submissive Urination

If your dog wets when he greets people or is disciplined, he isn't having a housebreaking problem. Uncontrollable and unconscious leaking of urine is common in puppies and certain breeds. If your dog has been given a clean bill of health by a veterinarian, extinguish this tendency by:

- Teaching commands so you can give orders that force your dog to focus on his responsibilities instead of his emotions
- Keeping your dog leashed to enable nonemotional, silent correction of misbehaviors
- Avoiding eye contact, talking, and touching during emotional states
- Making your entrances and greetings devoid of emotion
- Never yelling, striking, or showing anger toward him

Since living with this behavior can be exasperating, consider diapering your dog for the first month so you don't have to continually clean up. To diaper your dog, simply pin a bandanna or towel around his privates and teach him not to remove it. Acclimate your dog to wearing the diaper by umbilical cording and jerking the leash if he even sniffs at it. When he is totally uninterested in the diaper—usually after less than a week of umbilical cording—let him walk around the house unleashed as usual, without concern about dribbling.

Avoid vigorous petting, impassioned tones of voice, and strong eye contact. Only interact with a superficial, brief pat, calm word, or fleeting glimpses when his bladder is empty. When he consistently responds without tinkling, test his control after he's had water. Gradually try a warmer approach, but be ready to turn off the affection and issue a command if it pleases the pee out of him.

Car Riding

Restraining your dog by crating, tying, or seat belting reduces the chance that he'll act unruly in the car and ensures ease of correction when necessary. If your dog becomes disruptive, attach a leash to his collar to hold and jerk as you drive.

Teach carsickness-prone and reluctant riders to enter and exit the car on command. Leash him, open the car door or hatch, and command him to go in as you give him a boost. Immediately invite him out with a "chin touch okay" and repeat the procedure five times in a row, several times per day. Within a week he should be readily responding on command. The more relaxed your dog becomes about getting in the car, the less inclined he'll be toward motion sickness.

To make the car a more pleasurable place to be, arrange to have him sit in the car with a canine companion who likes riding. Or try building the positive association with food: If your dog is a fairly neat chowhound, feed him only in the parked car.

However, don't feed your dog for three hours before a ride if he has a tendency to get carsick. Experiment with placing him in different spots in the car. You may find a location that because of the view, air flow, or smoothness of the ride doesn't induce sickness. If motion sickness continues to be a problem, ask your veterinarian about using medication.

Begging

It often takes only one tidbit for your clever dog to be convinced that your meals are better than his and that you're willing to share if he begs. If you've fostered this bad habit, the dog's can be broken, but you probably can't be cured. On the other hand, if you've acquired a dog with a begging habit, keep him out of the room when food is near, enforce the "down stay," or teach him to go to his bed.

In addition, follow these feeding rules: feed him dog food in his dish and never share goodies or feed him from your hands or a plate. Finally, when you eat or prepare food, completely ignore him.

Stealing and Scavenging

If you were all alone in someone else's house, what would you do when you got bored? Would the thought of looking at their stuff or even rummaging through cabinets, closets, or the refrigerator tempt you?

Now you know how a dog feels. He is trapped and bored and has no hands with which to do arts and crafts, but he does have plenty of senses yearning to be indulged. When given too much freedom too soon, he will quickly discover the joys of hunting for household treasures too often left easily accessible by negligent humans.

Many dogs steal when you're home for amusement. They know the only guaranteed way to rouse you from the recliner is to show off the valuables they've confiscated.

Police the canine klepto by:

- Incarceration (crating)
- Chain gang (umbilical cording)
- Surveillance (keeping your eyes glued to him)
- Don't be a victim:
  Keep the garbage out of reach
  Close cabinets and closets and put laundry away
  Teach the "drop it" or "leave it" command
- Dispense justice fairly:
  Only correct crimes in progress; never correct stealing after the fact
  When you discover the infraction, leash your dog, invite him to make the same mistake, and correct it with a leash jerk

House Soiling

Not even keeping your dog in good health, neutering him, and committing to a lengthy and ever-watchful program of house-breaking and basic training will guarantee that house soiling will never be a problem.

Consider the experiences of these owners.

Jay's Bullmastiff Rollie had been housebroken for two years when he began lifting his leg on the corner of the bed. The neutered male's marking made Jay furious. Each time he found it, he would yell and go looking for Rollie, who was invariably parked in the kitchen awaiting Jay's entrance. Jay would grab his collar and try to drag the 130-pound canine watering pot to the bedroom; Rollie would brace himself and stare at Jay, daring him to repeat the familiar scolding, until finally he bit his owner.

Penny considered her Maltese Angel an ideal companion. Imagine her surprise, then, when a visitor hesitantly inquired about the strange odor in the living room. Embarrassed, Penny thought about those occasions once or twice a month when she would discover a pile, attributing it to having left Angel too long. Penny, offended by the visitor's comment, said, "The house doesn't smell. You probably just don't like dogs."

Months later, Penny replaced the carpeting throughout the house. Upon removing the old carpet, the installers discovered urine stains—the result of many years of accidents. Because small dogs have small accidents, the urine usually dried without being detected. Penny never realized her Angel was not fully housebroken.

As Jay discovered, after-the-fact corrections didn't stop Rollie's marking, but did make him defensive and untrusting. Penny, on the other hand, was unaware of habitual little accidents; she needed to face the fact that her ignorance had allowed a bad habit to take hold. House-training problems are frustrating but can be solved by treating the dog as totally untrustworthy, just as you would an eight-week-old pup, and doing daily vigorous obedience training so the dog is accustomed to taking direction from you.

If your dog has been in your house less than six months, it's likely he's been insufficiently supervised and confined, and you need to follow the plan outlined in the housebreaking chapter.

"What if umbilical cording doesn't work and my dog soils anyway?"

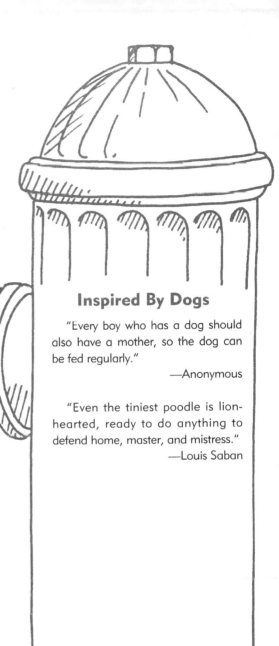

Inspired By Dogs

"Every boy who has a dog should also have a mother, so the dog can be fed regularly."

—Anonymous

"Even the tiniest poodle is lion-hearted, ready to do anything to defend home, master, and mistress."

—Louis Saban

An occasional dog will not be averse to going potty while he's umbilical corded. The advantage when working with this type is that, once he's trained not to go while umbilical corded, he will quickly become reliably housebroken. Simply carry a beanbag (a paper lunch bag containing a quarter-cup of dried beans) or other harmless bopper with you and give the appearance that the sky has fallen in by beaning him on the head or rear without saying a word if he attempts to let loose indoors.

"Will simply following the suggestions in the housebreaking chapter correct soiling problems?"

No. In addition, train him vigorously on new obedience routines and commands fifteen minutes every other day and give him vigorous exercise the other days to ensure he is optimally receptive to the program.

"How long will it take to correct this housebreaking problem?"

As long as he's been breaking good housebreaking habits, plan on *not* allowing him unsupervised freedom in the house. When he is out of confinement, keep your eyes riveted on him. If he begins any actions that precede soiling, such as sniffing or circling, don't yell. Instead, silently launch a shaker can or something equally startling at him so you don't draw attention to your part in this corrective procedure.

"How can I correct my dog if he never soils when I'm watching?"

To make your spying pay off, set him up so you can correct. Rub down another dog with a towel and drape the scented towel on a chair, bed or doorknob. The suspicion that another dog has been in his house may cause him to mark. This time, though, you'll be ready to stop him. Also, be on the defensive if you give him the opportunity to potty outdoors but he doesn't because he's distracted by rain, wet grass, or other adverse conditions. Instead of crating him, follow him around the house, waiting for him to consider going potty indoors. Distract or correct him if he starts sniffing or circling with intent. Say nothing and spray him with water, jerk the leash if it is attached, or toss a shaker can at his rear end.

If he only goes in a certain area when you aren't watching, such as behind the couch or upstairs, block off the area or booby trap it with balloons, mousetraps, or Scat Mats.

"When will I know my dog is becoming trustworthy?"

After weeks or months of following, when your dog has refrained from soiling the house and developed an aversion to going indoors, gradually allow him unsupervised freedom.

"How can I prevent my dog from having accidents when I can't supervise or confine him 100 percent of the time?"

Consider diapering as described under "Submissive Urination" so he cannot soil the house.

Crate Soiling

Although dogs normally won't mess in their crates, some do. Occasional accidents shouldn't concern you, but if it happens every other day or more, try these suggestions:

- Remove all bedding in hopes he'll be repulsed by having nothing other than his body to absorb the mess.
- Use a smaller crate so he only has enough room to turn in place.
- Teach him to enter and exit his crate on command (see the discussion of confinement, page 119).
- Put his food and water in the open crate to encourage a better association about being in there; remove it when he's enclosed.

Identify and halt rituals that precede soiling. Barring physical problems, crate soiling is always preceded by a ritual such as whining, barking, pawing, digging, chewing on bars, or circling, turning, sitting, standing, or lying down repeatedly.

To correct these rituals as soon as they begin, confine your dog when you are home. Stop noisemaking (barking, howling, or whining) and destructive behavior (chewing, digging, or pawing) by using a leash jerk or shaker can as suggested in "Crating Introduction," page 119. By concentrating on the most pronounced behavior first—barking before whining, or chewing before pawing—you'll find that minor noisemaking and destructive behaviors will decrease, too. As a result, the dog will relax, rest, and not soil.

Occasionally, all these suggestions fail to work, in which case you should save yourself aggravation by purchasing a grate. This allows urine and excrement to drop to the floor of the crate to facilitate cleanup, minimize odor, and keep your dog fresh-smelling.

Biting

Biting should always be considered a serious behavior problem. Whether it occurs because a dog is trying to get our attention, relieve frustration, or change our behavior, biting is never cute and rarely justifiable.

Unfortunately, some owners appreciate (consciously or unconsciously) a dog's aggression and reinforce it by rewarding it or denying its existence. Most dog-bite injuries and aggressive-dog euthanasia could have been avoided with proper supervision, socialization, training, and intervention by an owner who recognized the warning signs and instantly stopped inappropriate behavior. The signs of impending aggression include hard eye contact, stiffening, weight shifting forward, tail out, growling, fast whining, or signs of interest, excitement or arousal.

Whether it's playful, fear-driven or dominant, A-1 obedience skills are imperative. Aggressive tendencies always diminish as the owner's control of his dog increases. Through obedience training, owners have the opportunity to learn how to interpret their dog's mood and body English. It is that astute observation that enables owners to get control of the potentially aggressive dog well before he reaches a highly agitated state. If the owner intervenes too late—when the dog's adrenaline is peaking—he'll be oblivious to attempts to stop him. To raise your proficiency as a handler, enlist the help of an experienced professional trainer. Finally, a responsible owner never assumes his dog is "cured" and takes every precaution, no matter how well-trained the dog is.

Chewing on Things

If an older dog suddenly begins chewing on inappropriate items, give him plenty of exercise and Nylabones to chew, continue vigorous obedience, and return to crating and supervising. Also, consider setting your dog up as this student did.

Acupuncture for Dogs?

Veterinary acupuncturists in this country have been working on dogs and other animals for more than twenty years. They've been successful in relieving pain when other, more conventional treatments have failed. Acupuncture is a branch of Chinese medicine in which special needles are inserted into the patient's skin as therapy for various disorders, or to simply induce anesthesia. Traditional Chinese thought holds that chi, or life force, flows through the body along channels; blockage in one or more of these channels is believed to cause illness. Veterinary acupuncturists aim to restore health by inserting needles at the appropriate sites, known as acupuncture points, along the affected channel.

Western research suggests that acupuncture causes the release of natural painkillers known as endorphins, which help relieve discomfort, at least on a temporary basis. It has also been suggested that acupuncture works by inducing a state of hypnosis in the patient, or because the insertion of the needles stimulates peripheral nerves, acting as a distraction from the original pain.

Veterinary acupuncturists claim to be able to relieve pain in dogs, especially pain caused by arthritis or injury to the skeleton or musculature. Along with massage and chiropractic manipulation, acupuncture might be a viable alternative for the dog who has not responded to more conventional treatments.

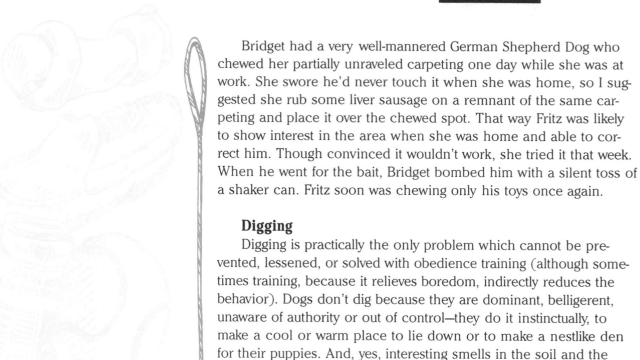

Bridget had a very well-mannered German Shepherd Dog who chewed her partially unraveled carpeting one day while she was at work. She swore he'd never touch it when she was home, so I suggested she rub some liver sausage on a remnant of the same carpeting and place it over the chewed spot. That way Fritz was likely to show interest in the area when she was home and able to correct him. Though convinced it wouldn't work, she tried it that week. When he went for the bait, Bridget bombed him with a silent toss of a shaker can. Fritz soon was chewing only his toys once again.

Digging

Digging is practically the only problem which cannot be prevented, lessened, or solved with obedience training (although sometimes training, because it relieves boredom, indirectly reduces the behavior). Dogs don't dig because they are dominant, belligerent, unaware of authority or out of control—they do it instinctually, to make a cool or warm place to lie down or to make a nestlike den for their puppies. And, yes, interesting smells in the soil and the wonderful feeling of vigorous burrowing and dirt in their toes is hard for any dog to resist. Therefore, monitoring your dog and correcting digging attempts is an on-going process—you aren't fighting your dog, you are fighting nature. Your best option is to never leave your dog unsupervised in an area with digging potential, but if you insist on correcting, here's what you'll need to do:

- When you can't supervise your dog leave him in a run or tied out on concrete, patio block, or a similar, undiggable surface.
- Provide a comfortable environment for him. Fresh water and shelter from heat, cold, wind, and rain must always be available.
- Exercise him vigorously and regularly so he doesn't seek aerobic activity from digging.
- Fill previously dug holes with dog feces. Most won't return to dig in that hole, although some dogs will simply dig new holes.

Correcting digging requires you to monitor your dog more closely than the Secret Service guards the President. Any time he begins digging, startle him without saying a word. If he is leashed, jerk it, then praise. If he is tied out, attach a second leash, long enough for you to hold and jerk. If he is in the back yard, create a sharp noise, spray him with water, or launch a shaker can at him.

Barking—in the Crate and at a Distance

Out of respect for other household members, neighbors, tenants, and anyone with a low tolerance for barking, correct this problem—otherwise, you may be forced to get rid of your dog or face eviction. Don't worry that your dog will stop barking altogether. Teaching barking inhibition increases his value as a watch dog because when he barks, you'll know it's for good reason.

To correct barking, even if it is only a problem in your absence, teach the dog to be "quiet" on command when he's standing next to you (see the section on "Other Commands"). If your dog will obey the "quiet" command without making you raise your voice or repeat yourself, no matter what the distraction, barking in your absence will usually subside. If it doesn't, you may be unintentionally reinforcing excessive barking—you may be attempting to silence a dog by petting him or giving him a toy, or you may be letting him be vocal without consequences. If you use the "quiet" command and never tolerate barking or try to appease him, but he continues to vocalize in your absence, find out exactly when and why he is barking. Record him with a tape recorder when you leave, ask a neighbor about his habits, and spy on him. If he isn't barking at outside noises, separation anxiety is probably the problem. Read and follow the suggestions in the section on "Separation Anxiety."

If he is barking at outside noises:

1. Teach him not to bark at outside noises when you are home. Keep his leash attached and periodically knock on the walls and create strange sounds. Say nothing as you run over to correct with bitter apple or to cuff him under the jaw.
2. Keep him in a covered crate in a noise-insulated room with a fan or other generated white noise in your absence. Occasionally crate him when you're home to confirm that he's peaceful when confined.
3. Although rarely necessary, investigate these options as a last resort:

- Antibark collars automatically emit a warning buzz when the dog vocalizes. The collar will deliver timely correction if the dog continues to make noise after the warning. The two most popular collars correct by delivering a mist of annoying citronella at the dog's muzzle or a mild electric shock.
- Antianxiety medication (see your veterinarian to find out if your dog is a good candidate and to discuss benefits and risks).
- Debarking, a surgical procedure, muffles the barking sound. Vocal cords can heal back together, and if they do, the dog's bark will return to normal.

Problem-Solving Aids

Miracle cures, gadgetry, and fads may look like easy solutions to difficult problems. Typically, attempts to solve problems with a single aid usually fail. For example: Using odor remover on your carpeting won't abolish house soiling, nor will applying repelling spray to your garbage prevent your dog from raiding it; using a no-pull harness won't teach your dog to heel. On the other hand, multipronged solutions are recommended and highly successful—such as ridding your carpet of odor and using the housebreaking advice in this book. A new word, projectile, or booby trap may be a beneficial addition to your training program if you understand why they work.

Gain Respect by Singing a New Tune

If your dog's response to "come" has been apathetic at best, and you get hoarse repeating it, why not select a new word, follow the steps outlined, and teach him to respond appropriately to the new word? Similarly, stop yelling "Quiet," "Off," and "Drop it" and instead start over teaching "Hush," "Paws," and "Out" so that this time they really mean something. It takes less time to get a reliable response by teaching a totally new association than by changing an old one.

Projectiles

Shaker cans are the most commonly used projectiles. They work well when the dog has been properly trained on leash and the shaker can is then used to stop a sneaky problem behavior. Unfortunately, instead of learning not to misbehave, many dogs only learn to figure out how to dodge the can. Others become immune to its effect and play with the can when you toss it. In either case, if you've used projectiles with limited success, stop using them at least until you do the following:

1. Set him up on-lead so that each time he makes the wrong decision, you can stop him with a jerk of the leash.
2. Prevent your dog from making mischief in your absence by crating, supervising, and umbilical cording
3. Teach one-command obedience around distractions.

Booby Traps

Want to be able to correct bad behavior even if you aren't watching your dog every second? Then consider setting booby traps so your dog corrects himself whenever he misbehaves. Mousetraps or Snappy Trainers (mousetrap-like paddles) can be strategically placed on furniture, garbage cans, and other areas your dog isn't allowed. Make the traps less obvious by covering them with a sheet of newspaper or other lightweight drape. Just make sure of the following:

- That the dog's misbehavior will trip the trap
- That you'll be able to reset the trap soon and without his knowledge, so that repeated attempts will yield consistent results

Booby traps are most successful with dogs who are generally well behaved and somewhat timid. If your dog is indeed very startled by booby traps, the training phase will be brief, and you'll soon be able to leave traps set while you're gone and therefore not able to reset them.

Scat Mats are pads that can be placed around forbidden objects such as plants, as well as on counters or furniture, to deliver an unpleasant but harmless sensation when they are stepped on or touched. They're relatively expensive but are very effective and are widely available at pet shops or by mail order.

Problem-Solving Options

Make changes in:

- The environment (close the window of opportunity for misbehavior)
- Your attitude (accept the inconvenience of training or the ramifications of not training)
- The dog (develop a problem-solving action plan with training techniques, setups, and corrections)

First and foremost, be consistent. Then you can cautiously and gradually increase your dog's freedom.

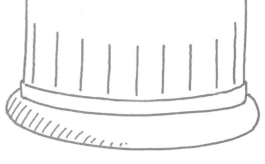

If your dog scratches doors or crawls behind the sofa, balloons can be a successful deterrent. Tape inflated balloons to the area of the door he scratches or place them in the crawl spaces you want to keep him out of.

If your dog jumps on counters or noses in the garbage, try a pyramid of shaker cans. Arrange them on a piece of cardboard atop an open garbage can or on the edge of a counter so that when he noses or jumps up, he'll hit the cardboard and get showered with shaker cans.

Booby traps are easy for clever dogs to detect and avoid. Still, when arranged by inventive owners, mousetraps, Scat Mats, balloons and shaker-can pyramids have been known to work wonders. Even after the dog has been reformed, the booby trap or a remnant of it should be left in place as a constant reminder.

Disfavored Aids

People often think dog problems are complicated and unique. Even dogs with severe problems are almost always responsive when conscientious owners use traditional training methods. In rare cases, though, it may be appropriate to use extreme measures. Radical alternatives include electronic collars, cutting vocal cords, extracting teeth from biting dogs, or giving drugs to alter behavior. Unless these are used in conjunction with a good training program under the guidance of a professional, I strongly advise against them.

"All in the Family" Problems

Training my dogs was hard enough, but watching my family do things that might diminish my training efforts was even harder. Since I wasn't allowed to have house dogs, opportunities for encouraging begging and overexcitability were, thankfully, minimal. And fortunately, my family paid relatively little attention to my dogs. Aside from not wanting to burden anyone with my responsibilities, I was terrified to let my family care for my dogs in my absence. In their limited interactions with the dogs, I found they were too casual and trusting. I worked hard to keep my dogs well-groomed, socialized, and mannerly. My family construed my conscientiousness as being cruel or overprotective. Consequently, they would occasionally, in their goodness, take the dogs out for a run in a burr-filled field, or fail to watch them closely around strange children, or not stop foolish adults from giving unfamiliar dogs bear hugs or staring them down while making growling and barking noises. They'd also leave the dogs outside unattended and unsupervised in the unfenced yard.

Frustrated as I was, my dogs and I survived. But what can you do if your family consists of difficult, contradictory personalities?

Perhaps one is a wimp who tries to talk you out of doing nasty obedience which will ruin the dog's free spirit; each time you enforce a rule, he commiserates with the dog. Maybe another is a loudmouth, giving what he thinks is much-needed training advice, demonstrating his expertise by yelling commands to you and the dog. Maybe there's a talker who is always jabbering and saying nothing, then wonders why the dog treats him like an inanimate object. Or perhaps there's a secret saboteur who watches what you do and then undoes your hard work by feeding table food during meals, letting the dog pull on the leash or hang his head out of the car window, or inviting him on the furniture.

I wish people problems were as easy to solve as dog problems. Each family situation is unique. But in general:

Express and demonstrate your concern for the dog's well being by taking charge of his training, housing, supervision and care, including health, exercise and grooming. Make arrangements for someone trusted to handle these tasks when you are unavailable.

Assign duties, with specific details as to how to perform them, to interested household members.

Remember:

- No matter how common your philosophies, no two people will agree 100 percent on how to raise a dog.
- Expect to be annoyed, sometimes, by family members.
- Understand that what others do can't sabotage your authority. The dog will learn what *you* expect from him by the way you react to his behavior in your presence.

Maintenance Program: Use It or Lose It

Dog training is a lot like showering. Thinking about showering or complaining about being stinky won't make you cleaner. You actually have to get wet and lather up. Even then, you don't stay clean forever. No matter meticulously you scrub and how carefully you attempt to avoid getting messy, you will never be free of the need to shower regularly.

Dog training, like showering, does work—but it must be repeated. Once your dog knows the basics, you can keep him in tiptop form in almost no time at all. Remembering and enforcing the "Ten Commandments of Dog Training" will ensure lifelong harmony with your canine companion:

1. Always enforce the "no pulling on leash" rule.
2. Only give one command for one action.
3. Only give commands that you are prepared to enforce.
4. Correct with firmness—not cruelty.

    Dogs live for the moment, so corrections must be instantaneous (not after the fact).

    When your dog's adrenaline rises, so does his pain tolerance. Adjust the strength of your corrections accordingly.
5. Remember that a dog is like a bank—it only gives you what you ask for.
6. Training is not necessarily what you try to teach—it is what a dog learns. Allowing a dog to misbehave *is* a form of training!
7. Say what you mean and mean what you say.
8. The more controlled your dog is, the more freedom he can enjoy.
9. Regression is a normal part of the learning process.

    View regression as an opportunity to improve the dog's understanding; the only way he can truly know what is right is by unsuccessfully attempting to do things the wrong way. Training through regression strengthens obedience.

    When the going gets tough, the tough simplify. Back up to a level of success, then progress again.
10. Love your dog and take pride in the relationship you've created, fostered, nurtured, and developed.

Chapter Six

YOUR BEST FRIEND!

Your Best Friend

If your dog is new to you, then you aren't even thinking about what you can do with him. A cock of his head, a little yip, his playing with your best pair of shoes—all seem like delights you never imagined. You walk around all day saying things like, "Isn't he the cutest!" Right now, aside from housebreaking, life is almost perfect.

But what will you and Rover do when he's all grown up? Do you have any plans for him? Is he just going to walk around the house all day and sleep while you are gone? Is his a life perpetually addicted to following toddlers around all day, licking their breakfast from their faces? Or worse yet, waiting in the wings to see what goodies will fall from the highchair? Certainly your dog, if not meant to star in movies, has some latent talent, no?

Of course he does! Dogs will do almost anything you ask them to, as long as you provide them with the training to perform it. A dog who loves you will give you his all. So, other than sleeping on the couch when he's not supposed to, or making a bed out of the dirty clothes you piled on the floor not thirty seconds ago, what are some of the fun things your dog can do with you?

Obviously, "fetch" is popular with most dogs, but that can be a little repetitive (not that they mind). However, there are a number of organized activities that you and Spot can join, should you decide that Spot needs to fulfill some higher destiny. No, I'm just joking. But seriously, if you want to have some fun with your dog, there are countless activities you can engage in. In this chapter we'll look at fun things you can do, and even some that are organized by rules set forth by the AKC. Many of these require plenty of training on your part. The activities are not that particularly hard, but all require time. And all are fun.

These are some of the things that you can do with your dog:

Dog shows (AKC)
Performance events (AKC)
Canine Good Citizen (AKC, but open to mixed breeds)
Hiking
Camping
Swimming
Travel
Teaching tricks

Dog Shows

So, you're a consummate stage mother? Maybe you bought Fido because he came from championship lines, and you wanted to try your hand at showing? Maybe you've been to a dog show and it looks like fun? Or maybe it's just something you want to try once. Believe me, you're not alone. There are somewhere around twenty thousand dog shows per year, twelve to thirteen thousand of which conform to AKC recognized standards. Millions of people compete in these events, and an even larger number attend as spectators. This is called the "sport of dogs" by show people.

Now, first, let me caution you. Dog showing is very competitive. You are not the first yahoo who went out and bought a pet, and thought, "Gee, wouldn't it be fun to show Rover?" Dog-show people can be snotty. Many are very dedicated to their "sport" and don't take dabblers very seriously. In some cases, they actually loathe them. You will have to attend many shows in your breed before some of them talk to you without looking down their noses. Many will first ask you if you bred the dog yourself, or whom you bought it from. You have to understand, many people who compete are breeders whose livelihood, or at least some part of it, comes from dogs. You're just one more obstacle for them to overcome.

That said, there are also many lovely people in the sport, and the camaraderie and competition are fun. It's also fun because you'll be talking to many people who have dogs just like yours, and you'll trade all kinds of information and learn that much more. And the spectators are right there and also fun to talk to. They will all want to pet your dog and talk to you. And Rover will have fun, too!

Let's take a look at how shows work, and how the show world works.

So You Want to Be a Star!

Dog shows are not run by the AKC. Rather, they are sponsored by a specific organization, who will conform to the AKC's recognized standards. Now, you have to understand that breed clubs, such as the German Shorthair Pointer Club of America,

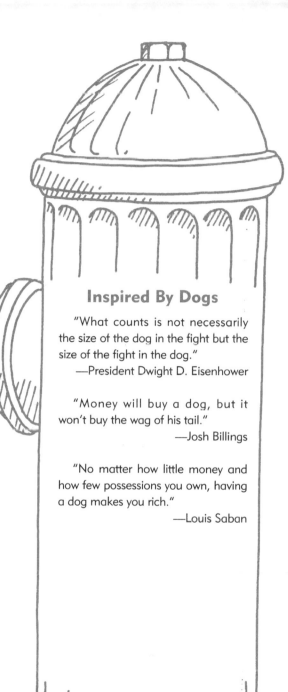

Inspired By Dogs

"What counts is not necessarily the size of the dog in the fight but the size of the fight in the dog."
—President Dwight D. Eisenhower

"Money will buy a dog, but it won't buy the wag of his tail."
—Josh Billings

"No matter how little money and how few possessions you own, having a dog makes you rich."
—Louis Saban

are recognized by the AKC as the authorities on each breed. The club sets the "breed standard," and the AKC recognizes and honors that standard. The standards are modified over the years to one extent or another, to recognize new markings or colors, etc. One pending example is that the German Shorthair Club of America doesn't recognize black and white German Shorthairs. However, these dogs are shown and confirmed in England, Australia, and in many other parts of the world. Someday, the club, and therefore the AKC, will allow black and white German Shorthairs into the show ring. This kind of modification is not that unusual.

OK, so now we're at an event. How does this all work? Let's follow a typical show as if you were a contestant. So, let's see, where are we? First, we'll compete at the breed stage. Do you have a dog or a bitch? That matters, because they're separated. Dogs and bitches compete in their own groups before they compete against each other. This isn't sexist. You have to remember, these shows are set up to reward good breeding. Essentially, they're very much like a livestock competition at a state fair. (Many dog people will not like that analogy.)

It is important to note that very little goes on at a dog show other than judging. The dogs will not be judged on talent, for example. If you've taught old Fido to shoot basketballs or to roll over and play dead, or some other fun, imaginative thing, then you're better off calling the *David Letterman Show*, because the AKC doesn't recognize tricks.

The groups are each broken down into five major classes:

Puppies (6 to 9 months and 9 to 12 months)
Novice
Bred by Exhibitor
American-Bred
Open

The dogs are judged on general appearance, which includes things such as head, neck, forequarters, hindquarters, coat, color, gait, and temperament. The dogs are not judged one against another: "This dog is prettier than that dog." *No!* The dogs are each judged by a person well-versed in the breed who decides whether this dog is the best possible representation of what the ideal dog of the breed should look like.

In the next level, the winners are all brought in, and the judge picks out the best dog from all the winners. This is called the "winners dog." Several dogs are picked as "reserve winners." The bitch group is also judged in the same way. The reserve winners are placed in order of finish, as in horse racing—second, third, and fourth. These selections are made partly in case the "winners dog" is disqualified for any reason later on. The winners dog and bitch both receive points toward their championships.

The day's not over yet. I hope you're not getting tired!

In the next level, you start all over again. You're winners dog—you've won the group that showed. But now, in this next section, any dog that has finished his or her championship at any other show is welcome to compete. The competition is mixed now. Now, you go through the same exercise all over again. The judge looks over the field, where the competition is much tougher, and he or she judges them, putting them in some kind of order similar to what we just went through. At this point the judge picks a Best of Breed award. This can be either male or female. Then he picks a Best of Opposite Sex (in other words, he picks a male as Best of Breed, then he picks a female as Best of Opposite Sex, or vice versa).

Now, sometimes, if this is a breed-only event, that's it. The day is over. They showed German Shorthaired Pointers all day, and when the smoke cleared, you walked away with some big-time championship points, and Spot is thrilled. You're exhausted. However, today we are not at a breed-only show, so there's more to do.

At a full show, other breeds will be showing at the same time as you. All 144 recognized breeds are competing. You get a small breather here, and then you go back on stage. The next competition is the group competition. You remember when we looked at the various breeds in Part 1? All the dogs were separated out by group—Herding, Sporting, Working, Non-Sporting, Toy, Terrier, and Hound. Since you own a German Shorthair Pointer, you will be judged in the Sporting Group. The Best of Breed of each breed, that one dog only (and that's you!), will compete against all the other Best of Breeds who won in this group. In other words, you'll be competing against the Best of Breed of the Golden Retrievers, Labrador Retrievers, etc. Again, do they pick these dogs because a German Shorthaired Pointer is prettier than a Labrador? *No!* An experienced

Sporting Group judge will judge each animal against the ideal of what that breed should be. Each dog is rated against its breed's standard. Is this Lab a better representation of a Lab than this Pointer is an example of a Pointer?

Now, you were lucky to get out of the Sporting Group alive. Now, each group has been judged in the same way. So, here we are, and it's the final run around the ring. You are with the six other dogs who have won their groups. Yet another judge looks you all over, and in the same way the groups were judged, he or she chooses a winner, which will be crowned Best in Show.

You're certainly thrilled. What an exciting experience! And it only took a couple of days. You see, something as big as an all-breed show takes several days to complete. These shows are usually held outside at a large fair grounds. The competitions, depending on the breed, can take all day. But if you like dogs (and apparently you do), then you just had more fun than you ever imagined.

Handlers

There are people in the dog-show industry called handlers. These people make a living showing other people's dogs in competitions. Many breeders use handlers because they cannot be all around the country, showing their many dogs. Some breeders will have more than one dog on the road. In situations like these, some breeders don't see their dogs for months and months at a time. They will sometimes fly into a city just to visit their dog and handler and watch the show, and then leave the dog with the handler and fly back home. This is the life of a championship dog for people who are serious about dog shows.

Now, it is a lot of fun showing your dog yourself. You drive to strange cities, stay in motels that allow dogs, and hang out with dog people for several days. It's this time spent with your dog that makes it the most fun. But if you are serious about winning, you may want to consider a handler. These people travel from show to show and know the many ins and outs of the ring. They know tricks of the trade and are very astute about the politics of the show ring. They are not cheap—they have many expenses to cover. Some of the recommended books listed in the back of this book will give you much more in-depth coverage of what you need to compete and win if you are serious about showing.

Performance Events

The AKC sanctions and different clubs sponsor a variety of events which are much more active than showing. These performance events are sometimes very general in their competition, and some are breed- or group-specific. For example, Obedience and Agility trials are open to all breeds, but you'd be hard-pressed to enter your Labrador Retriever into Herding Trials, or your herding dog into a Field Trial event.

However, these events are a lot of fun to compete in. They do require plenty of repetitive training on your part and your dog's. However, if you like spending active time with your dog, it will give some structure to the fun you're hoping to have. And the competition, against other people who are having fun, too, is a flat-out hoot. These folks are not snotty at all. However, they are still very serious about competing and completing the titles that these events award.

These events are open only to purebred dogs. The various trials break down like this:

Obedience Trials
Agility Trials
Tracking
Field Trials and Hunting Tests
Herding
Lure Coursing
Earthdog Tests

Obedience, Agility, and Tracking

We'll look at Obedience, Agility, and Tracking Trials first, because those competitions are open to all purebred dogs. The idea of obedience is to help meld you and your dog into a working team. This should be fun for both you and your dog, and will make him a better pet and you a better owner in the process. Agility stresses teamwork, expert training, and athleticism. And tracking requires not just a good nose, but an understanding of what is required in what might become a very serious profession.

Obedience

The idea is to be able to train your dog so that he can eventually be trained to comprehend and act on commands, regardless of

distance or interference. This is the most popular of all trials among nonbreeders, as these are things which will make life easier for most owners. There are actually Puppy Kindergarten classes which will take dogs as young as three months. And there are prenovice groups as well. Both these classes work with you and your dog on lead. In Obedience, there are three levels of increasing difficulty: Novice, Open, and Utility. In any trial, the dog must score 170 or more of the possible 200 points to earn his or her title.

Novice is the first group where you can earn a title. The title one earns is called a CD, which stands for Companion Dog. There are six simple tasks your dog needs to complete before he can have this title conferred upon him: stand for confirmation, heel on lead, free heel, long sit, recall, and long down. These are all off-lead.

Open is a little more difficult. The exercises required are retrieve (usually a dumbbell) over flat route, retrieve over high jump, free heel, drop on recall, broad jump, long sit, and long down. For completing this course, your dog will earn a CDX, which stands for Companion Dog Excellent.

Utility work is ranked as the hardest for good reason. These are some of the most advanced trials there are. There are five events: ability to distinguish between two scents, a signal event, group examination, directed retrieve, and directed jumping. If your dog finishes this course with a passing grade, he receives a UD, or Utility Dog, certificate. Of course, there are those overachievers who have qualified for UDX (yes, you've guessed it—Utility Dog Excellent) and even the OTCh (overall Obedience Champion).

Agility Trials

This is slightly more fun than obedience, but obviously not quite as useful. Agility teams you and your dog together as a pair who needs to perform a certain number of tasks or exercises. It's a lot of fun to train and is very much like playing with your dog. The idea is that not only does Spot have to complete the exercise correctly (a feat in and of itself), but he also has to race against the clock. It can get exhausting. But it's very rewarding and often hilarious. The dogs seem to have more fun at these trials than in any other.

The dogs are broken out by size. No one expects a toy dog to make the same jumps as a Doberman Pinscher. As in Obedience, there are levels. In Agility, there are four:

Novice Agility (the title you earn is NA)
Open Agility (the title you earn is OA)
Agility Excellent (the title you earn is AX)
Master Agility Excellent (the title you earn is MX)

Basically, your dog needs to complete an obstacle course. In order to gain the title, he must complete the course three times (at least one must be completed under a different judge). In these exercises, the dogs are required to run through and around poles, make a series of jumps, climb, balance, and race through tunnels.

It's scored very much like the Obedience Trials. Top score is 200 points. Infractions are deducted. This is fast becoming one of the most popular of all trials, first because anyone can enter, and second because it's tremendous fun. You'll laugh and be astounded. It's always an exceptional show.

Tracking

This is exactly what it sounds like. A course is made up over a large field or a series of fields, as well as across roads and through woods. A dog is given a scent and has to track that scent. The only thing is, in this case, the humans know where the scent is, because the judges mark the field. So when the dog goes off-course, the judge knows it. Sometimes while the judges lay the scent they create what are known as "tricks" in the field. They might make a hard right or left, or sometimes might crisscross a path with the scent. Along the path are things that must be retrieved and returned to the judges by the dog.

This competition is open to all breeds. It is surprising how many breeds participate. There are four levels of certificates, including Tracking Dog (TD); Tracking Dog Excellent (TDX); Variable Surface Tracking Test (VST); and Champion Tracker (CT). Of course, the various trials become more difficult at each

What about the Rest of Us?

What if your dog isn't a purebred? Or what if your dog is a purebred, but its breed isn't recognized by the AKC?

There are other organizations that sponsor very similar Obedience and Agility Trials. They are sponsored by the UKC. For years, many Pit Bulls, Jack Russell Terriers, and other dogs have competed for the UKC's titles. The good news is that you don't have to be a purebred. Mixed breeds are encouraged to compete and complete as well.

stage. Many dogs that start out in this competition may go on to search-and-rescue work or police work.

Breed-Specific Competitions

These are competitions which more or less are aimed at groups. The Field and Hunting Trials are aimed at the Sporting group (and a few hounds); Herding is aimed at the Herding group; Lure Coursing is mainly for Sight Hounds; and Earthdog tests tend to be for Terriers and Dachshunds. However, if you have any breeds in these categories, or are just plain interested in dogs, it really is a lot of fun to go and see one of these events, let alone enter them!

Field Trials and Hunting Tests

Art Buchwald once said that he'd never heard certain colloquial phrases used with their real meaning until he went to his first field trial. Sayings like "That dog won't hunt" suddenly had new meaning. He also pointed out that some field trials were tracked by folks on horseback, because they covered so much ground so quickly, following the dogs. The crowd on horseback was called the gallery and was constantly pushing forward. The judges were afraid that the spectators might interfere, so once, one called out, "Gentlemen, hold your horses!" You probably get the idea—field trials have been going on a long time.

There are two distinct types of competitions. Field Trials are for pointing dogs, especially pointers (any kind), retrievers, and spaniels. The idea is that these dogs go into a field and spot game, marking it for their companion hunters and the other dogs. These are very competitive events. The dogs are tested and judged against one another. There are two titles awarded in Field Trials—Amateur Field Champion (AFC) and Field Champion (FC).

Hunting tests tend to be more open and involve many of the sporting dogs as well as Beagles, Basset Hounds, and Dachshunds. Here, the dog is judged against a level of performance. Although hunting tests are a little less competitive, they are still an excellent means of judging dog and hunter alike. There are three titles for hunting: Junior Hunter (JH), Senior Hunter (SH), and Master Hunter (MH).

Herding Trials and Tests

The relationship with herding dogs is one of the oldest relationships humans have. Herding trials exercises are used to gauge the development of what is still a very important job for many herding dogs. It's also lot's of fun! The AKC separates herding dogs into four distinct groups: Shepherd (usually used with sheep and usually lead a flock); Drover (works livestock from behind, usually sheep or cattle); Livestock Guarding (they do not move livestock, but guard it from other predators); and All-Round Farm Dogs (these usually can respond quickly to different situations and can perform a number of different jobs).

The first few exercises are called tests. These test the general inborn instincts of your animal and his ability to be trained. After that, you're off to the pasture. There are six different levels to achieve.

The first two tests are Herding Tested (HT) and Pre-Trail Tested (PT). In these, your dog's abilities are judged, again, based on inborn reaction as well as certain trained functions. The next levels are progressively harder. The idea is that a dog must keep ducks, sheep, or cattle together, sometimes under very difficult circumstances. The four remaining certificates to be achieved are Herding Started (HS); Herding Intermediate (HI); Herding Excellent (HX); and Herding Champion (HCh).

Lure Coursing

This is probably one of the best spectator sports in all of dogdom. These are the sight hounds. Over an open, but rigged, course, sight hounds (used by man to hunt over open plains since the time of the Pharaohs), chase a flag at speeds which seem unimaginable. Yes, sight hounds hunt by sight. The dogs included are Afghan Hounds, Basenjis, Borzoi, Greyhounds, Ibiza Hounds, Rhodesian Ridgebacks, Salukis, Scottish Deerhounds, and Whippets. A lure, or prey (which in most cases is a fluttering plastic bag), is pulled very quickly along a series of wires. The dogs give chase. The dogs are judged on overall ability, quickness, endurance, follow, and agility. There are three titles to be earned: Junior Courser (JC), Senior Courser (SC), and Field Champion (FC).

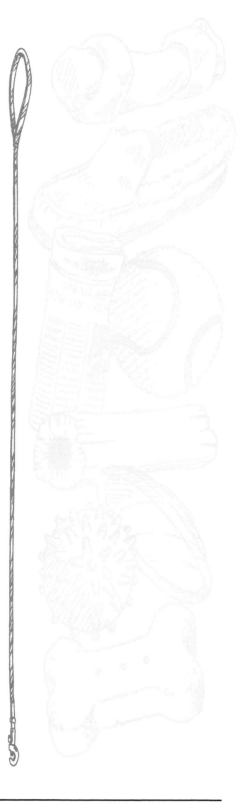

Earthdog Tests

Here's what the entry-level test for this is: two large mice or rats are placed safely in a cage at the end of a long underground tunnel. Your terrier is let loose. The dog is judged on his desire to do everything necessary to get to those two rodents trapped in a cage underground. The rodents are safe, as the dogs cannot get to them. This is called Introduction to Vermin—remember, many of these terriers were called "ratters" and were used for ridding farms and factories of unwanted small vermin.

There are three earthdog titles: Junior Earthdog (JE), Senior Earthdog (SE), and Master Earthdog (ME). If you are a terrier person, you will marvel at this event!

Other Open Competitions

Some other competitions may be breed-specific but are not AKC-sanctioned. The AKC sponsors the Canine Good Citizen, which is an excellent program encouraging good canine behavior, and includes both purebred and mixed-breed dogs. Of course, there are other types of competitions. There are dog sledding events, protection events, scent hurdle racing, flyball, freestyle obedience (or canine freestyle), and Frisbee (or flying disk) events.

Canine Good Citizen R

This is one event that the AKC sponsors that applies to all dogs, purebred and mixed-breed. The idea is that the dogs who complete these ten tests are certified to be good canine citizens who can behave themselves whether they're alone with their owner, with other people, or with other dogs. These events are usually sponsored by local clubs or community-minded organizations.

These are the ten tests:

1. The dog accepts a friendly stranger.
2. The dog accepts being petted by a friendly stranger.
3. The dog accepts inspection and grooming.
4. The dog demonstrates heeling while on a loose lead.
5. The dog displays that he can move through a crowd properly.

Inspired By Dogs

"A door is what a dog is always on the wrong side of."

—Ogden Nash

"To his dog, every man is Napoleon, hence the constant popularity of dogs."

—Aldous Huxley

"My father was a Saint Bernard, my mother was a collie, but I am a Presbyterian."

—Mark Twain

"The more I see of men, the more I like dogs."

—Mme. De Staël

6. The dog completes a long sit or down.
7. The dog shows that he can immediately calm down after play.
8. The dog shows that he can accept other dogs politely, with no show of dominance.
9. The dog must react calmly to sudden distractions.
10. The dog displays that it can be left alone and still exhibit good manners.

If you intend on making your dog a significant part of your life (especially if you live in an urban or suburban area), then taking advantage of Canine Good Citizen R testing is a very good idea. It's not only fun to learn and do, but it's valuable to be able to trust your dog and how he interacts with others. To find out more information about Canine Good Citizen R, call the AKC at (919) 233-9767.

Therapy Dogs

These dogs aren't in need of therapy—they help give it. They *are* the therapy. It's well known in the medical community that animal visits to long-term care facilities (nursing homes, mental illness facilities, etc.) often bring about tremendous reactions from the patients. Therapy dogs can usually get patients who are socially closed off to interact and help them to create personal relationships. In other words, therapy dogs are therapeutic. The dogs that make the grade for these types of assignments must be well-behaved and love affection. You need to have a dog that could pass the Canine Good Citizen test (though that is not a prerequisite).

If you enjoy doing nice things for others, many different therapy dog programs are run throughout the country. This is a great way to train your dog and help others at the same time. You both will feel better for doing it.

Dog Sledding

You'd think this one was popular only in Alaska, right? Wrong! More and more clubs are starting up all over the United States and all over the world. Many spitz breed fans have joined forces, and with the help of new technologies (sleds on wheels) and a devotion to the sport, have brought about new ways to train and compete with dog-sled teams in areas not covered by snow and ice. But

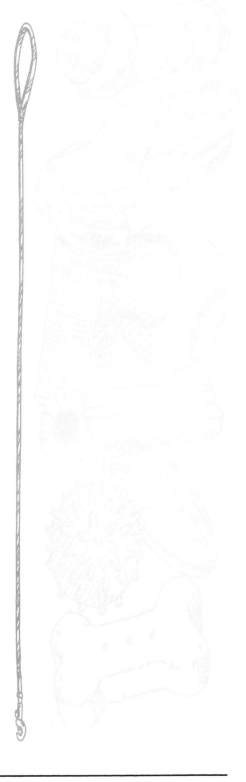

here's the fun news—other breeds are being teamed up and are competing.

The premiere guiding force in all of this is the International Sled Dog Racing Association. And they are all over. There are even some clubs as far south as Virginia and North Carolina!

Schutzhund or Protection Events

All right, for all of you out there who have heard about Schutzhund, here it is. Schutzhund is German for "protection dog." Today, different levels of schutzhund training have been assigned to help qualify dogs for police work as well as for protection. This sport combines aspects of tracking, obedience, and protection. Schutzhund requires tremendous hours of training and requires a dog who is calm and self-assured. A hyper or anxious dog, one that lacks confidence or is easily distracted, is probably not a good candidate for schutzhund.

Although there are many people who are qualified for this type of training, the most notable dogs in this sport tend to be dogs used for police work.

Scent Hurdle Racing

If you have ever seen a relay race—for example, at a swim meet—that's basically what this is. The dogs are held at one end. On command, they must race over a series of hurdles, retrieve a dumbbell, and then leap the hurdles again with the dumbbell in their mouths, until they turn it over to their owners. Dogs usually compete two at a time in this type of race. Of course, some dogs, anxious to win their praise, either scoot under and go around the hurdles. They have to start all over again. It's so fast and so funny, it's no wonder this sport is growing by leaps and bounds.

Flyball R

This is very much like scent hurdling, except that the dog, after racing over the hurdles, runs to a flyball box. Here, he depresses a lever that shoots a tennis ball up into the air. He must catch the ball, then leap the hurdles back. It's not uncommon for dogs to steal each other's tennis balls, or to fail to race correctly back to that starting point. But it is common for people and dogs to have a riotously good time at these events. The sport is governed by the

North American Flyball Association, and it confers three different titles: Flyball Dog (FD); Flyball Dog Excellent (FDX); and Flyball Dog Champion (FbDCh).

Canine Freestyle (or Freestyle Obedience)

This is the weirdest thing you ever saw—but it's also very cool. It's the newest thing to hit the obedience circuit. In this competition, the handler and the dog have developed a very intricate routine that needs to satisfy a particular number of feats. The routine is then set to music. Sometimes costumes are used. Many dog people compare it with ice dancing. A horse person might point out its likeness to dressage competitions.

Frisbee (or Flying Disk) Events

This one isn't difficult to figure out. Many folks do this all the time with their pets out in the parks, right? Wrong! This stuff is fast, furious, and wicked. To see some of the top Frisbee dogs do their stunts and tricks, and compete against others, is as amazing as it gets. There are competitions all over the country.

You and Your Dog in the Great Outdoors

OK, so you're an active person and you want to take your dog with you into the great big outdoors. Certainly it's a lot of fun to go out into nature with man's best friend to tread well-worn paths and to blaze new ones, all with your trusty companion right there beside you. We have many friends who do this with their dogs. All of them have both funny stories and horror stories. It's the wild, folks. Smokey the Bear is not going to roll out the red carpet for you. Forests are just as dangerous as city streets. You have to be prepared. Just remember Dorothy and the gang as they carefully tiptoed through the forest—"Lions, and tigers and bears! Oh, my!" Oh, yes.

Preparing for the Great Outdoors

When people take their dogs hiking or camping, there are plenty of things they take for granted—but they shouldn't. One of those things is their dog's health. Make sure you take your dog for a thorough examination. The one thing that Cheryl S. Smith advises in her classic book *On the Trail with Your Canine Companion* is to make sure your dog is healthy. She ought to know—hers is the best book on the subject. She insists that not only should you get a check-up—you should get a certificate of health from your vet. Many campsites require such paperwork before they will let a dog in.

It's also important to have papers proving that your dog has been vaccinated for rabies. Although few, if any, campsites require Canine Good Citizen certificates, if they are on the fence, Ms. Smith argues, they may be swayed if you produce this document.

Another important thing is identification. It's very important. If you're really out there, and Rex decides he's going to chase some deer and suddenly becomes separated from you, you're going to want to know that his tags with identification and information are on him. Make sure the tags are not temporary ones, but strong ones made of very hard impact-tested plastic, or better yet, metal. Make sure they are very firmly fastened to the collar and that the collar is secure.

More than anything, you need to get your dog in shape. Don't assume that just because he can outrun your big fanny, he's in shape. Make sure to take him for some long walks in the weeks leading up to the trip. That's all you need in the middle of your trip—for your dog-turned-weekend-warrior to come up lame in the middle of a hiking expedition. Or worse, to realize that your dog was getting sick before the trip started, and that illness has blossomed while you're somewhere deep in the heart of the woods. Make sure to exercise your dog several weeks prior to leaving.

You will find that in the woods, as in the city, training is invaluable. Because the dog has descended from the wild, we assume that he knows how to act and what certain things are. However, may I remind you—we, too, are descended from wild animals, and we don't have a clue, either. A well-trained dog comes when called. If your dog sees some wildlife, he may start to give chase or track it. You need to be able to recall him on a moment's notice. It's in these situations when you realize how important good

training is. Work on the basics: come, sit, stay, down—and the long down.

And as you might have for yourself, make sure you bring a first-aid kit, with enough of the right supplies for both you and your dog. Many a dog has cut his foot or hurt himself racing through the forest like a rollercoaster in summer. A first-aid kit will help you keep your dog healthy and infection free, and it may save your dog's life as well as your trip.

Travel

I have to be honest—when my wife and I travel with the dogs in our station wagon, we don't use crates. However, I do believe that crates are the best possible way to go. They are not always practical, given your specific destination. But if it's at all possible, you should bring your dog's crate and use it.

Now, if you have a station wagon, and you want to put the dog(s) in the back, that's perfectly fine. A space separator or gate is a good idea. It keeps the dogs from trying to hop over the seat and reduces the room they have to move around. They will tend to lie down more often, knowing that there's nowhere else to go. This is also good because, if you're in an accident, the dogs should be safe all the way back there.

If you don't have a station wagon, SUV, or truck with a cargo area, then you will definitely want to station Spot in the back seat. We use a relatively short lead which we attach to a spot in the center of the car. The dogs are not tied down uncomfortably. There is enough slack that they can sit up, but not enough for them to pace. This is also good in case of an accident. Your pets are safer back there.

Finally, let's talk about windows. Yes, dogs love to stick their heads out of windows and let their tongues hang out. But if everybody's dog jumped off the Brooklyn Bridge, would you let yours? It's not good for Fido, so put an end to it fast. The windows in back should be rolled down far enough to let a good amount of air in, but not so far that the dog can stick his or her head out the window.

What to Pack for Spot:

Certificate of health
Rabies papers
Food and water bowls
Some towels (for the dog)
First-aid kit (with supplies for dog and yourself)
Some toys
A leash and collar

Hiking

Hiking presents all kinds of problems we'll only touch on lightly here. First and foremost, you need to be wary in the woods for your dog's safety. Don't assume that he knows what he's doing. Try to keep him in sight at all times. Make sure he'll come to you if called.

There are many things you need to watch out for in the forest. First, there are other animals, especially animals such as skunks, raccoons and porcupines. Encounters with these can really ruin a trip, if not end it. The skunk might only add a whole new dimension to your hiking and camping experience, but encounters with raccoons and porcupines can be fatal.

Raccoons are very powerful animals and tenacious fighters. They may also have rabies. If your dog has an encounter with a porcupine, your trip is over. You really shouldn't attempt to remove the quills yourself. You should find the help of a veterinarian immediately. Pulling out the needles incorrectly might cause more harm and pain than when they went in.

Other animals to fear are deer and bears. The bear is a formidable foe for any animal, wild or domestic. If your dog is game enough to take him on, you may be in for some real problems. Deer are not such easy prey, either. Especially if there are females in season or competing males, your dog will find out the hard way that Bambi's more than capable of taking care of himself. Many a dog has attacked a buck and been gored to death. And last but not least, wild boars also present problems. They are not very big, but they have razor-sharp tusks. These pigs are some of the angriest wildlife in North America, and they present a danger to people and animals.

The last major animal you should be aware of is other dogs. If your dog doesn't get along with other dogs, then you might want to keep him on a short lead. Be careful—you don't want to be sued because your dog attacked someone else's dog, or vice versa.

Those are the main animals to be concerned about. Actually, there are many more than we can list here, because

Do I Have to Keep My Dog on His Leash While We're Hiking?

In most state parks the answer is an unequivocal yes! You should call ahead to learn the rules and regulations, as they vary from state to state and from park to park. Also, depending on the location, you might need to worry about the foot traffic. We've been hiking with our dogs in some areas where there were more people than birds running around up and down a small mountain. Our dogs were on lead all day. And this was in Vermont!

There are some wonderful leads called Flexi-leads. They come in handy during trips like these. They expand and contract on command. That gives your dog some leeway in exploring the local fauna, and gives you a certain amount of control. Otherwise, you may need to use a short lead.

Regardless, no lead is going to save you from some calamity unless Rover is well trained. A leash is not a substitute for good training—it's just a safeguard.

some are only regional. You may want to consult local wildlife management or parks authorities where you'll be traveling before you leave home.

Certainly the other things we need to worry about are plants and other humans. I usually get poison ivy once a year. I never go deep into the woods without being fully protected. However, my dogs don't step lightly when they see it. They are completely oblivious. There are many such situations which present themselves in the forest. Be careful and try to direct your dog away from any poisonous plants whenever possible. Also, dogs are known to chew all kinds of grasses. Try to discourage this, especially in the woods.

Make sure your dog is friendly with other humans. If you happen on a stranger in the woods, you don't want to see your fellow hiker with his arm half-devoured by Spot. Make sure your dog is stranger friendly, especially in these environs, where you're never sure how or when you'll run into other human beings.

Swimming

No dog on Earth is as crazy about swimming as our German Shorthaired Pointer, Exley. Once, in Connecticut, he swam across the Mianus River. By the time we drove to the other side to retrieve him, he had swum back to the other bank. This is not something you want to experience.

Make sure to keep an eye on your dog. Don't let him swim out too far. Don't let him swim in waters that don't look clean or are overrun with algae. And be careful of rough waters. Some dogs are good swimmers, but others are not. Try to exercise some common sense and know your dog's limits.

Camping

Once at a campsite, you may want to find a way to station your dog while you set up camp. Many manufacturers make stakes that are designed for just this kind of temporary use. Many look like giant corkscrews. This is a good way to give everyone some down time, including Rover.

One of the things I must suggest strongly is that you let your dogs sleep in the tent with you. Although I'm sure your dog is an

impassioned protector, he's more than likely to get hurt if night predators arrive. These animals only want your food and are not interested in fighting. However, if they're provoked, a bloody mess may occur.

Remember to keep the dogs far away enough from the fire. Dogs sometimes get too close because their fur insulates them from the heat of the flames. There is nothing more disgusting than the smell of burnt fur. Remember, you're supposed to cook the weenies, not the dogs!

Chapter Seven

YOUR DOG'S HEALTH AND FITNESS

An Ounce of Prevention

You love your dog, so of course you want him to be healthy—alert, bright-eyed, with a lustrous coat and sweet breath. It's no fun for you or your dog if he suffers with constant itching, hair loss, vomiting or diarrhea, or stinky dog breath. Believe it or not, it doesn't take repeated visits to the veterinarian or costly drugs to have a healthy dog. All it takes is common sense and vigilance. All it takes is regular preventive care.

What does *preventive care* mean? It means taking care of your dog the way you take care of yourself. It means:

- Brushing him regularly
- Checking his eyes, ears, and mouth regularly
- Keeping his toenails short
- Feeding him a high-quality food
- Making sure he always has access to cool, clean water
- Keeping his environment clean
- Giving him the attention and exercise he needs
- Spaying or neutering your dog
- Keeping him current on all his vaccines
- Taking him for a regular veterinary check-up at least once a year

Preventive care means you're in touch with your dog's physical and mental condition. Let's look at each of the areas of preventive care mentioned above and see how they benefit you and your dog.

Regular Brushing

Regular brushing accomplishes so many things! First, it removes dead hair and stimulates new hair growth. It invigorates the skin and coat, adding shine while removing any knots that may be forming and any dirt or dead skin that's sitting in the coat. Brushing feels good to your dog, and he will look forward to having his coat brushed gently and thoroughly. Because your dog will enjoy being brushed regularly, you'll enjoy brushing him. Grooming sessions are great bonding sessions! But even more important, they're your opportunity to check your dog's skin and coat for any problems.

Did you know the skin is the largest organ in the body? We'll talk more about common skin problems later in this chapter, but for now, it's enough to say that because it's the largest organ, it's the most exposed part of the body, and is therefore subject to the greatest onslaught of environmental elements. Your dog's skin and coat are prime targets for ticks, fleas, prickly seed pods, sharp objects such as barbed wire or splinters, all sorts of allergens, and the hosts of bacteria that are everywhere.

By brushing your dog regularly, you'll be able to spot fleas or the tell-tale sign of their presence, "flea dirt," which is the digested blood fleas excrete after a meal. Flea dirt looks like little flecks of pepper sprinkled on your dog's skin. If you wet a paper towel and rub the "dirt" with it, you'll find it dissolves to a rusty red color—blood. If you see flea dirt on your dog, the fleas are not far away, and you'll need to take immediate action to rid your dog and your home of the problem. (Learn how to deal with fleas later in this chapter.)

Brushing will also expose any ticks that may have gotten onto your dog. There are all different kinds and sizes of ticks, carrying various diseases. Of course, you must remove any tick you find on your dog right away (learn how later in this section), but the sooner you find it, the less likely it is that there will be an infection. You'll also notice cuts, scrapes, and patches of red, swollen, or hairless skin if you brush your dog regularly. Again, the sooner you find them, the sooner you can treat and relieve them.

Checking Eyes, Ears, and Mouth

Eyes

It doesn't take a lot of work to check your dog's eyes—after all, if you're like me, you spend so much time looking into them already that it's no big deal. But to keep your dog's eyes free from infection, you need to see beyond his best-begging look or his I-love-you-madly look and notice whether there's a buildup of secretion in the corners of his eyes, or any swelling

or redness around the eye. It's even possible for your dog to scratch his cornea on sharp grass. To remove secretory buildup around the eyes, use gentle materials such as tissues or a soft towel and cleansers specially formulated for use around the eye. Soap stings dogs' eyes, too! If you notice redness, swelling, or scratches, a trip to the veterinarian is warranted.

Ears

Does your dog have floppy ears or erect ears—long, hairy ears or cropped ears? If you have a prick-eared or cropped-eared dog, you will have to worry less about dirty ears that can lead to infected ears, because more air gets into the inner surfaces of the ear flaps. If your dog has floppy ears, no matter the length or thickness of fur on them, you'll need to make sure you check the inner surfaces frequently. The warm, moist environment under the dog's ear is the perfect host to dirt and bacteria buildup. Proper ear-cleaning procedures are described in Part 3, in the grooming section. Study them and make a point of looking under your dog's ears every few days.

Mouth

Isn't doggy breath the worst? Make sure your family never has to suffer from it by taking proper care of your dog's teeth and mouth. Dogs form plaque and tartar just as we do, but until we can teach them how to use a toothbrush, they need our help to keep their pearly-whites spick-and-span. Don't despair—it's easy to do. There are all sorts of brushes and doggy toothpastes available, or you can use a moist scrap of cheesecloth sprinkled with baking soda and get the same results. Don't use human toothpaste on your dog! What you want to do is just run a toothbrush or the cheesecloth over your dog's teeth near the gum line so you loosen the particles. No need to rinse—your dog will do that when he drinks some water.

Another reason you want to check your dog's mouth regularly is to spot problems such as chipped teeth, swollen gums, or any cuts. If you notice any of these, call your veterinarian.

Toenails

Keep those toenails short! Overgrown toenails can cause your dog's feet to splay, can lead to bone and joint problems, and can even grow so long that they curl under the foot and into the foot pads. Not good! There are a variety of doggy nail clippers you can use. Experiment to see which you're most comfortable with. (How to clip nails is explained in detail in Part 3, in the Grooming section.)

The Importance of Diet

A thorough discussion of diet and the kinds of foods available for dogs was presented in Part 3. You may want to review it to remind yourself just how important it is to the overall health of your dog. Like us, a dog is what he eats. If he's eating doggy junk food, his whole body will suffer. If he's eating a high-quality food, his whole body will benefit.

Cool, Clean Water

Would you want to drink the lukewarm, slobbery water left in the bottoms of people's water glasses after a meal? No way! Well, your dog doesn't know enough not to drink the canine equivalent that's often left in his bowl, and because he needs to drink to stay hydrated, he'll drink it anyway. So if you only fill the water bowl once a day or when you get around to it, don't be surprised if your dog gets an upset stomach or diarrhea occasionally. He needs fresh water all day long. Change the water in his bowl several times a day, and make sure to wash the bowl.

Environment

When was the last time you washed your dog's bed? How about picking up after your dog in the yard—do you do it regularly? If you don't keep your dog's environment clean, it will affect not only him, but your whole family. You don't want your dog tracking feces in on his paws when he comes in from the yard, and you don't want a smelly, dirty dog bed in the middle of your family room. So keep your dog's environment clean and you'll all feel better for it.

Attention and Exercise

If you don't provide enough of these, you'll be spending a lot of time reading Part 5 of this book and trying to solve common behavior problems. It's a fact: Dogs are social animals. Hey, we domesticated them, so it's our own fault that they want to be with us all the time— that they're happiest when we're with them, stroking their heads or curling up on the couch together. But don't forget they're animals, and

even a Toy breed needs to have his body and mind exercised. Take your dog for a walk. Play ball with him in the back yard. Teach him some tricks. Make sure he minds his manners. All these things keep his mind and body active—two key elements of health.

Spaying or Neutering Your Dog

Consider spaying your female or neutering your dog as preventive care for a number of reasons. Healthwise, a spayed female is far less prone to diseases of the reproductive system, because she does not have a uterus, fallopian tubes, or ovaries. A neutered male, one without testicles, is immune to testicular and prostate cancers. As for behavior, you'll be spared the mess of the female's biannual "season," and your male will be less likely to lift his leg in your home, roam in search of females in heat, or engage in aggressive behavior.

Vaccines and Your Veterinarian

From the time your dog was a wee pup he received vaccinations to protect him from major infectious diseases such as distemper, parvovirus, leptospirosis, hepatitis, and of course, rabies. Don't desert him now! Your dog needs his vaccines updated regularly, and there's no excuse for missing them. Your veterinarian will make sure you know when your dog's due, so make the appointment and take your dog in for his shots. The organisms responsible for some of these diseases can also infect people, so the health of your dog and your family is at stake.

Your veterinarian will want to see your dog at least once a year—not just to make sure he's up on his shots, but to give his professional opinion on the overall health of your dog. The vet will examine your dog from head to tail, including his eyes, ears, mouth, feet, limbs, chest, back, and anus. He will ask you about any lumps or bumps he might detect, or any swellings or tender spots. He'll let you know if your dog's teeth need a scraping (as ours do occasionally), and he'll advise you about your dog's weight and overall condition. If you've been following the preventive measures described here, you will be proud to hear your veterinarian tell you how healthy your dog looks and acts. Way to go! That's a compliment to the kind of care you're giving your best friend. Keep it up.

Basic Care for Your Dog

Let's face it—even with the best preventive care, things are going to happen to your dog. He's going to get fleas, he'll cut himself, he may develop a cough. He'll start limping or scratching or throwing up. Then what are you going to do? Don't despair—you'll find the answer in the following pages. We're going to cover all these:

Vaccines and what they protect against

Combating and controlling ticks and fleas

What to do about worms

First aid and emergencies

Common problems of the skin, eyes, ears, mouth, nose, digestive system, respiratory system, circulatory system, nervous system, musculoskeletal system, urinary system, and reproductive system

Vaccines and What They Protect Against

A vaccine is intended to work with the immune system to fight against invasive infections of bacteria and viruses. The injection contains a harmless amount of the organism the body may someday need to fight off. This "jump-starts" the immune system to respond to that organism again if it enters the body. Without vaccines, dogs are far more susceptible to contracting infectious diseases from other dogs and other animals.

Veterinarians typically begin a vaccination schedule for a puppy at about six weeks of age. At this time the pup receives a shot for distemper and measles. Approximately eight weeks later, at fourteen to sixteen weeks of age, the pup needs his DHLPP shot, a combination vaccine for distemper, hepatitis, leptospirosis, parainfluenza virus, and parvovirus. The veterinarian may also vaccinate the pup against rabies at this time. Expect to take your dog in for his DHLPP shot every year thereafter, and for his rabies shot as necessary, depending on which vaccine your veterinarian uses (some need to be boostered more often than others). In some parts of the country, veterinarians recommend that dogs receive a vaccine for the tick-borne Lyme disease, too.

The next sections describe the deadly diseases you're protecting your dog against with his shots.

Distemper

This is a viral disease that attacks a dog's gastrointestinal (digestive), respiratory, and nervous systems. It can strike at any age, but is most deadly if acquired young, which is why it's one of the first shots a pup receives. A dog with distemper will secrete a thick, yellowish discharge from his nose and eyes. He'll run a fever and he will not want to eat. The pneumonia, encephalitis, and dehydration that can result can be deadly.

Infectious Canine Hepatitis

Another viral disease, hepatitis attacks body tissue, particularly the liver, and most often strikes dogs under twelve months of age. Symptoms are mild and include increased thirst, loss of appetite, abdominal discomfort, and lack of energy. Death is sudden and there is no specific treatment.

Canine Leptospirosis

Lepto strikes the liver and also the kidneys, but this disease is caused by bacteria. Severe infections cause shock and death, but if it's caught early, aggressive treatment with antibiotics can fight it off. Symptoms include vomiting, excessive thirst with decreased urination and dehydration, and abdominal pain. Lepto is highly contagious, and an infected dog can also pass the bacteria through his urine for some time, even after treatment. The disease is also contagious to people.

Parainfluenza Virus

Parainfluenza is one of the germs involved in what's commonly called "kennel cough," a respiratory condition that results in a harsh, dry cough. Kennel cough is highly contagious and is so named because it is usually acquired where many dogs live together, such as in a kennel. Kennel cough can be treated with antibiotics, rest, and the proper environment. Affected dogs must be isolated from other dogs, and especially from puppies, who are more severely stricken than older dogs.

Parvovirus

This viral infection manifests itself as an inflammation of the intestinal lining, causing sudden vomiting, bloody diarrhea, a high fever, and rapid weight loss. It is transmitted through the feces and can survive outside a dog's body for three to six months. The disease is extremely debilitating and rapidly lethal; treatment is intensive and often unsuccessful.

Rabies

The rabies virus attacks the central nervous system, causing unpredictable and often aggressive behavior. This erratic behavior is what, in turn, can cause the virus to spread, because it is through the bite of an infected animal that another animal is infected. Rabies can be transmitted from species to species, too, making it a health hazard to domesticated animals and people. This is why all states require that dogs and cats be vaccinated against rabies. Rabies is common in the northeastern United States, where there are large populations of skunks, raccoons, foxes, bats, and groundhogs. If you observe erratic behavior in any of these animals, call your local animal warden immediately.

Lyme Disease

Lyme disease is a tick-borne viral disease that causes often-debilitating joint pain. Although a vaccine exists to protect against Lyme, check with your veterinarian for his or her opinion about whether your dog would really benefit.

Combating and Controlling Fleas

Fleas have been annoying humankind and animals for centuries, and they're almost as tough to control today as they were in the days of ancient Rome. The flea's exoskeleton is amazingly resilient, and fleas can jump several hundred feet to land on an unsuspecting host.

The Flea Life Cycle

Despite what many dog owners believe, fleas do not spend most of their lives on their pets. In fact, fleas only stay on dogs to feed and breed. They feed by biting the dog and sucking its blood. Because fleas often harbor tapeworm larvae in their systems, fleas can transmit tapeworm disease to the animal through the bloodstream or by being eaten when a dog tries to chew the fleas off himself. When fleas mate, the females lay hundreds of eggs. These drop off the dog and into the environment. Larvae hatch from the

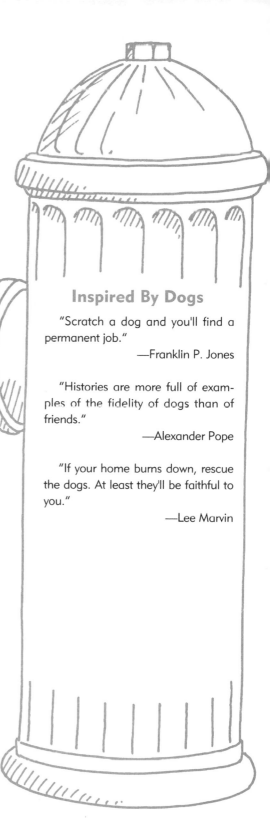

Inspired By Dogs

"Scratch a dog and you'll find a permanent job."
—Franklin P. Jones

"Histories are more full of examples of the fidelity of dogs than of friends."
—Alexander Pope

"If your home burns down, rescue the dogs. At least they'll be faithful to you."
—Lee Marvin

eggs in two to three weeks, and these feed on environmental debris such as human or animal dandruff, mold, and other protein and vegetable matter. From the larval stage, the flea develops a cocoon shell in which it matures. In the cocoon stage, the flea can live with no nutrients for almost a year. Then all it takes is the slight vibration of an animal's passing for the cocoon to release the adult, which jumps onto its host and begins the life cycle all over again.

Does Your Dog Have Fleas?

Your dog can pick up fleas almost anywhere—outdoors, in a neighbor's house, even from another dog. Chances are, by the time you spot adult fleas on your dog, you have an infestation in your home and/or yard.

You'll know you and your dog are in trouble when you see him itching or licking himself suddenly and with real purpose. To confirm your suspicions, part your dog's hair to the skin or brush it backwards and see if you notice any black specks. The specks can be dense around the dog's groin area, in the hair at the base of the tail, and around the ears and neck. With a moist paper towel, wipe the specks. If they turn red, they're flea dirt—particles of digested blood the flea has excreted.

What to Do?

Now that you know your dog has fleas, you will have to be diligent about removing them from the dog *and* the environment. If you only remove the fleas from your dog without eliminating the flea eggs, larvae, and cocoons from the environment, you are guaranteed a continuing problem.

Dog owners are fortunate to have a wide range of flea-fighting products to choose from, ones that are safer than ever for dogs and the environment. You should consult with your veterinarian before waging a war on the fleas that have infiltrated your happy home; you'll want to be sure that the products you select for use on your dog and your home are appropriate for your dog's age, weight, and skin type, and that the ingredients don't clash with a product you choose for your home and yard.

The active ingredient in many of the topical flea products on the market these days is pyrethrin, a natural compound that's toxic to fleas but won't harm pets or people. There are also formulations that stop flea eggs from developing, interrupt the reproductive cycle, and break down the flea's tough skeleton.

Once you've selected the flea-fighters you'll need, plan a systematic approach to ridding your dog, home, and yard of all stages of the flea life cycle. Take every step seriously if you want to completely eliminate the problem. You'll need to vacuum thoroughly, using several vacuum-cleaner bags and disposing of them all in airtight plastic bags. You'll need to wash all the dog's bedding in very hot water. This may include your family's bedding, too, if the dog shares anyone's bed. Any place that your dog passes through or sleeps in can be considered a flea "hot spot" and potentially infested. Concentrate your efforts here.

To remove fleas on your dog, wash with a flea-killing shampoo, then comb thoroughly with a fine-toothed flea comb. Dip the comb in a large glass of soapy water to drown any fleas that survived the bath. Dry your dog thoroughly, and don't let him roll in his favorite hole in the yard or lie down in his usual spot on the porch—these are possible hot spots, too, and need to be treated with an outdoor insecticide.

Once you've treated the dog, house, and yard, you'll never want to repeat the process, so you'll need to step up your preventive measures.

Preventing a Flea Problem

Figuring your dog can get fleas any time he steps out of your home and into a well-populated area, you should check him regularly before coming inside. Run a flea comb through his fur. This will snag any freeloaders before they start breeding. Kill them on the comb by crushing them with your fingernail or immersing the comb in a glass of soapy water. During the warm months, when fleas are at their worst, bathe your dog regularly with a flea-preventive shampoo, and ask your veterinarian about other products designed to keep fleas from settling on your pet. Vacuum your home frequently, and make sure to keep your pet's bedding fresh and clean.

Flea Bite Sensitivity

Many dogs are allergic to the saliva that fleas inject into their skin when they bite them, or are particularly sensitive to fleas living on them. These dogs can develop serious skin ailments from their

allergies and sensitivities, which often linger even after the flea problem has been eradicated. The excessive scratching, licking, and fur-biting they indulge in to get at the fleas leaves their skin damaged, causing further itching and, often, infection. The infection can leave the skin swollen or patchy and can lead to permanent hair loss. Besides being unsightly, a flea allergy or sensitivity is extremely irritating to your dog. Your veterinarian will advise you on how best to treat this many-symptomed problem.

Combating and Controlling Ticks

There are many types of ticks throughout the United States, the most common being the brown tick, the wood tick, and the deer tick. All adult ticks seek out dogs and other animals as hosts for feeding and breeding. The brown tick is typically the size of a match head or small pea when engorged. The wood tick is a larger tick that, when full, swells to the size of a kernel of corn. The deer tick is a tiny tick that even when engorged is no larger than a speck. The brown tick is known to transmit Rocky Mountain spotted fever, while the deer tick is the carrier of Lyme disease, both of which can be deadly.

Ridding Your Dog of Ticks

The sooner you spot a tick or ticks on your dog, the better. You need to remove the tick(s) immediately, then monitor the spot from which you removed it. To take a tick off your dog, first wet a cotton ball with alcohol or a dab of petroleum jelly. Apply this to the tick to suffocate or numb it. Then, with tweezers or with gloves on your hands, pull the tick gently off the dog. Deposit the tick in a jar filled with alcohol or nail polish remover. If your dog comes out of a trip to the woods loaded with ticks, you may want to get a tick dip from your veterinarian to help remove them all at once.

Tick bites rarely become infected, but you'll want to keep an eye on your dog's skin in the area from which the tick was pulled off, especially if it was a deer tick. Often a red, circular rash will develop around the bite—an early indicator of Lyme disease. If you notice any redness or swelling in the area of a tick bite, make an appointment to have it checked by the veterinarian.

Long-Lasting Help?

Unfortunately, it's almost impossible to keep ticks off your dogs if you spend any time outdoors with them. Your best bet, yet again, is preventive care: bathing your dog with a flea and tick shampoo formulated for his needs, taking your veterinarian's advice about what products work best to keep ticks off your dog, and always checking your dog thoroughly when you return from an outdoors adventure.

What to Do about Worms

Like the infectious diseases that are easily avoided by proper vaccinations, worms (intestinal parasites) are another potentially deadly enemy of your dog's health that are easily avoided by proper care, hygiene, and attention.

There are several types of worms that infect dogs. Tapeworms, whipworms, roundworms, hookworms, and heartworms are the most common.

Dogs become infected by worms by contact with contaminated soil; raw, contaminated meat (such as a dead animal in the woods); or ingestion of an infected host (such as a flea). That's why it's so important to clean up after your dog in the yard and around the house, and to have fecal exams performed by the veterinarian regularly (microscopic examination is often the only way to detect the presence of internal parasites).

Treating Worms

You might suspect your puppy or dog has worms if his appetite decreases, he has an upset stomach, he loses weight, and you see blood or mucus in his stools. These symptoms are characteristic of an advanced state of parasitic infection; dogs can have a slight infection and appear normal until your veterinarian detects worms in his feces. For common infestations, safe, effective, and fast-acting worming medications are available.

Heartworm

The heartworm is a particularly deadly parasite because it infests and grows in the canine heart. Left untreated, heartworms literally strangle the heart, causing it to fail and the dog to die.

Heartworm is transmitted by infected mosquitoes. When they land on a dog to bite, heartworm larvae are deposited on the skin. The larvae burrow their way through the dog's skin, growing into small worms as they go. When they finally reach a blood vein, the worms travel to the heart, where they mature. Heartworms can grow

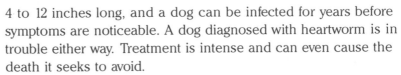

4 to 12 inches long, and a dog can be infected for years before symptoms are noticeable. A dog diagnosed with heartworm is in trouble either way. Treatment is intense and can even cause the death it seeks to avoid.

Today's dog owners are extremely fortunate to have heartworm preventive medication readily available. In some parts of the country veterinarians suggest giving dogs the preventive daily or monthly (depending on the type) only in seasons in which the mosquito is most active; in other parts of the country, veterinarians keep dogs on the preventive all year round as a safety precaution. Ask your veterinarian what's best for your dog and stick with the program. If you take your dog off of preventive for more than several months, he must be tested for the presence of heartworm before being allowed to go back on it.

Common Problems of Particular Systems

The Skin

The dog's skin is a dynamic and vital organ. No matter if your dog is short- or longhaired, his skin is always shedding dead cells and replacing them with new ones. The skin is made of two layers: the epidermis, or outer layer of skin cells, and the dermis, or second layer. A dog's skin is prone to many problems that can affect either or both layers of skin—most notably, itching, hair loss, swelling and inflammation, and flaking. Because skin problems are often the most visible and pronounced of ailments afflicting dogs, it's not surprising that they represent a large percentage of the overall cases referred to veterinarians.

Scratching and Itching

While all animals occasionally scratch themselves (including us humans!), excessive or constant scratching or itching is the sign of a problem. The most common causes are fleas, hypersensitivity (an immunologic or allergic reaction), and pyoderma (a bacterial infection). If the underlying cause isn't determined, the condition can grow increasingly worse.

At the first signs of itching, check your dog for fleas. As described earlier in this chapter, you can do this by moving the fur backwards and looking for fleas themselves, or for "flea dirt"—the digested blood fleas excrete that indicates their presence. If your dog has fleas, you will need to remove them from his body and from the environment.

Some dogs are so sensitive to flea bites that they develop flea allergy dermatitis. The dog develops an immunologic hypersensitive reaction to the saliva injected by the flea when it feeds on the dog. By constantly licking, scratching, and chewing at his skin, the dog develops areas of hair loss, which can further progress to open sores that lead to infection. The area most affected seems to be the base of the tail and lower back.

Flea allergy dermatitis typically develops when a dog is three to five years old, and it can be extremely tough to reverse, even if your dog is flea-free! The sooner your veterinarian can diagnose the condition, the sooner you can begin treatment and hope to alleviate the symptoms. Treatment will involve being vigilant about keeping your dog and home flea-free, the use of special shampoos, dips, or ointments to prevent itching, and possibly a prescription for anti-inflammatory drugs.

Dogs can also develop immunologic hypersensitivities to foods—anything from beef to wheat to dairy. This is why so many premium diets feature ingredients such as lamb, rice, or turkey.

Allergies

A hypersensitivity reaction to things in the environment, such as certain fabrics, detergents, molds, or fungi, usually means the dog is allergic to that thing. Symptoms usually develop when the dog is one to three years old and begin to show in the spring or fall. Areas of the body most affected include the face, stomach, paws, and, oddly enough, the creases of the elbows. If your dog is constantly rubbing his face, licking and scratching his paws, or itching his tummy or elbows, you should suspect an allergic hypersensitivity. Left untreated, the itching will lead to areas of broken, exposed skin that are ripe for infections. Often, paw licking will develop into a behavioral habit, perpetuating the condition.

Because of the enormous number of potential allergens in the dog's environment, your veterinarian will need to evaluate your dog's symptoms carefully and perform blood and skin tests to try to determine the allergen. Once this is pinpointed, elimination of the source is necessary, and you will probably need to use special shampoos and ointments to alleviate itching.

Infections

Bacterial infection is the result of skin that's under attack and losing the battle. The skin of a healthy dog has certain bacteria that live on its surface and within the hair's follicles. This "good" bacteria wards off infection by "bad" bacteria. But when something happens to disrupt the balance, harmful bacteria invade and proliferate, causing serious infection and some severe and very painful problems.

Hot Spots

These are quarter-sized areas of red, moist, swollen sores, typically found on longhaired dogs during warm, humid weather. They can be caused by the dog's licking itself in response to some other problem such as a parasitic infection, or general hypersensitivity. Often the cause goes undiscovered. Treatment involves applying antibiotic ointment to the wound and using an Elizabethan collar on the dog so he cannot reach the spot to continue licking or chewing at it.

Skin-Fold Pyoderma

Dogs with areas of thick folded skin on their bodies, such as Chinese Shar-Pei, Bloodhounds, Mastiffs, Pugs, and others, can develop infections in between the folds. That's because the fold creates a warm, moist spot—prime breeding grounds for bacteria. Regular inspection of the folds can help prevent infection, and antibiotic ointment can help treat it.

Another spot bacteria may breed rapidly is between the toes, and this is only exacerbated by the dog's licking. Scratches or cuts to the skin between the toes often go unnoticed, which can also lead to infection. Again, good grooming habits can go a long way toward preventing this condition.

Seborrhea

When there is an imbalance of new cell growth to replace dying cells, the result is a thickening of the skin with noticeable shedding

of the dead cells. This is called seborrhea. Symptoms include extreme flakiness, an overall greasiness to the skin and coat, an unpleasant and persistent odor to the coat, itchiness, and bald patches of thick skin. The causes of seborrhea include hormonal imbalance, parasitic infection, excessive bathing or grooming, and nutritional disorders—all factors that contribute to the skin's not being able to properly regulate itself. Diagnosis is fairly simple, but treatment can be quite involved and may necessitate antibiotics, special shampoos, and anti-inflammatories.

Common Problems of the Eyes, Ears, and Mouth

Eyes

Eyes and their surrounding tissues are susceptible to a number of problems. Dogs have three eyelids: top and bottom, and a third eyelid called the nictitating membrane, an extra layer of protection against the elements. The eyelids and the nictitating membrane all produce tears to lubricate the eye.

If one or both of your dog's eyes is tearing excessively, suspect a problem. It could be that a speck of dust or dirt or a grass seed has lodged between the eyelid and the eyeball. If you can see the particle, you can try to remove it with blunt tweezers or a moistened paper towel or cotton ball. To help the eye heal, apply some antibiotic ophthalmic ointment such as Neosporin just inside the lower lid.

Likewise, if an eye appears red or swollen, the dog may have an infection caused by a foreign body. It is best to consult your veterinarian if such a condition exists.

Entropion and Ectropion

Sometimes eye irritation is caused by the eyelashes rubbing against the eye. If the eyelid rolls inward, causing the eyelashes to aggravate the eye, the condition is called entropion. When the eyelid rolls outward the condition is known as ectropion. Dogs with ectropion have exposed eyelid tissue that's particularly prone to damage and infection. Entropion and ectropion are both common congenital defects that require surgical repair.

Conjunctivitis

The membrane that lines the inner sides of the eyeball up to the cornea is called the conjunctiva. If it becomes infected, you'll notice

a discharge from the corner of the dog's eye. The discharge may be clear and watery or opaque and thick. Typically this is the result of a bacterial infection. Your veterinarian can give you the best diagnosis.

Eye Problems of Older Dogs

As your dog ages, he becomes prone to dry eye and cataracts. As the name implies, dry eye is a condition in which the surface of the eye appears dull instead of shiny and bright. Dry eye is a condition of the tear glands, indicating that something is at fault with them. Consequently, they cannot supply the moisture necessary to lubricate the eye properly, which in turn leads to infection. Your veterinarian may be able to stimulate the tearing mechanism, or artificial tears will be prescribed.

Cataracts are clouding of the cornea that lead to blindness. They usually appear as milky colored or bluish-gray spots in the dog's eye. All older dogs are prone to developing cataracts. Other dogs at risk are diabetic dogs and dogs with a congenital problem that causes cataracts to form early.

Ears

Dogs' ears come in all shapes and sizes, from small and erect to long and pendulous. The most common problems they're susceptible to are cuts, hematomas, and infections. Many breeds' ears are cropped both to enhance appearance and to reduce the incidence of ear infection.

The Inner Ear

The skin of a healthy inner ear should be pink with some waxy light-brown secretion in the ear canal. If you notice your dog scratching at his ears, excessively rubbing the side of his face against the floor or other surfaces, or whining with discomfort when you stroke around his ears, suspect an infection or other problem. The skin that lines the ear canal is the perfect host for bacteria, which thrive in warm, moist environments. Dogs who swim regularly, who live in humid environments, who have long, hairy ears, or whose ears are not regularly inspected for excessive dirty wax buildup can easily develop an infection. Your veterinarian will diagnose it and give you instructions for treatment.

Ear mites can be another source of itchy, inflamed inner ears. These microscopic parasites also like warm, moist environments, where they feed on skin flakes. A scraping at the vet's office will confirm this diagnosis.

The Outer Ear

Ear flaps are most prone to cuts, bites, and hematomas. As long as a cut is not deep, it is simple to treat by cleaning it thoroughly and applying antibiotic ointment. Often dogs involved in a fight will get their ears bitten. If the bite is deep, take the dog to the veterinarian; otherwise, wash it thoroughly, apply antibiotic ointment, and monitor it for infection.

Hematomas are the result of a pooling of blood in the ear flap. This can happen after a dog shakes his ears violently, scratches them excessively, or knocks them against a sharp object. Consult your veterinarian about the best way to deal with a hematoma.

Deafness

Some breeds of dogs have genetic defects that cause them to either be born deaf or develop deafness at an early age. Conscientious breeders will test their dogs if they suspect a problem and remove affected dogs from their breeding programs. This is most common in Dalmatians and some terriers. Older dogs often lose some or all of their hearing. They still manage to get around in familiar, safe environments, but special care should be given to them.

Nose

First of all, forget the folk remedy that says a dog with a warm, dry nose is sick. Yes, a dog's nose should typically be cool and moist, and if it's not, the dog may have a fever. But some sick dogs will have cool, runny noses. Regardless, the nose is an all-important organ to the dog. Smell is his most acute sense; through it he learns the most about his environment and the other creatures in it.

Runny Nose

Because the nose itself doesn't have any sweat glands, when a dog is excited or sick, the nasal mucous membrane will secrete water. Only secretions that persist for several hours indicate a problem.

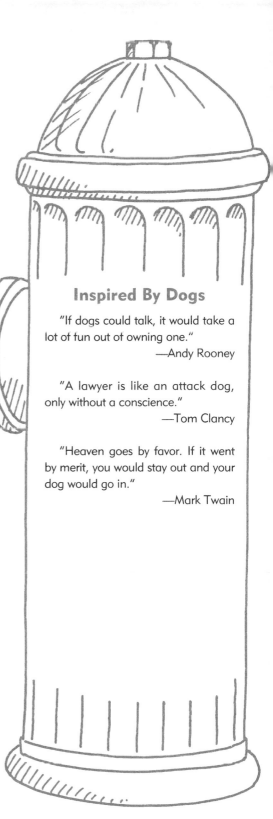

Inspired By Dogs

"If dogs could talk, it would take a lot of fun out of owning one."
—Andy Rooney

"A lawyer is like an attack dog, only without a conscience."
—Tom Clancy

"Heaven goes by favor. If it went by merit, you would stay out and your dog would go in."
—Mark Twain

Sneezing

This indicates an irritation to the front of the nasal cavity (coughing or gagging means the irritation is further back). It could be the inhalation of dust or dirt, which would cause the dog to sneeze several times and then stop, or it could indicate a fever or infection if it persists. If the sneezing is accompanied by discharge from the nose and/or eyes, see your veterinarian.

Mouth

The dog's mouth is made up of the lips, teeth, gums, and tongue. It is the passageway to the esophagus. While the lips and tongue can be injured by cuts or burns, injury and disease most commonly affects the teeth and gums, and it is on these that we will concentrate.

Teeth

The average adult dog has 42 teeth in his mouth (this can vary by breed, with shorter-faced breeds having less teeth). With improper oral hygiene, the teeth can become encrusted with plaque and tartar, leading to smelly (dog) breath, inflamed or infected gums, tooth loss, and general deterioration of the mouth.

Because of the high incidence of dogs suffering from periodontal disease, veterinarians and others in the pet industry have gone out of their way to educate owners and provide them with materials that make taking care of their dogs' teeth easy.

Healthy puppies and young dogs have bright white teeth and pink gums. It is possible to keep your dog's teeth looking almost as good as they did when he was a pup. This requires regular brushing, proper feeding and chew toys, and inspection for problems.

Get your dog used to having his mouth handled by regularly lifting his lips and gently opening his mouth. Look at his teeth and gums. Is the gum line red or swollen? Are the teeth white all the way to the gums? Do you see any chipped teeth?

You should brush your dog's teeth several times a week. To do this, you can purchase one of several types of doggy toothbrushes on the market. Some even come with their own doggy toothpaste that's specially flavored so dogs like the taste. Remember, never use human toothpaste on your dog. He won't like it, and it's bad for him. If you don't want to try the special toothbrushes and paste, you can wrap a small strip of gauze or cheesecloth around your finger to use as a scrubber. Use a paste of baking soda and water as the dentrifice. To brush, lift your dog's lip and brush or rub against the teeth with your finger. Try to get the brush or your finger all the way to the back of the mouth to reach the molars. Open the mouth and move the brush or your finger along the inside of the teeth along the gum line. Work quickly, gently and thoroughly. The whole process should only take a few minutes. When you're finished, reward your dog with a crunchy snack—dogs love those miniature carrots!

During your annual check-ups at the veterinarian's office, the doctor can advise you whether your dog's teeth need to be surgically scraped to have any lingering or stubborn tartar removed. Since this procedure requires anesthesia, discuss it with your vet at length before subjecting your dog to it.

Gums

As previously stated, healthy gums are pink and should be firm. Red, swollen, painful gums are a sign of gingivitis and require immediate attention. Your veterinarian will probably need to scrape your dog's teeth to remove offending tartar, after which you'll need to aggressively brush and inspect your dog's teeth. Severe gingivitis can lead to infection and tooth decay.

Choking and Gagging

If your dog starts to choke or gag, there may be something caught in the back of his mouth. If possible, try to remove the object yourself. If it's lodged too firmly and your dog is struggling and choking, take him to the veterinarian immediately. Try to calm and reassure the dog.

The Digestive System

This system is made up of the esophagus, stomach, small intestine, liver, gall bladder, spleen, colon, rectum, and anus. The problems most typically associated with this system are:

Vomiting
Bloat
Diarrhea
Constipation
Flatulence
Anal sac disorders

Every dog will experience upsets of the digestive system in the course of his life; most problems are easily treated and symptoms resolve within hours or days.

Vomiting

If your dog is vomiting, there is definitely something wrong with him. Determining what that something is, however, is trickier than you might think. You'll need to take special note of what he vomits and how he vomits to figure out what's wrong.

The most common cause of vomiting is simply overeating, or eating so quickly the food is gulped down and then comes back up again. Dogs will also commonly vomit after eating grass, and some dogs get carsick and vomit in the car. If your dog vomits what's obviously partly digested food or chewed grass and only vomits once or twice, or is distressed by the car, don't worry about it. If you notice blood in the vomit, or if the vomiting is severe and frequent, make an appointment to see the veterinarian. These are signs that your dog is truly not well.

Bloat

This condition is also called gastric dilatation, which is exactly what it is: a swelling up of the stomach due to gas, fluid, or a combination. When the stomach fills up this way, it is prone to twisting, which quickly leads to shock and death. Dogs can develop bloat by eating too much dry kibble; exercising vigorously after eating, or gulping their food or their water. Some breeds seem prone to it, and it appears to run in some breed lines. Dogs experiencing bloat become restless, drool heavily, try to vomit or defecate unsuccessfully, and cry in pain when their stomachs are palpated. It is imperative to get your dog to the veterinarian as soon as possible if you suspect bloat.

Diarrhea

Like vomiting, the type and consistency of diarrhea vary depending on what's really wrong with the dog. When all is normal, the dog eats and drinks and his digestive system absorbs nutrients from the food and water and passes along undigested materials in the stool, which should be firm and consistent in color. Any irritation to the intestines or the bowel will trigger diarrhea. These irritations can vary from a change in food or water, to overexcitement, to eating something that can't be digested or is toxic, or that produces an allergic response. The color, consistency, odor, and frequency of the diarrhea can help you and your veterinarian determine the underlying cause and set about providing the proper treatment.

Constipation

If you notice your dog straining to defecate, or even whimpering or whining while doing so, with the result being no passing of stool, your dog is constipated. Most cases of constipation are caused by inappropriate diet, which causes stools to form improperly and either block the colon or be painful to pass. Try giving your dog one-half to two tablespoons of a gentle laxative such as milk of magnesia. Take the dog out often so you don't risk an accident in the house. If you don't get results in twelve to twenty-four hours, consult your veterinarian.

Flatulence (Passing Gas)

Having an overly flatulent dog is no fun! Through no fault of his own, a dog who passes gas can clear an entire room in no time. Peeyew! Chalk your dog's flatulence up to inappropriate diet yet again. A diet high in meats, fermentable foods such as onions, beans, or even some grains, or dairy products can lead to excess gas. Review your dog's diet carefully, including the ingredient list of his dog food, and slowly integrate a diet change. If this doesn't yield results, your veterinarian can help.

Anal Sac Disorders

Dogs have two anal sacs, one on each side of the rectum at about 5 and 7 o'clock, commonly called "scent sacs." They secrete a distinctive odor that leaves the dog's scent when he defecates. If the sacs become blocked, they can become sore and infected and will need to be expressed. If your dog frequently scoots across the floor dragging his bottom or wants to lick the area often, suspect an anal sac problem and ask the vet to show you how to handle expressing them to relieve the buildup.

The Respiratory System

Dogs breathe through their respiratory system, a series of airways that comprise the nasal passages, throat, windpipe, and bronchial tubes that lead to the lungs. Any of the following symptoms indicate a problem in the system:

Rapid breathing
Noisy breathing
Coughing

Rapid Breathing

Dogs will breath heavily and rapidly in a number of circumstances, such as after strenuous exercise, in excessive heat, or if they're excited or stressed. If your dog is breathing rapidly while at rest and you can't attribute any of these other factors to his condition, consult your veterinarian.

Noisy Breathing

This includes wheezing, sneezing, labored breathing, hoarseness, and any odd sound the dog makes while trying to breathe. Owners of some short-faced breeds live with this problem. Their dogs have shorter airways and will regularly snort, snore, or breathe heavily. For other dogs, noisy breathing is generally due to an obstruction, though it can also indicate a lung disease or heart failure. It's best to have your veterinarian listen and look.

Coughing

Coughing results from the effort to extricate an obstruction in the airways, whether it's a bone chip, a collapsed windpipe, or a fluid buildup in the lungs caused by a respiratory disease such as kennel cough. Kennel cough is highly contagious between dogs and can spread rapidly at a dog show or in a kennel. There is a vaccine to help prevent kennel cough, and if it's caught early, treatment is successful.

The Circulatory System

At the center of the circulatory system is the all-important heart, a muscle that pumps blood to the rest of the body. Diseases that affect the canine heart include birth defects, aging, infectious disease, and heartworms. Heartworm is a condition that can be deadly, but is easily avoided by giving regular preventive heartworm medication, as discussed earlier in this section.

The Nervous System

All activity in the nervous system generates from the brain, the spinal cord, and the peripheral nerves. Spinal cord diseases, seizures, head injuries, and paralysis are some of the problems that can result from injury or disease of this system.

Seizures and Epilepsy

A seizure is caused by a sudden burst of electrical activity in the brain, affecting the entire body by causing uncontrolled convulsions: foaming at the mouth, jerking of the limbs, snapping of the jaws, rolling of the eyes. Depending on the seizure's severity, the dog may collapse and slip into unconsciousness. Seizures can be caused by trauma to the brain or the healing associated with it, or by an hereditary condition.

Epilepsy is a state of recurrent and similar seizures that typically happen in three phases: sudden restlessness accompanied by champing or foaming at the mouth; falling to the ground with head thrown back and pupils dilated, slobbering and drooling; and a recovery phase in which the dog is disoriented. The more violent phases, one and two, happen in just a few minutes; the recovery phase may last hours. You must consult with your veterinarian and your dog's breeder if your dog has epilepsy.

Paralysis

Complete paralysis is the result of permanent damage to the spinal cord. But a dog can experience partial paralysis due to a spinal cord disease or infection. Lyme disease is a form of tick paralysis in which the effects of the tick bite come on slowly, impairing movement to the point of paralysis. A speedy diagnosis is key to recovery. Normally the paralysis resolves with treatment by antibiotics.

The Musculoskeletal System

Bones and muscles support the body and protect the internal organs. All dogs, regardless of size, have an average of 319 different

bones in their bodies. The bones are connected by ligaments and surrounded by muscles.

If your dog is limping or is favoring a particular leg (lame), chances are he's got a bone or joint disease, a strained muscle or tendon, or possibly a broken bone. The causes range from something as severe as a congenital disorder, such as hip or elbow dysplasia, to something as ordinary as a strained muscle or age-related as arthritis. Your veterinarian should give you a professional diagnosis.

Hip Dysplasia

Canine hip dysplasia (often referred to as CHD or just HD) is a disorder of the hip socket. In a healthy hip, the head of the thigh bone (femur) should fit snugly in the hip socket (acetabulum). If the ligaments around the socket are loose, the head of the femur will start to slip from the socket. This causes gradual hind-end lameness and pain. Treatment varies depending on the age of the dog, the severity of the condition, and the options available to dog and owner. Rapid advances are being made in the treatment of hip dysplasia.

While a specific cause of CHD has not been identified, it is suspected to be an inherited disorder, and breeders are encouraged to X-ray their dogs before breeding and to only breed dogs that have been certified free of the disease. It has happened, however, that CHD-free parents have produced pups that develop hip dysplasia. Weight, nutrition, and environment have all been implicated in the possible exaggeration or development of CHD, which normally manifests at an age of rapid growth.

The Urinary System

The components of the urinary system are the bladder, prostate, and urethra, as well as the kidneys and ureters. The system works together. The two kidneys' jobs are to siphon excess waste created by ordinary metabolism, yet regulate water and minerals. Wastes are deposited into the ureter, which empties into the bladder. Urine passes from the bladder to outside the body via the urethra (in the male, the urethra also transports semen).

If all is functioning well, your dog will urinate regularly (not frequently), and his urine will be clear and yellow in color. A problem of the kidneys, bladder, urethra, or prostate will be evident as straining to urinate, blood-tinged or cloudy urine, excessive drinking accompanied by excessive urination, or pain upon urination. The problem could be something as minor as dehydration or as complicated as renal failure. You must consult your veterinarian for a diagnosis.

The Reproductive System

Of the Female

This includes two ovaries, a uterus, and fallopian tubes. A spayed female will have all of these removed. Intact females will experience regular heats and are prone to false pregnancies and infection of the uterus, called pyometra. As advised earlier in this chapter, you and your female dog will be happier and healthier if she is spayed. Some believe that a spayed bitch is prone to obesity. While it is true that she will not be under the same hormonal influence that keeps an intact bitch in form, with regular exercise and the proper diet a spayed bitch can be kept in top shape.

Of the Male

The male dog's reproductive system includes the testicles, penis, and prostate gland. Intact males are prone to damage or injury of the penis or scrotum, cancer of the testes, and inflammation, enlargement, or cancer of the prostate. Once again, you and your dog will live happier, healthier lives if the dog is neutered. Neutering is the surgical removal of the testicles. The empty scrotum eventually shrinks and leaves no scar. Neutering not only guarantees the male won't develop testicular cancer or prostate problems, it also lessens a male's territoriality, making him (with proper care and training) a friendlier pet. Neutering does not significantly change a dog's temperament, however; if you have an aggressive male, neutering will not solve the problem, but combined with training, it can certainly help.

Handling an Emergency

Emergencies elicit two states that don't help matters any—shock and/or fear in the dog, and panic in the owner. When dealing

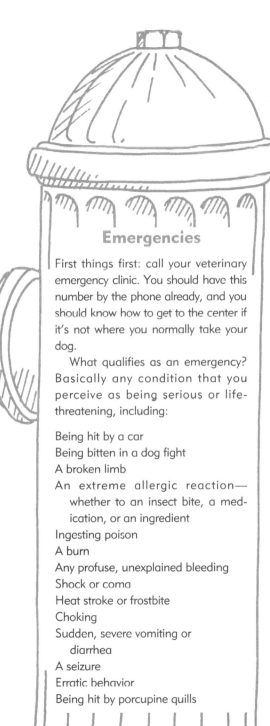

Emergencies

First things first: call your veterinary emergency clinic. You should have this number by the phone already, and you should know how to get to the center if it's not where you normally take your dog.

What qualifies as an emergency? Basically any condition that you perceive as being serious or life-threatening, including:

Being hit by a car
Being bitten in a dog fight
A broken limb
An extreme allergic reaction—
    whether to an insect bite, a med-
    ication, or an ingredient
Ingesting poison
A burn
Any profuse, unexplained bleeding
Shock or coma
Heat stroke or frostbite
Choking
Sudden, severe vomiting or
    diarrhea
A seizure
Erratic behavior
Being hit by porcupine quills

with an emergency, keep reminding yourself to stay calm and stay focused on what you can do for your dog. Ideally, you should have someone drive you to the clinic while you handle the dog.

After you've called the veterinary clinic, as well as someone to come help you if you're alone with the dog, follow these steps:

1. Evaluate the dog's condition and deliver any first-aid procedures, such as reducing bleeding, putting on a muzzle so the dog doesn't bite you or someone else, applying any ointment, or wrapping a wound.
2. Keep your dog still and warm by reassuring him while down and keeping a blanket on him.
3. Make preparations to transport him so he experiences as little turbulence and commotion as possible.

Find a Veterinarian

This is by no means a complete discussion of the health conditions that affect dogs, or their diagnosis or treatment. There are of course professional-level books far more detailed than this one. The authors suggest you consult other books for more detailed information, and most importantly, find a veterinarian you can trust and rely on. He or she will be the person you should turn to for detailed advice.

Chapter Eight

YOUR OLDER DOG

You think it's never going to happen: The rambunctious puppy who chewed through three armchairs and took three years to train to heel is starting to slow down! You begin to notice at around age five or six (depending on the breed), and next thing you know, you have a canine senior citizen.

There are a lot of wonderful things about this time in your dog's life. You and he have a strong bond, and you know what to expect from each other. Your dog listens more. He sleeps more, even though he still loves to go to the beach or for walks, and can play with the family for hours.

In fact, these may be some of the most enjoyable years you'll spend with your dog. He'll love going for car rides with you and will wait patiently while you do your quick errands. He'll be the first out the door if you let him know you want to play ball, but he'll be ready to stop when you tire of the game.

The Aging Process

A dog's body ages in some of the same ways as a human's: metabolism slows, the immune system slows, arthritis may set in, vision, hearing, and smell can be impaired, there may be loss of bladder and bowel control, and there is usually an overall slowing down.

It's tough to see your dog go through these changes, and sometimes it's tough for you and your family, too. Your older dog may not be able to hold it through the night, and you may wake up to find accidents in the house. Older dogs know these are mistakes and may look at you with real apology in their eyes. Take pity on your older dog and let him know you understand. You may want to set your alarm an hour or so earlier in the morning so that your dog won't have to wait as long at night.

Tending to Your Older Dog's Needs

You live with your dog, so you know when something is affecting him. As he enters and goes through his senior years, it's especially important that you pay attention to signs that he may be hurting.

Just as we stressed preventive care in the health chapter, we'll stress it again here. You can fend off so many major problems by being alert and attentive to your dog's overall health every day.

Aching and Stiffness

If your dog is having trouble getting up and down stairs, or takes some lame steps every once in a while, you can suspect an arthritis problem. Your veterinarian can suggest something to alleviate the pain, such as buffered aspirin. If the pain seems more intense, a visit to the vet is called for.

Suspicious Lumps and Bumps

Many dogs develop lumps and bumps over their bodies as they age. If you notice any on your dog, you should have them examined by the veterinarian as soon as possible. Most are simply fatty growths, but some can be tumors, and it's important, in those cases, to have them biopsied to determine if they're cancerous.

Sight and Sound

Other functions you'll want to monitor are your dog's vision and hearing. Most dogs develop cataracts (clouding of the eye lens) as their vision deteriorates, but not all do. Your dog may be losing his sight and you may not notice. Dogs with impaired vision are still able to get around almost normally, especially in familiar territory, because they are so familiar with their homes and immediate vicinity. The same can be true of hearing loss. Your dog may not respond to you as quickly, but if he sees you calling to him or knows that when you come home he gets his dinner shortly thereafter, he'll still respond. The veterinarian can perform more conclusive tests if you suspect your dog is losing his sight or hearing.

Teeth and Gums

If you haven't been keeping your dog's teeth and gums clean and healthy until now, you're in trouble. The accumulated plaque and tartar of a lifetime can have serious effects on the teeth and gums. Your dog may start to lose his teeth, which exposes the mouth to infection. He will probably have bad breath, which will make him a less lovable companion in close quarters (through no fault of his own!). His gums may become so sore that he isn't able to eat the kibble that is his best food source.

If you've been keeping up with regular veterinary visits, you should know whether your dog's teeth and mouth are in good shape. Your dog may even have needed to have his teeth cleaned under anesthesia. The thing is, you don't want to subject an older dog to this procedure if you don't have to, because older dogs are more prone to the ill effects of anesthesia. Keep brushing!

Nutritional Needs

One of the major influences in overall geriatric health is nutrition. If your senior citizen is eating too much fat and not enough fiber, not only does he risk becoming obese, but he may become constipated or have other gastrointestinal upsets. Also, just as we become allergic to things as we get older that didn't affect us when we were young, the same thing happens with dogs. The tried-and-true food you gave him for most of his life may now be causing him to itch or sneeze, or it may bother him in other ways.

The levels of proteins, fats, carbohydrates, vitamins, and minerals that a dog needs vary according to age. A growing puppy or an active dog in his prime is going to need a lot more to keep his body going than will a semiretired, couch-loving senior dog. Discuss your dog's activity level with your veterinarian to determine the best diet. There are now specific dog foods for growth, maintenance, and senior years, including special diets for allergies and "lite" foods.

Another temptation is to spoil your older pal by giving him special treats. Spoiling the ones we love is natural; just remember, the more weight your dog carries around, the poorer his overall health is going to be. You may be indulging him in the short run, but those indulgences could mean less time with your dog in the long run. If you give a special treat, just cut back on his regular diet for a day or so. Ideally, you'll have kept your dog fit and trim throughout his lifetime, in which case it'll be easier to maintain this same condition into his senior years.

Exercise for Today and Tomorrow

Your dog may be slowing down, but that doesn't mean he shouldn't get out. In fact, he'll be happier and healthier if you keep him exercising. This doesn't mean going on the same five-mile runs you did when he was six or seven. Take into consideration the fact that his joints are stiffer, his energy level is lower, and his systems are working harder to keep up. A five-mile walk would be more like it. Of course, all dogs are individuals, and the amount of exercise they can handle varies with the dog's breed, his age, his regular activity level, and so on. The point is, you know your dog and you know what he's capable of. Don't push him, but don't sell him short, either.

The Geriatric Physical Exam

When your dog turns eight or so, you should take him to the veterinarian for a senior examination. Even if he seems as healthy as ever, your veterinarian can take whatever tests he may think are necessary to evaluate your dog's condition. These can include blood tests, urine tests, vision and hearing tests, etc. Your veterinarian should know your dog already and can provide objective commentary on his overall state that can assist you in knowing what to do or beware of going forward.

Around the House

There are a number of things you can do around the house to make your older dog more comfortable.

If you know his sight and/or vision are deteriorating, put off any major redecorating or remodeling plans. Your old dog can navigate around familiar sofas, chairs, or tables and will know the smells of familiar carpets or other floor surfaces. Making major changes to the layout of familiar rooms such as dens or kitchens will thoroughly confuse a blind dog, which will further stress him and make his condition worse.

Don't yell at a dog who can't hear well. Communicate more through sight and touch. Pet your dog to get his attention, then beckon him to where you want him to be. Use the hand signals you taught him over the years to help him understand what you want.

If your dog is having trouble getting up and down the stairs, or can't jump up on to sofa to watch TV with you, or has trouble getting in and out of the car, you should lift or carry him if you can. If your dog weighs too much for you to be able

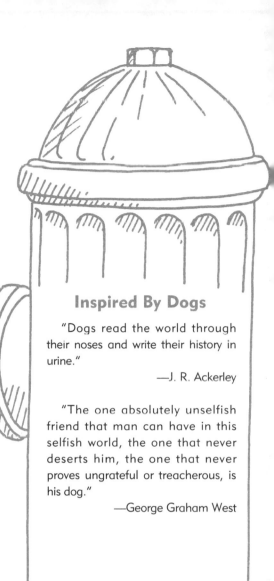

Inspired By Dogs

"Dogs read the world through their noses and write their history in urine."

—J. R. Ackerley

"The one absolutely unselfish friend that man can have in this selfish world, the one that never deserts him, the one that never proves ungrateful or treacherous, is his dog."

—George Graham West

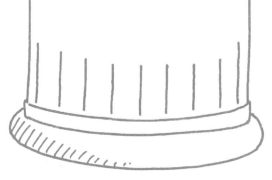

to do this, consider building some simple ramps to help him. The ramps will need to be covered with some kind of non-slip material. Your dog will be so much happier if he is not banned from his favorite spots because of his failing health.

Speaking of favorite spots, these are usually the softest, most cozy places in the house. Older dogs especially appreciate them. A flip through any dog supply catalog will show that there are all sorts of beds made to make geriatric dogs more comfortable, from egg-carton foam beds to specially heated pads. These are designed to relieve arthritic joints and to keep calluses from forming on the joints.

You should also provide your older large dog with raised food and water bowls from which to eat and drink. This makes eating and drinking easier on his back, neck, and shoulders.

Saying Good-bye

No matter how well you take care of your dog throughout his life, old age will eventually catch up to him. It may be a slow decline or a rapid decline. There may be good days—those during which your dog wakes with his renowned zest for life, eats well, and wags his tail enthusiastically when you talk to or pet him—and bad days—those during which your dog won't even want to get out of bed for his favorite toy or treat. The good days will renew your hopes, and the bad days will break your heart.

As your dog's caretaker and friend, it's up to you to determine when the bad days can't go on and decide if it's time to put your dog to sleep. When our old friends suffer at the end of their lives, euthanasia is the gift we can give them to bring their lives to a peaceful close with us by their side. It is a terribly painful decision to have to make, but it is a wise and humane one.

Discuss putting your dog down with your family so everyone can be prepared for it. Call your veterinarian and talk to him or her about your decision. Ask to come to the office when it will be quiet so you won't have to wait a long time and the doctor won't be extremely busy. If it is going to stress out your dog to

Pampering Your Pal

Count every day you have with your old friend as a blessing; they go by far too fast. To help your dog feel special, remember that he has special needs at this time in his life. He will particularly appreciate all this:

Soft, cozy, clean bed
Regular walks
A consistent schedule
Being kept clean and warm
Some extra treats (but watch his weight!)
All the petting you can give

Include your old friend in family outings and gatherings just as you always did. That's the best treat of all.

take him to the vet's, ask for a mild sedative you can give before you come over, then go pick it up so you can give it to your dog at the right time.

Think about what you want to do with your dog's body when he is no longer. If he's small enough, do you want to bury him near your home? Do you want to bury him in a pet cemetery so you can visit his gravesite for many years to come? Do you want the veterinarian to have him cremated? Make a decision that's right for you and that you won't regret later.

Euthanasia is a painless procedure in which a lethal dose of anesthesia is injected into a vein. As the drug enters the bloodstream, the dog loses consciousness and dies within seconds. You can be assured that all he feels is the slight prick of the needle.

You should be with your dog until the very end. Talk to him and tell him what a good friend he's been and how much you'll miss him. It's normal to cry, so don't be embarrassed. Your veterinarian will certainly understand if you want to be with your dog for a few minutes after he passes away.

When Your Friend Is Gone

You may be surprised at how deeply you are affected by the loss of your dog. When you think about it, even though you may have known deep down that this time was coming, you were still trying to be strong and optimistic, if only to give your dog hope. Now that your friend is truly gone, you will not only grieve for his loss, but you will find a release for all the days, possibly years, of hanging on that you did for his sake.

Your home will not be the same without your dog there, and everything will remind you of him—his old bed, his old bowls, his old collar, favorite toys, favorite spots. We are lucky to live in a time when it's acknowledged how deeply people love their dogs; in fact, some people feel stronger love

Support Groups

Here's a list of some phone numbers for those who feel the need for counseling while grieving over the loss of their friend.

University of California, Davis,
School of Veterinary Medicine
Davis, CA
(916) 752-4200

Michigan State College of Veterinary Medicine
Lansing, MI
(517) 432-2696

Ohio State University Veterinary Teaching
Hospital
Columbus, OH
(614) 292-1823

Tufts University New England Veterinary
Medical Center
North Grafton, MA
(508) 839-7966

Virginia–Maryland Regional College of
Veterinary Medicine
Blacksburg, VA
(540) 231-8038

Web Sites

Austin Humane Society and SPCA
http://www.austinspca/homepage.html
Offers chapter's Pet Loss Support Group

AVMA
American Veterinary Medical Association
http://www.avma.org
Have section on pet loss.

Bide-A-Wee
http://www.inch.com/~bideawee/index.html
This animal welfare site offers bereavement services.

Pet Loss and Rainbow Bridge
http://www.primenet.com/~meggie/bridge.htm
Entire Web page is dedicated to those grieving the loss of their pets.

International Association of Pet Cemeteries
http://www.petrest.com/iapc.html
All the practical questions are answered. A sad but very good site.

for their dogs than for other people in their lives, so naturally they are going to feel their loss more deeply. Your family will also be grieving, and it's important to allow everyone to grieve in their own way and time, and to talk about those feelings.

If you or anyone in your family are having a particularly difficult time, or if you just want to know that there are others who have gone through similar pain, you can find books on coping with the loss of a pet in your book store or library or on line. A particularly good one is Dr. Wallace Sife's *The Loss of a Pet*. Speaking with other dog owners can help, too, since chances are they've had a similar experience and understand what you're going through. There are also pet-loss hotlines you can call to speak with people who can lend a kind ear. It's important to honor the memory of your friend. Your heart will heal with time, and you know he will always be with you.

"Other Dogs" and Old Dogs

Is it a good idea to get a younger dog or a puppy when your dog starts getting old? Will this new addition reinvigorate your canine senior citizen, or will it send him into an irreversible funk and bring on a quicker death? Will you find yourself so involved in caring for the new dog that you somehow neglect your old friend when he may need you most?

These are all things to think about before you add another dog to your household while your own dog is in his golden years. He may, in fact, find a new friend invigorating and revert to a kind of second puppyhood. Or he might withdraw altogether. Puppies are truly irresistible, while older dogs have their share of problems that are not always pleasant to deal with. Even unconsciously, you may find yourself giving all your attention to the newcomer, which will not make your older dog feel good.

Before you get another dog, sit down and really think about how your dog may react. Don't get a puppy so there will be another dog in the house when your old dog's time comes. Don't get another dog if your dog is used to being Number One and is not particularly well socialized.

Dog Life Expectancies

The average dog will live to be twelve to fifteen years old. Of course, there are no guarantees that your dog will live to be that old, or that young! Dogs have been known to live for more than twenty years and as few as four or five (or less with some genetic disorders). Some giant breeds such as Newfoundlands and Great Danes generally have shorter lifespans (six to eight years), while some small breeds such as Lhasa Apsos or Yorkshire Terriers can live into their late teens. And while some will argue that mixed breeds are prone to the fewest health problems and may therefore live the longest lives, there is no proof for this claim.

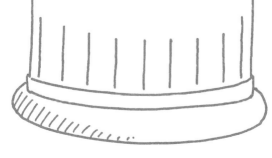

Chapter Nine

CANINE RESOURCES

Listed below are addresses and/or telephone numbers for a number of different resources. Included are magazines, books, videos, and dog catalogs. Make sure to check the Web site guide for more resources as well as URLs.

Magazines

AKC Gazette
American Kennel Club
51 Madison Avenue
New York, NY 10010

Bloodlines Journal
United Kennel Club
100 E. Kilgore Road
Kalamazoo, MI 49001

Canine Review
(Canadian show journal)
Canadian Kennel Club
89 Skyway Avenue, Suite 200
Etobicoke, ON M9Q 6R4
Canada

Dogs in Canada
Canadian Kennel Club
89 Skyway Avenue, Suite 200
Etobicoke, ON M9Q 6R4
Canada

Dog Fancy
Fancy Publications
3 Burroughs
Irvine, CA 92718

Dog World
MacLean Hunter Publishing Corp.
29 N. Wacker Drive
Chicago, IL 60606
or:
9 Tufton Street
Ashford, Kent TN23 1QN
United Kingdom

Dogs Monthly/Our Dogs
5 Oxford Road Station
Manchester M60 1SX
United Kingdom

Dogs Today
Pet Subjects Limited
Pankhurst Farm, Bagshot Road
West End, Near Working,
Surrey GU24 9QR
United Kingdom

Good Dog!
P.O. Box 10069
Austin, TX 78766

Kennel Gazette
1-5 Clarges Street
Piccadilly
London W1Y 8AB
United Kingdom

Mushing Magazine
Stellar Communications, Inc.
P.O. Box 149
Ester, AK 99725-0149

National Dog
P.O. Box 670
Seven Hills NSW 2147
Australia

New Zealand Kennel Gazette
Private Bag 50903
Porirua 6220
New Zealand

Pet View Magazine
National Pet Health and Care Network
P.O. Box 160581
Sacramento, CA 95816

Shelter Sense
(a publication of the HSUS)
2100 L Street NW
Washington, DC 20037

Books

General

The Complete Dog Book, by The American Kennel Club (Howell Book House)
The Complete Dog Book for Kids, by The American Kennel Club (Howell Book House)
Dogs: A Historical Journey, by Lloyd M. Wendt (Howell Book House)
Dogs on the Web, by Audrey Pavia and Betsy Sikora Siino (MIS Press)
The Intelligence of Dogs, by Stanley Coren (Free Press)
The Lost History of the Canine Race, by Mary Elizabeth Thurston (Avon)

The Most Complete Dog Book Ever Published, by Andrew DePrisco and James B. Johnson (TFH)
Pack of Two, by Caroline Knapp (The Dial Press)
Pet Sitting for Profit, by Patti J. Moran (Howell Book House)
Selecting the Best Dog for You, by Chris Nelson (TFH)
The Quotable Dog, by Greg Snider (Contemporary Books)
Through Otis's Eyes, by Patricia Burlin Kennedy and Robert Christie (Howell Book House)

Adoption and Rescue

The Adoption Option, by Eliza Rubenstein and Shari Kalina (Howell Book House)
Save That Dog!, by Liz Palika (Howell Book House)
Second-Hand Dog, by Carol Lea Benjamin (Howell Book House)

Health

The Consumer's Guide to Dog Food, by Liz Palika (Howell Book House)

Dog Doctor, by Mark Evans (Howell Book House)

Dog Owner's Home Veterinary Handbook, by Delbert G. Carlson, DVM, and James M. Giffin, MD (Howell Book House)

Home Remedies for Dogs and Cats, by *Prevention* Magazine (Rodale)

Training and Behavior

Back to Basics: Dog Training by Fabian (Robinson), by Andrea Arden (Howell Book House)

Dog Behavior, by Ian Dunbar (TFH)

Dog Perfect, by Sarah Hodgson (Howell Book House)

Dr. Dunbar's Good Little Dog Book, by Ian Dunbar (James & Kenneth Publishers)

Dual Ring Dogs, by Amy Ammen and Jacqueline Frasier (Howell Book House)

How to Be Your Dog's Best Friend (The Monks of New Skete), by Job Michael Evans (Little, Brown)

People, Pooches & Problems, by Job Michael Evans (Howell Book House)

Surviving Your Dog's Adolescence, by Carol Lea Benjamin (Howell Book House)

Training by Bash, by Bashkim Dibra (Dell)

Training in No Time, by Amy Ammen (Howell Book House)

When Good Dogs Do Bad Things, by Mordecai Siegel (Little, Brown)

Pet Loss

The Loss of a Pet, by Dr. Wallace Sife (Howell Book House)

When Your Pet Dies, by Jamie Quakenbush (Simon & Schuster)

Videos

American Kennel Club
AKC/Video Fulfillment
5580 Centerview Dr.
Suite 200
Raleigh, NC 27606
The American Kennel Club produces videos on all breeds of dogs as well as on training, health, and activities such as hunting tests and field trials. Write for more information.

"Training the Companion Dog" and/or
"SIRIUS Puppy Training"
by Ian Dunbar
James & Kenneth Publishers
2140 Shattuck Avenue #2406
Berkeley, CA 94704

Dog Resource Guide

Black Ice
Dog Sledding Equipment
3620 G Yancy Avenue
New Germany, MN 55367

Cherrybrook
Route 57
P.O. Box 15
Broadway, NJ 08008
(908) 689-7979
1-800-524-0820

Dog Lover's Bookshop
(212) 369-7554

Direct Book Service
Dog & Cat Book Catalog
P.O. Box 2778
Wenatchee, WA 98807
(509) 663-9115
1-800-776-2665

In the Company of Dogs
P.O. Box 7071
Dover, DE 19903
1-800-924-5050

J-B Wholesale Pet Supplies
5 Raritan Road
Oakland, NJ 07436
1-800-592-7847

Oken Shaw Grange
Doncaster Road
Crofton, Wakefield
West Yorkshire
United Kingdom

Pet-Pak Inc.
P.O. Box 982
Edison, NJ 08818
(908) 906-9200
1-800-217-PETS

Pet USA
P.O. Box 128
Dept. #508
Topsfield, MA 01983
1-800-4-PETUSA

Pet Supply House Ltd.
373 Wyecroft Road
Oakville, ON L6K 2H2
Canada

RC Steele
P.O. Box 910
Brockport, NY 14420
(716) 637-1408
1-800-872-3773
1-800-424-2205 in Canada

Reigning Cats & Dogs
5617 H Street
Sacramento, CA 95819
(916) 455-5619

Ringpress Books Ltd.
Dogs Today Breeds
PO Box 8
Lydney
Gloucs GL15 6YD
United Kingdom

Sugarum Dog Centre
20 Boronia Drive
Hillside, Victoria 3037
Australia

Organizations and Associations

Animal Advocacy
American Humane Association
63 Inverness Dr. East
Englewood, CO 80112
(303) 792-9900

ASPCA
424 East 92nd Street
New York, NY 10128-6804
(212) 876-7700

Delta Society (for Therapy Dogs)
P.O. Box 1080
Renton, WA 98057
(206) 226-7357

Doris Day Animal League
900 2nd Street NE, Suite 303
Washington, DC 20002
(202) 842-3325

Friends of Animals, Inc.
P.O. Box 1244
Norwalk, CT 06856
(203) 866-5223

The Humane Society of the United
States
2100 L Street, NW
Washington, DC 20037
(202) 452-1100

National Humane Education Society
521A East Market Street
Leesburg, VA 22075
(703) 777-8319

Pets Are Wonderful Council
(P.A.W.)
500 N. Michigan Avenue
Suite 200
Chicago, IL 60611
(312) 836-7145

Project BREED
Network for Ani-Males and Females
18707 Curry Powder Lane
Germantown, MD 20874-2014
(301) 428-3675

Therapy Dogs International
6 Hilltop Road
Mendham, NJ 07945
(201) 548-0888

United States Agility Association, Inc.
P.O. Box 850955
Richardson, TX 75085-0955
(214) 231-9700

Breed Registries

United States and Canada
American Kennel Club
51 Madison Avenue
New York, NY 10010
(212) 696-8200

American Kennel Club
5580 Centerview Drive
Raleigh, NC 27606-3390
(919)233-9767

American Mixed Breed Obedience
Registry
205 1st Street SW
New Prague, MN 56071

American Rare Breed Association
100 Nicholas Street NW
Washington, DC 20011

Canadian Kennel Club
Commerce Park
88 Skyway Avenue, Suite 100
Etobicoke, ON M9W 6R4
Canada

Mixed Breed Dog Club of America
1937 Seven Pines Drive
St. Louis, MO 63146-3717

States Kennel Club
P.O. Box 389
Hattiesburg, MS 39403-0389

United Kennel Club
100 East Kilgore Road
Kalamazoo, MI 49001-5598
(616) 343-9020

World Kennel Club
P.O. Box 60771
Oklahoma City, OK 73146
(405) 570-7929

AKC-Affiliated Breed Clubs

American Brittany Club, Inc. (M)
Corres. Secretary: Joy Searcy, 800 Hillmont Ranch
Road, Aldeo, TX 76008
Breeder Contact: Ms. Velma Tiedeman, 2036 N. 48th
Ave., Omaha, NE 68104, (402) 553-5538

American Pointer Club, Inc. (M)
Secretary: Lauri Shroyer, 7208 Sugar Maple Ct.,
Rockville, MD 20855
Breeder Contact: Lauri Shroyer, 7208 Sugar Maple Ct.,
Rockville, MD 20855, (301) 926-1599

German Shorthaired Pointer Club of America (M)
Secretary: Patte Titus, 4103 Walnut Street, Shaw AFB,
SC 29152-1429, checksix@cpis.net
Breeder Contact: Ann King, 11946 NYS Rt. #34N, Cato,
NY 13033, (315) 626-2990

German Wirehaired Pointer Club of America, Inc. (M)
Corres. Secretary: Karen Nelsen, 25821 Lucille Ave.,
Lomita, CA 90717
Breeder Contact: Mrs. Nancy Mason, 826 Cinebar Rd.,
Cinebar, WA 98533, (360) 985-2776

American Chesapeake Club, Inc.(M)
Corres. Secretary: Dyane Baldwin, RD2 Box 287A,
Newport, PA 17074, pondholo@igateway.com
Breeder Contact: For a puppy information packet,
please send a $3.00 check payable to the American
Chesapeake Club, Inc. (to cover duplication and
postage costs) to: Janet Cole, American Chesapeake
Club, P.O. Box 523, Florissant, MO 63032-0523

Curly-Coated Retriever Club of America (L)
Corres. Secretary: Marilyn Smith, 251 NW 151 Ave.,
Pembroke Pines, FL 33028, Tootsye@aol.com
Breeder Contact: Sheila Callahan-Young, 3 Roberts
Court, Gloucester, MA 01930, (508) 281-3860,
wing@tiac.net

Flat-Coated Retriever Society of America, Inc. (M)
Recording Secretary: Kurt Anderson,42 Drazen Drive,
North Haven, CT 06473, 73210.136@compuserve.com
Breeder Contact: Kathy Barton, 5325 Ann Hackley Dr.,
Fort Wayne, IN 46835-1413, (219) 486-5905
katefire@aol.com

Golden Retriever Club of America (M)
Secretary: Linda Willard, P.O. Box 20434, Oklahoma
City, OK 73114
Breeder Contact. Anne McGuire, (281) 861-0820

Labrador Retriever Club, Inc. (M)
Secretary: Christopher Wincek, 12471 Pond Road,
Burton, Ohio 44021 Rodarbal@aol.com
Breeder Contact: Judy Meyer, P.O. Box 454,
Chesterland, OH 44026-0454, (216) 729-2064

English Setter Association of America, Inc. (M)
Secretary: Mrs. Dawn S. Ronyak, 114 S. Burlington
Oval Dr. Chardon, OH 44024
Breeder Contact: Mrs. Dawn S. Ronyak,
114 S. Burlington Oval Dr. Chardon, OH 44024,
(216) 285-4531, settereng@aol.com

Gordon Setter Club of America, Inc. (M)
Corres. Secretary: Nikki Maounis, P.O. Box 54,
Washougal, WA 98671
Breeder Contact: Ms. Phyllis Tew, 9707 N. Kiowa
Road, Parker, CO 80134, (303) 841-2015

Irish Setter Club of America, Inc. (M)
Corres. Secretary: Mrs. Marion Pahy, 16717 Ledge
Falls, San Antonio, TX 78232-1808
Breeder Contact: Mrs. Marilee Larson, 27371 Whitmor,
Pioneer, CA 95666, (209) 295-1666

American Water Spaniel Club (M)
Secretary: Ann Potter, HR 3 Box 224,Johnson City, TX
78636
Breeder Contact: David and Kelly O'Pool, 629 Westhill
Ave., Idaho Falls, ID 83402, 1-800-555-AWSC

Clumber Spaniel Club of America, Inc. (M)
Secretary: Ms. Barbara Stebbins, 2271 SW Almansa
Ave, Port St. Lucie, FL 34953
Breeder Contact: Edythe Donovan, 241 Monterey Ave.,
Pelham, NY 10803, (914) 738-3976

American Spaniel Club, Inc. (M)
Corres. Secretary: Ellen Passage, 35 Academy Road,
Hohokus, NJ 07423-1301
Breeder Contact: Dorothy Mustard, 30 Cardinal Loop,
Crossville, TN 38555, (931) 484-5030,
mustdo@midtenn.net

English Cocker Spaniel Club of America, Inc. (M)
Secretary: Kate D. Romanksi, P.O. Box 252, Hales
Corners, WI 53130
Breeder Contact: Kate D. Romanksi, P.O. Box 252,
Hales Corners, WI 53130, (414) 529-9714

English Springer Spaniel Field Trial Association, Inc. (M)
Corres. Secretary: Cheryl Sligar, 5180 N. Dapple Gray
Rd., Las Vegas, NV 89129, CSligarESS@aol.com
Breeder Contact: Cheryl Sligar, 5180 N. Dapple Gray
Rd., Las Vegas, NV 89129 (702) 656-7116,
CSligarESS@aol.com

Field Spaniel Society of America (M)
Corres. Secretary: Lynn Finney, Box 247, Lyndell, PA
19354, bttrblu@worldaxes.com
Breeder Contact: Sharon Douthit, 1905 Ave. J., Sterling,
IL 61081, (815) 625-0467, sushar@cin.net

Irish Water Spaniel Club of America (M)
Secretary: Evelyn Van Uden, 3061 Moore Road,
Ransomville, NY 14131
Breeder Contact: Evelyn Van Uden, 3061 Moore Road,
Ransomville, NY 14131, (716) 791-4335

Sussex Spaniel Club of America (L)
Corres. Secretary: Sylvia Schlueter, 383 Blane Ct.,
Dawson, IL 62520
Breeder Contact: Sylvia Schlueter, 383 Blane Ct.,
Dawson, IL 62520, (217) 364-9603

Welsh Springer Spaniel Club of America, Inc. (M)
Corres. Secretary: Karen Lyle, W254 N4989 McKerrow
Dr., Pewaukee, WI 53072-1300
Breeder Contact: Pat Pencak, 135 Old Forrestburg Rd.,
Sparrow Bush, NY 12780, (914) 856-4533

Vizsla Club of America, Inc. (M)
Corres. Secretary: Mrs. Florence Duggan, 451
Longfellow Ave., Westfield, NJ 07090
Breeder Contact: Mrs. Florence Duggan, 451 Longfellow
Ave., Westfield, NJ 07090, (908) 789-9774

Weimaraner Club of America (M)
Exec. Secretary: Dorothy Derr, P.O. Box 2907,
Muskogee, OK 74402-2907
Breeder Contact: Ms. Rebecca Weimer, 324 Sundew
Dr., Belleville, IL 62221, (618) 236-1466

American Wirehaired Pointing Griffon Association (L)
Corres. Secretary: Patricia Loomis, 7920 Peters Rd.,
Jacksonville, AR 72076, patloomis@aol.com
Breeder Contact: Suzzette Wood, 3056 Partin
Settlement Rd., Kissimee, FL 34744, (407) 846-0484

Hound Group
Afghan Hound Club of America (M)
Corres. Secretary: Norma Cozzoni, 43 W. 612 Tall
Oaks Trl. Elburn, IL 60119
Breeder Contact: Norma Cozzoni, 43 W. 612 Tall Oaks
Trl. Elburn, IL 60119, (630) 365-3647

Basenji Club of America (M)
Secretary: Anne L. Graves, 5102 Darnell, Houston, TX
77096-1404
Breeder Contact: Melody E. Russell, 2714 NE 110th St.,
Seattle, WA 98125-6739, (206) 362-4202

Basset Hound Club of America, Inc. (M)
Secretary: Melody Fair, P.O. Box 339, Noti, OR 97461-
0339, HEIRLINE@aol.com
Breeder Contact: Lisa Lamoreux, 409 Easy Street,
Concord, NC 28027, (704) 792-9672

National Beagle Club (M)
Secretary: Susan Mills Stone, 2555 Pennsylvania NW,
Washington, DC 20037
Breeder Contact: Julie Fulkerson, 2781 Wheat Rd.,
Lenoir City, TN 37771 (540) 752-0507

American Black & Tan Coonhound (L)
Secretary: Stan Bielowicz, 222 Pate Rogers Rd.,
Fleming, GA 31309
Breeder Contact: Cheryl Speed, 3508 Berger Rd., Lutz,
FL 33549, (813) 963-2033

American Bloodhound Club (M)
Secretary: Ed Kilby, 1914 Berry Ln., Daytona Beach, FL
32124
Breeder Contact: Ed Kilby, 1914 Berry Ln., Daytona
Beach, FL 32124, (904) 756-0373

Borzoi Club of America, Inc. (M)
Corres. Secretary: Karen Mays, 29 Crown Dr., Warren,
NJ 07059-5111, zencor@bellatlantic.net
Breeder Contact: Karen Mays, 29 Crown Dr., Warren,
NJ 07059-5111, (908) 647-3027, zencor@bellatlantic.net

Dachshund Club of America, Inc. (M)
> Secretary: Carl Holder,1130 Redoak Dr., Lumberton, TX 77657
> Breeder Contact: Jere Mitternight, 2301 Metairie Heights Ave., Metairie, LA 70001, (504) 835-1025, jerem@juno.com

Greyhound Club of America (M)
> Corres. Secretary: Margaret Bryson,15079 Meeting House Ln., Montpelier, VA 23192
> Breeder Contact: Margaret Bryson, 15079 Meeting House Ln., Montpelier, VA 23192, (804) 883 7800

American Foxhound Club (L)
> Corres. Secretary: James M. Rea, P.O. Box 588, Clarkesville, GA 30523

Harrier Club of America
> Secretary: Kimberly Mitchell, 301 Jefferson Lane, Ukiah, CA 95482
> Breeder Contact: Kimberly Mitchell, 301 Jefferson Lane, Ukiah, CA 95482, (707) 463-0501

Ibizan Hound Club of the United States (M)
> Secretary: Stephanie Bonner, 3098 Elm Road, Duluth, MN 55804, sbonner@duluth.infi.net
> Breeder Contact: Elizabeth Binney, 1999 Gripp Road, Sedro-Wooley, WA 98284-9216, (360)856-2139

Irish Wolfhound Club of America (M)
> Secretary: Mrs. William S. Pfarrer, 8855 U.S. Route 40, New Carlisle, OH 45344
> Breeder Contact: Mrs. William S. Pfarrer, 8855 U.S. Route 40, New Carlisle, OH 45344, (937) 845-9135

Norwegian Elkhound Association of America, Inc. (M)
> Corres. Secretary: Debra Walker, 3650 Bay Creek Rd., Loganville, GA 30249
> Breeder Contact: Debra Walker, 3650 Bay Creek Rd., Loganville, GA 30249, (770) 466-9967

Otterhound Club of America (L)
> Corres. Secretary: Dian Quist-Sulek, Rt.#1, Box 247, Palmyra, NE 68418
> Breeder Contact: Dian Quist-Sulek, Rt.#1, Box 247, Palmyra, NE 68418, (402) 441-7900

Petit Basset Griffon Vendeen Club of America (M)
> Secretary: Ms. Shirley Knipe, 426 Laguna Way, Simi Valley, CA 93065
> Breeder Contact: Ms. Shirley Knipe, 426 Laguna Way, Simi Valley, CA 93065, (805) 527-6327

Pharaoh Hound Club of America (L)
> Corres. Secretary: Rita L. Sacks, P.O. Box 895454, Leesburg, FL 34789-5454
> Breeder Contact: Rita L. Sacks, P.O. Box 895454, Leesburg, FL 34789-5454, (352) 357-8723

Rhodesian Ridgeback Club of the United States, Inc. (M)
> Corres. Secretary: Dawn Sajadea, P O Box 5215, River Forest, IL 60305-5215, dsajadea@tezcat.com
> Breeder Contact: Deborah Hopper-Danford, 2032 US 401 Hwy S, Louisburg, NC 27549-9801, (919) 496-3389

Saluki Club of America (M)
> Secretary: Judy Tantillo, 208 Forked Neck Road, Shamong, NJ 08088, fax (609)268-3455, asuwish@cyberEnet.net
> Breeder Contact: Diane Thompson, 581 Classen Drive, Dallas, TX 75218, (214)503-0039, ThompsonD@marykay.com

Scottish Deerhound Club of America, Inc. (M)
> Secretary: Mr. Tom Gentner, 3477 Flanders Dr., Yorktown Heights, NY 10598, tgentner@aol.com
> Breeder Contact: Bette Stencil, 1328 South Riverside Ave., St. Clair, MI 48079-5133, (810) 329-3841

American Whippet Club, Inc. (M)
> Secretary: Mrs. Harriet Nash Lee, 14 Oak Cir., Charlottesville, VA 22901
> Breeder Contact: Mrs. Harriet Nash Lee, 14 Oak Cir., Charlottesville, VA 22901, (804) 295-4525

Working Group

Akita Club of America (M)
> Secretary: Sandi Soto, 5602 N. Church St., Tampa, FL 33614 Fax: (813) 889-0668, akitainu@cyberspy.com
> Breeder Contact: Mrs. Debbie Stewart, 17945 Jo Ann Way, Perris, CA 92570-8961, (909) 943-1811

Alaskan Malamute Club of America, Inc. (M)
Corres. Secretary: Stephen Piper, 3528 Pin Hook Road, Antioch, TN 37013-1510, spiper@nashville.net
Breeder Contact: Cap Schneider, 21 Unneberg Ave., Succasunna, NJ 07876, (973) 584-7125

Bernese Mountain Dog Club of America, Inc. (M)
Secretary: Ms. Roxanne Bortnick, P.O. Box 270692, Fort Collins, CO 80527
Breeder Contact: Ms. Ruth Reynold, 5265 E. Fort Rd., Greenwood, FL 32443, (904) 594-4636

American Boxer Club, Inc. (M)
Corres. Secretary: Mrs. Barbara E. Wagner, 6310 Edward Dr., Clinton, MD 20735-4135
Breeder Contact: Mrs. Lucille Jackson, 11300 Oakton Rd., Oakton, VA 22124, (703) 385-9385

American Bullmastiff Association, Inc.
Secretary: Linda Silva,15 Woodland Lane, Smithtown, NY 11787
Breeder Contact: Ms. Barbara Brooks-Worrell, 16045 SE 296th, Kent, WA 98042-4529, (206) 630-4342, bbrooks@u.washington.edu

Doberman Pinscher Club of America (M)
Corres. Secretary: Nancy Jewell, 13451 N. Winchester Way., Parker, CO 80134
Breeder Contact: Mrs. Tommie F. Jones, 4840 Thomasville Rd., Tallahassee, FL 32308

Giant Schnauzer Club of America, Inc. (M)
Secretary: Kathy DeShong, 7855 Whistling Winds Lane, Brighton, IL 62012, (618) 466-6768, GSCAMERICA@aol.com
Breeder Contact: Robin Greenslade, 12 Walnut Ter., Salem, NH 03079, (603) 894-4938

Great Dane Club of America, Inc.
Corres. Secretary: Kathy Jurin, 1825 Oaklyn Dr., Green Lane, PA 18054

Great Pyrenees Club of America, Inc. (M)
Corres. Secretary: Maureen Maxwell-Simon, 7430 Jonestown, Harrisburg, PA 17112
Breeder Contact: Janet Ingram, 204 Wild Partridge Ln., Radford, VA 24141, (540) 731-0229, jlingram@usit.net

Komondor Club of America, Inc. (M)
Corres. Secretary: Linda Patrick, 4695 Peckins Rd. Chelsea, MI 48118, Cords4me@provide.net
Breeder Contact: Linda Patrick, 4695 Peckins Rd. Chelsea, MI 48118, (734) 433-0417, fax (734) 433-0527, Cords4me@provide.net

Greater Swiss Mountain Dog Club of America, Inc. (B)
Corres. Secretary: Dori Likevich, 11713 Duncan Plains Road, Johnstown, OH 43031
Breeder Contact: Dori Likevich, 11713 Duncan Plains Road, Johnstown, OH 43031, twinpine01@aol.com

Kuvasz Club of America (M)
Corres. Secretary: Susan Gilmore, P.O. Box 90, Braceville, IL 60407, kcasecy@aol.com
Breeder Contact: Patricia Zupan, 1018 N. 250 E., Chesterton, IN 46304-9332, (219) 921-1529, IndyZee@Mail1.nitco.com

Mastiff Club of America, Inc. (M)
Corres. Secretary: Karen McBee, Rt.#7, Box 520, Fairmont, WV 26554, mmcbee@access.mountain.net
Breeder Contact: For a packet please send a $5.00 check payable to the MCOA (to cover duplication and postage costs) to: BRL, 15235 N 40th Lane, Phoenix, AZ 85023-2524

Newfoundland Club of America, Inc. (M)
Corres. Secretary: Steve McAdams, PO Box 370, Green Valley, IL 61534
Breeder Contact: Rebecca Cieniewicz, 341 Carter's Gin Rd., Toney, AL 35773, (205) 852-7015

Portuguese Water Dog Club of America, Inc. (M)
Corres. Secretary: Ms. Joan-Ellis Van Loan, 99 Maple Ave., Greenwich, CT 06830
Breeder Contact: Sandra Overton, 1395 SE 8th Ave., Oak Harbor, WA 98277, (360) 675-9539, fax (360) 240-0292, soverton@whidbey.net

American Rottweiler Club (M)
Corres. Secretary: Doreen LePage, 960 S. Main St., Pascoag, RI 02859, doreen@ids.net
Breeder Contact: Lauri Ladwig, 1184 E. Fleetwood Ct., Boise, ID 83706, (208) 424-1304

Saint Bernard Club of America, Inc. (M)
Corres. Secretary: Penny Janz, 33400 Red Fox Way, No. Prairie, WI 53153
Breeder Contact: Penny Janz, 33400 Red Fox Way, No. Prairie, WI 53153, (414) 392-2852, pmjanz@global-dialog.com

Samoyed Club of America, Inc. (M)
Corres. Secretary: Lori Elvera, 3017 Oak Meadow Drive, Flower Mound, TX 75028, Kenoshasam@aol.com
Breeder Contact: Lori Elvera, 3017 Oak Meadow Drive, Flower Mound, TX 75028, Kenoshasam@aol.com

Siberian Husky Club of America, Inc. (M)
Corres. Secretary: Fain Zimmerman, 210 Madera Dr., Victoria, TX 77905, slcdog@tisd.net
Breeder Contact: Carol Himes, 38945 CR 653, Paw Paw, MI 49079, (616) 657-2175, cadohi@net-link.net

Standard Schnauzer Club of America (M)
Secretary: Joan Sitton, 160 Carmel Riviera Dr., Carmel, CA 93923
Breeder Contact: Darlene Cornell, 4 West Stone Street, Newburgh, NY 12550, (914) 565-4604, schnz@juno.com

Terrier Group

Airedale Terrier Club of America (M)
Corres. Secretary: Mrs. April Stevens, 4078 Hickory Hill Rd., Murrysville, PA 15668
Breeder Contact: Corally Burmaster, 20146 Gleedsville Rd., Leesburg, VA 20175, (703) 779-8030

Staffordshire Terrier Club of America (M)
Secretary: Dr. H. Richard Pascoe, 785 Valley View Rd., Forney, TX 75126

Australian Terrier Club of America, Inc. (M)
Corres. Secretary: Ms. Marilyn Harban, 1515 Davon Ln., Nassau Bay, TX 77058
Breeder Contact: Sabine Baker, P.O. Box 30, Cobbs Creek, VA 23035, (804) 725-9439

Bedlington Terrier Club of America (M)
Corres. Secretary: Mr. Robert Bull, P.O. Box 11, Morrison, IL 61270-7419
Breeder Contact: Mr. Robert Bull, P.O. Box 11, Morrison, IL 61270-7419, (815) 772-4832

Border Terrier Club of America, Inc. (M)
Secretary: Pattie Pfetter, 801 Los Luceros Dr., Eagle, ID 83616
Breeder Contact: Judy Donaldson, 135 Westledge Rd., W. Simsbury, CT 06092, (860) 651-0140

Bull Terrier Club of America (M)
Corres. Secretary: Mrs. Becky Poole, 2630 Gold Point Cir., Hixson, TN 37343
Breeder Contact: Mrs. Becky Poole, 2630 Gold Point Cir., Hixson, TN 37343, (423) 842-2611, rockytp@voyageronline.net

Cairn Terrier Club of America (M)
Corres. Secretary: Christine M. Bowlus, 6152 Golf Club Road, Howell, MI 48843
Breeder Contact: Christine M. Bowlus, 6152 Golf Club Road, Howell, MI 48843, (517) 545-4816

Dandie Dinmont Terrier Club of America, Inc. (M)
Secretary: Mrs. Gail Isner, 151 Junaluska Dr., Woodstock, GA 30188
Breeder Contact: Mrs. Lloyd Brewer, 1016 Mars Dr., Colorado Springs, 80906, (719) 473-9560

American Fox Terrier Club (M)
Secretary: Mr. Martin Goldstein, P.O. Box 1448, Edison, NJ 08818
Breeder Contact: Mrs. Billie Lou Robison, 17408 N.E. 195th St., Woodinville, WA 98072-6674, (206) 483-6177

Irish Terrier Club of America (M)
Corres. Secretary: Cory Rivera, 22720 Perry St., Perris, CA 92570
Breeder Contact: Jeanne Burrage, 103 N. Frazier Ave., Florence, CO 81226, (719) 784-0931

United States Kerry Blue Terrier Club, Inc. (M)
Corres. Secretary: Gene Possidento, 1 Park Lane, West Nyack, NY 10994
Breeder Contact: Lisa Frankland, 1699B 9th St., Langley AFB, VA 23665 (757) 766-8097, lisaf@exis.net

United States Lakeland Terrier Club (M)
Secretary: Mrs. Edna Lawicki, 8207 E. Cholla St., Scottsdale, AZ 85260
Breeder Contact: Mrs. Edna Lawicki, 8207 E. Cholla St., Scottsdale, AZ 85260, (602) 998-8409

American Manchester Terrier Club (M)
Secretary: Ms. Sandra Kipp, Box 231, Gilbertsville, IA 50634
Breeder Contact: Ms. Diana Haywood, 52 Hampton Rd., Pittstown, NJ 08867, (908) 996-7309

Miniature Bull Terrier Club of America (L)
Corres. Secretary: Kathy Schoeler, 8111 N. W. 46th Street, Ocala, FL 34482

American Miniature Schnauzer Club, Inc. (M)
Secretary: Jane Gilbert, 5 Salt Meadow Waye, Marshfield, MA 02050, JMJRGlbrt@aol.com
Breeder Contact: Amy Gordon, 802 Upland Road, W. Palm Beach, FL 33401, (561) 366-1038, aragonms@worldnet.att.net

Norwich and Norfolk Terrier Club (M)
Corres. Secretary: Heidi H. Evans, 158 Delaware Ave., Laurel, DE 19956
Breeder Contact: Mrs. Susan Ely, 85 Mountain Top Rd., Bernardsville, NJ 07924, (908) 766-3468

Scottish Terrier Club of America (M)
Corres. Secretary: Polly O'Neal, 4058 Stratford, Abilene, TX 79605
Breeder Contact: Polly O'Neal, 4058 Stratford, Abilene, TX 79605, (915) 672-4229, pbo@camalott.com

American Sealyham Terrier Club (M)
Secretary: Judy E. Thill, 13948 N. Cascade Rd., Dubuque, IA 52003
Breeder Contact: Mrs. Patsy Underwood, 3206 W Cortez Ct. Irving, TX 75062, (972) 255-3581

Skye Terrier Club of America (M)
Corres. Secretary: Karen J'Anthony, 1667 E. Lebanon Rd., Dover, DE 19901
Breeder Contact: Donna C. Dale, 180 Marsh Creek Road, Gettysburg, PA 17325, (717) 334-0303 (phone), (717) 334-0710 (fax), gleantan@mail.cvn.net

Soft Coated Wheaten Terrier Club of America (M)
Corres. Secretary: Genie Kline, 585 Timberlane Road, Wetumpka, AL 36093
SCWTCA Public Information: (650) 299-8778

Staffordshire Bull Terrier Club, Inc. (M)
Corres. Secretary: Catherine Swain, P.O. Box 5382, Montecito, CA 93150
Breeder Contact: Marilyn Atwood, 24451 Dartmouth St., Dearborn Heights, MI 48125, (313) 277-3716

Welsh Terrier Club of America, Inc. (M)
Corres. Secretary: Derry Coe, 26841 Canyon Crest Rd, San Juan Capistrano, CA 92675
Breeder Contact: Derry Coe, 26841 Canyon Crest Rd, San Juan Capistrano, CA 92675, (714) 488-0178

West Highland White Terrier Club of America (M)
Corres. Secretary: Judith White, 8124 Apple Church Road, Thurmont, MD 21788
Breeder Contact: Gale McDonald, 3502 NW Half Mile Rd., Silverdale, WA 98383, (360) 697-4972, 0-700-4WESTIE (AT&T access)

Toy Group

Affenpinscher Club of America (M)
Secretary: Sharon I. Strempski, 2 Tucktaway Ln., Danbury, CT 06810
Breeder Contact: Barbara Sayres, 1064 Doctor Jack Rd., Conowingo, MD 21918, (410) 378-4075

American Brussels Griffon Association (M)
Secretary: Denise Brusseau, 5921 159th Lane NW, Anoka, MN 55303
Breeder Contact: Terry J. Smith, 221 E. Scott St., Grand Ledge, MI 48837, (517) 627-5916

American Cavalier King Charles Spaniel Club (L)
Secretary: Martha Guimond, 1905 Upper Ridge Rd., Green Lane, PA 18054
Breeder Contact: Yarrow Morgan, 5506 Trading Post Trail South, Afton, MN 55001, (612) 436-8326

Chihuahua Club of America, Inc. (M)
Corres. Secretary: Diana Garren, 16 Hillgirt Rd., Hendersonville, NC 28792
Breeder Contact: Josephine DeMenna, 2 Maple St., Wilton, CT 06897, (203) 762-2314

American Chinese Crested Club, Inc. (M)
Corres. Secretary: Kathleen Forth, Rt. 3 Box 157, Decatur, TX 76234
Breeder Contact: Janet Kiczek, 79 S New Boston Rd., Francestown, NH 03043, (603) 547-2804

English Toy Spaniel Club of America (M)
Corres. Secretary: Ms. Susan Jackson, 18451 Sheffield Ln., Bristol, IN 46507-9455
Breeder Contact: Ms. Christine Thaxton, 801 Greenwood Ave., Suite E, Waukegan, IL 60087, (847) 662-1000

Italian Greyhound Club of America, Inc. (M)
Corres. Secretary: Teri Dickinson, 4 Hillcrest Dr., Allen, TX 75002, fax: (972) 396-8993, tdickinson@compuserve.com
Breeder Contact: Lilian Barber, 35648 Menifee Rd., Murrieta, CA 92563, (909) 679-5084

Japanese Chin Club of America (M)
Secretary: Retha Hopkins, 3637 Pamelia Dr., Lauderdale, MS 39335, chinmom@netdoor.com
Breeder Contact: Mary Cooper, 222 S. Young St., Sparta, TN 38583, (615) 836-8150, airenchin@blomand.net
Breeder Contact: Chuck Fletcher, 17915-K Kings Point Dr., Cornelius, NC 28031, (704) 892-3447, japchin@charlotte.infi.net

American Maltese Association, Inc. (M)
Corres. Secretary: Pamela G. Rightmyer, 2211 S. Tioga Way, Las Vegas, NV 89117
Breeder Contact: Pamela G. Rightmyer, 2211 S. Tioga Way, Las Vegas, NV 89117, (702) 256-0420

American Manchester Terrier Club (M)
Secretary: Sandra Kipp, Box 231, Gilbertsville, IA 50634
Breeder Contact: Ms. Diana Haywood, 52 Hampton Rd., Pittstown, NJ 08867, (908) 996-7309

Miniature Pinscher Club of America, Inc. (M)
Corres. Secretary: Mrs. Janice Horne, 3724 88th SE, Mercer Island, WA 98040
Breeder Contact: Betty J. Cottle, 332 MacArthur Circle, Cocoa, FL 32927, (407) 632-6547

Papillon Club of America, Inc. (M)
Corres. Secretary: Mrs. Janice Dougherty, 551 Birch Hill Rd., Shoemakersville, PA 19555
Breeder Contact: Mrs. Janice Dougherty, 551 Birch Hill Rd., Shoemakersville, PA 19555, (610) 926-5581

Pekingese Club of America, Inc. (M)
Secretary: Mrs. Leonie Marie Schultz, Rt. #1, Box 321, Bergton, VA 22811
Breeder Contact: Mrs. Judith Pomato, 535 Devils Ln., Ballston Spa, NY 12020, (518) 885-6864

American Pomeranian Club, Inc. (M)
Corres. Secretary: Brenda Turner, 3910 Concord Place, Texarkana, TX 75501-2212
Breeder Contact: Jane Lehtinen, 1325 9th St. S, Virginia, MN 55792, (218) 741-2117

Poodle Club of America, Inc. (M)
Corres. Secretary: Mr. Charles R. Thomasson II, 503 Martineau Dr., Chester, VA 23831-5753
Breeder Contact: Mr. Charles R. Thomasson II, 503 Martineau Dr., Chester, VA 23831-5753, (804) 530-1605

Pug Dog Club of America, Inc.(M)
Secretary: Mr. James P. Cavallaro, 1820 Shadowlawn St., Jacksonville, FL 32205
Breeder Contact: Mary Ann Hall, 15988 Kettington Road., Chesterfield, MO 63017-7350, (314) 207-1508 n2pugs@worldnet.att.net

American Shih Tzu Club, Inc. (M)
Corres. Secretary: Bonnie Prato, 5252 Shafter Ave., Oakland, CA 94618
Breeder Contact: Mrs. Andy Hickok Warner, 2 Big Oak Rd., Dillsburg, PA 17019, (717) 432-4351

Silky Terrier Club of America, Inc. (M)
Secretary: Ms. Louise Rosewell, 2783 S. Saulsbury St., Denver, CO 80227
Breeder Contact: Ms. Louise Rosewell, 2783 S. Saulsbury St., Denver, CO 80227, (303) 988-4361

Yorkshire Terrier Club of America, Inc. (M)
Secretary: Mrs. Shirley A. Patterson, 2 Chestnut Ct., Star Rt., Pottstown, PA 19464
Breeder Contact: Mrs. Shirley A. Patterson, 2 Chestnut Ct., Star Rt., Pottstown, PA 19464, (610) 469-6781

Non-Sporting Group

American Eskimo Dog Club of America (L)
Corres. Secretary: Vivian Toepfer, 2206 Idaho Ave., Stockton, CA 95204
Breeder Contact: Carolyn Jester, Rt. #3, Box 211B, Stroud, OK 74079, (918) 968-3358

Bichon Frise Club of America, Inc. (M)
Corres. Secretary: Mrs. Bernice D. Richardson, 186 Ash Street, N. Twin Falls, ID 83301
Breeder Contact: Jane Lagemann, Hounds Ridge Rd., Lewisville, NC 27023, (910) 945-9788

Boston Terrier Club of America (M)
Corres. Secretary: Marian Sheehan, 8130 E. Theresa Dr., Scottsdale, AZ 85255
Breeder Contact: Jean Craig, 5648 East 23rd St, Indianapolis, IN 46218, (317) 356-1140

Bulldog Club of America (M)
Secretary: Toni Stevens, P.O. Box 248, Nobleton, FL 34661
Breeder Contact: Susan Rodenski, 480 Bully Hill Dr., King George, VA 22485, (540) 775-3015

Chinese Shar-Pei Club of America, Inc. (M)
Secretary: Georgette Schaefer, 210 White Chapel Court, Southlake, TX 76092-8500
Breeder Contact: Jocelyn Barker, P.O. Box 113809, Anchorage, AK 99511, (907) 345-6504

Chow Chow Club, Inc. (M)
Corres. Secretary: Irene Cartabio, 3580 Plover Pl., Seaford, NY 11783
Breeder Contact: Mary Wuest, 229 Kings Mill Road, Mason, OH 45040, (513) 398-0206

Dalmatian Club of America, Inc. (M)
Corres. Secretary: Mrs. Sharon Boyd, 2316 McCrary Rd., Richmond, TX 77469
Breeder Contact: Mrs. Gerri Lightholder, 6109 W. 147th St., Oak Forest, IL 60452, (708) 687-5447

Finnish Spitz Club of America (M)
Secretary: Bill Storz, 34 Sunrise Drive, Baltic, CT 06330
Breeder Contact: Kimberley Johnson, P.O. Box 556, Roy, UT 84067, (801) 774-9045

French Bulldog Club of America (M)
Corres. Secretary: Gail Pehlke, 20756 S. River Road, Shorewood, IL 60431, REGAILS@aol.com
Breeder Contact: Mr. Harry Dunn, Jr., 3638 Mayfair Dr., Tuscaloosa, AL 35404-5408, (205) 553-3817

Keeshond Club of America, Inc. (M)
Corres. Secretary: Tawn Sinclair, 11782 Pacific Coast Hwy., Malibu, CA 90265
Breeder Contact: Pat Yagecic, 4726 Grant Ave., Philadelphia, PA 19114, (215) 637-7731

American Lhasa Apso Club, Inc. (M)
Secretary: Esther DeFalcis, 3691 Tuggle Rd., Buford, GA 30519
Breeder Contact: Leslie Baumann,137 North 250 West, Valparaiso, IN 46385, (219) 462-9520, dbaumann@mail.icongrp.com

Poodle Club of America, Inc. (M)
Corres. Secretary: Mr. Charles R. Thomasson II, 503 Martineau Dr., Chester, VA 23831-5753
Breeder Contact: Mr. Charles R. Thomasson II, 503 Martineau Dr., Chester, VA 23831-5753, (804) 530-1605

Schipperke Club of America, Inc. (M)
Corres. Secretary: Dawn Hribar, 70480 Morency, Romeo, MI 48065
Breeder Contact: Margi Brinkley, 3245 8th St. S, Lebanon, OR 97355, (541) 259-3826

National Shiba Club of America (L)
Corres. Secretary: Liz Kinoshita, 2417 Ramke Pl., Santa Clara, CA 95050, lyzk@concentric.net
Breeder Contact: Dave Boykin, P.O. Box 3024, Carson City, NV 89702, (702) 265-7135, shibas@nanosecond.com

Tibetan Spaniel Club of America (M)
Corres. Secretary: Valerie Robinson, 103 Old Colony Dr., Mashpee, MA 02649
Breeder Contact: Valerie Robinson,103 Old Colony Dr., Mashpee, MA 02649, (508) 477-7637, deetree@capecod.net

Tibetan Terrier Club of America (M)
Secretary: Sharon Harrison, P.O. Box 528, Pleasanton, TX 78064
Breeder Contact: Mrs. Trudy Erceg, 356 Laurel Park Pl., Hendersonville, NC 28791, (704) 692-5007

Herding Group

Australian Cattle Dog Club of America (L)
    Secretary: Katherine Buetow, 2003B Melrose Drive,
    Champaign, IL 61820, ACDCA@cattledog.com
    Breeder Contact: Katherine Buetow, 2003B Melrose
    Drive, Champaign, IL 61820, (217) 359-0284

United States Australian Shepherd Association (L)
    Secretary: Andrea Blizard, 34 Deckertown Tpke.,
    Sussex, NJ 07461
    Information Chair: Sharon Fontanini,
    slfonta@us.ibm.com

Bearded Collie Club of America, Inc. (M)
    Corres. Secretary: Amber L. Carpenter, 541 Crestwood,
    Camden, AR 71701
    Breeder Contact: Amber L. Carpenter, 541 Crestwood,
    Camden, AR 71701, (870) 837-2930

American Belgian Malinois Club (M)
    Corres. Secretary: Marcia Herson, 209 Harrison
    Avenue, Harrison, NY 10528, mhcil@aol.com
    Breeder Contact: Ms. Sonya Tuovila, P.O. Box 339,
    Cobbs Creek, VA 23035, (804) 725-7512,
    bratpack@inna.net

Belgian Sheepdog Club of America, Inc. (M)
    Corres. Secretary: Carilee Cole, 11071 E. Stanley,
    Davison, MI 48423, cecole@juno.com
    Breeder Contact: Carilee Cole, 11071 E. Stanley,
    Davison, MI 48423, (810) 653-3842, cecole@juno.com

American Belgian Tervuren Club, Inc. (M)
    Corres. Secretary: Diane Schultz, Rt. 1 Box 759,
    Pomona Park, FL 32181
    Breeder Contact: Gail Cooper, 111 Sleepy Hollow
    Drive, Marble, NC 28905-8700, gailcoop@dnet.net

The Border Collie Society of America
    Corres. Secretary: April Quist, 2854 Kennedy Street,
    Livermore, CA 94550-8003

American Bouvier des Flandres Club, Inc. (M)
    Corres. Secretary: Dorothy Kent, 10520 West 102nd Pl.,
    Westminster, CO 80012-3717
    Breeder Contact: Dorothy Kent, 10520 West 102nd Pl.,
    Westminster, CO, 80012-3717, (303) 466-1242

Briard Club of America, Inc. (M)
    Corres. Secretary: Dianne Schoenberg, 3215 NE 89th,
    Seattle, WA 98115, diannes@u.washington.edu
    Breeder Contact: Ronni Balzarini, 283 Gates Ave.,
    Gillette, NJ 07933-1709, (908) 647-7329,
    RBalzarini@aol.com

Canaan Dog Club of America, Inc.
    Secretary: Sally Armstrong-Barnhardt, 2300 Crossover
    Rd., Reno, NV 89510-9354, K9TEACHER@aol.com
    Breeder Contact: Cynthia Grupp, 2367 Soda Canyon
    Rd., Napa, CA 94558, (707) 226-3353,
    CANAANDOG@aol.com

Collie Club of America, Inc. (M)
    Secretary: Mrs. Carmen Louise Leonard, 1119 South
    Fleming Rd, Woodstock, IL 60098
    Breeder Contact: Mrs. Carmen Louise Leonard, 1119
    South Fleming Rd, Woodstock, IL 60098, (815) 337-
    0323, SECCCA@aol.com

German Shepherd Dog Club of America, Inc. (M)
    Corres. Secretary: Blanche Beisswenger, 17 West Ivy
    Lane, Englewood, NJ 07631
    Breeder Contact: Blanche Beisswenger, 17 West Ivy
    Lane, Englewood, NJ 07631, (201) 568-5806

Old English Sheepdog Club of America, Inc. (M)
    Corres. Secretary: Allene Black, 220 Elm Street.,
    Enfield, CT 06082, gwynedd@tiac.net
    Breeder Contact: Ms. Joan Long, 5704 Greenwood,
    Shawnee, KS 66216, (913) 631-5614, longhome@gvi.net

Purebred Rescue/Adoption Clubs

Affenpinscher Club of America
Bernadine "Birdee" Hills, (608) 455-1611, fax (608) 455-
    1828, Wisconsin

Afghan Hound Club of America
Judy Fellton, (770) 971-1533, Georgia

Airedale Terrier Club of America
Barbara Curtiss, (860) 927-3420, New England
Lou Swafford, (301) 572-7116, Mid-Atlantic
Linda Baake, (919) 726-7703, South
Carol Domeracki, (616) 276-6390, Midwest
Melissa Moore, Chair, (602) 996-9648, fax (602) 953-0340,
    Southwest
Becky Preston, (817) 485-7041, Texas
Connie Turner, (503) 399-9819, Northwest

Akita Club of America
Nancy Baun, (973) 427-5985,
New Jersey,
Nancyb@intercall.com

Alaskan Malamute Club of America
Virginia A. Devaney, (505) 281-3961,
New Mexico

American Eskimo Dog Club of America
Bob Davis, (614) 889-5683, Ohio

(American) Staffordshire Terrier Club of America
Melanie Tierney, (716) 234-DOGS,
New York

American Water Spaniel Club
Elizabeth Pannill, DVM, (512) 357-2591, Texas, goatdoc@axiom.net

Australian Cattle Dog Club of America
Amy Berry, (619) 366-3593, California

Australian Shepherd
Kyle Trumbull-Clark, (800) 892-2722,
California

Australian Terrier Rescue
Barbara Curtis, (970) 482-9163,
Colorado, Bcgreyrock@aol.com

Basenji Club of America
Judith Holiday, (303) 795-5382,
Colorado

Basset Hound Club of America, Inc.
Mrs. Barbara Wicklund, (908) 874-0508, New Jersey

Bearded Collie Club of America
Paul Glatzer, (516) 724-0871, New
York

Bedlington Terrier Club of America
Ruth Mary Schneider, (804) 232-3748,
Virginia

American Belgian Malinois Club
Kathy Greenwood, (918) 371-3846,
Oklahoma

Belgian Sheepdog Club of America
Sharon Roundy, (708) 343-3358,
Illinois
Robin Barfoot, (517) 627-2549,
Michigan

American Belgian Tervuren Club
Cindy Simonsen, (414) 642-2286,
Wisconsin

Bernese Mountain Dog Club of America
Beth Friichtenicht, (309) 596-2633,
Illinois

Bichon Frise Club of America
Laura Fox-Meachen, (414) 878-4446,
Wisconsin

American Black and Tan Coonhound Club
Chris Hooker, (919) 776-7375, North
Carolina

American Bloodhound Club
Ed Kilby, (904) 788-0137, Florida

Border Collie Rescue Organization
Val Maurer, (330) 877-6566, Ohio

Border Terrier Club of America
Jo Ellen Wolf, (706) 863-0951,
Georgia

Borzoi Club of America
Carol Backers, (888) 264-8898

Boston Terrier Club of America
Linda Trader, (724) 883-4732,
Pennsylvania,
btcaresc@greenepa.net

American Bouvier des Flandres Club
Mrs. Dale Cuddy, (508) 948-5110,
Massachusetts

American Boxer Club
Chair: Tracy Hendrickson, (918) 250-9004, Oklahoma
West Coast: Alice Dalton, (619) 747-5712, California
South Central: Cheri Bush, (972) 881-1104, Texas

Central: Jeanette Everette, (815) 653-9016, Illinois
Northwest: Susan Bell, (360) 691-5601,
Washington
East Coast: Jean Loubriel, (973) 768-6627, New Jersey
Southeast: Mary Ellen Crawford, (904)
322-6969, Florida

Boxer Rescue: Dayton, OH and
Surrounding Area
Rachel Osborn, (937) 277-4652
Delma Robinson, (937) 426-9744

Briard Club of America
Merry Jeanne Millner, phone: (910)
869-5490, fax: (910) 841-7392,
North Carolina,
SENDERO869@aol.com

American Brittany Club
Rhonda Carlson, (510) 582-2714
(home), (510) 549-2527 (work)
California

American Brussels Griffon Association
Marjorie Simon, (713) 783-8887,
Texas

Bulldog Club of America
James and Diane Young, (210) 340-0055, Texas

American Bullmastiff Association
Virginia Rowland, (508) 939-5300,
Massachusetts

Bull Terrier Club of America Welfare Foundation
Norma Shepherd, (800) BTBT-911,
(401) 231-0927,
Rhode Island

Cairn Terrier Club of America
Mary Lou Wilde, (303) 779-0137,
Colorado

Cardigan Welsh Corgi Club of America
H. Pamela Allen, (703) 836-1963,
Virginia

Chihuahua Club of America
Sharon Hermosillo, (408) 251-0470,
California

Chinese Shar-Pei Club of America
Eastern Region: Charlene Rogers,
(203) 747-6397, Connecticut
Central Region: Deb Cooper, (708)
848-2226, Illinois
Western Region: Louise Watson,
(303) 772-7325, Colorado

Dominion Chinese Shar-Pei Club
Laura Prudom, (757) 473-3587,
Virginia

Chow Chow Club
Vicky DeGruy, (608) 756-2008,
Wisconsin

Clumber Spaniel Club of America
Sue Carr, (908) 580-1055, New Jersey

*American Spaniel Club (Cocker
Spaniels)*
Becki Zaborowski, (770) 974-7931,
Georgia

Collie Club of America
Ruth Ayres, (412) 364-5742,
Pennsylvania

*Curly Coated Retriever Club of
America*
Sheila Callahan-Young, (508) 281-
3860, Massachusetts

Dachshund Club of America
Emina Jean Stephenson, (412) 846-
6745, Pennsylvania

Dalmatian Club of America
Tina Thomas Smith, (919) 269-4683,
North Carolina

Dandie Dinmont Terrier Breed Rescue
Sandra Stuart, (770) 975-3773, Georgia

Doberman Pinscher Club of America
Gwen Lucoff, (310) 457-4460,
California

*English Cocker Spaniel Club of
America*
Marcia Wallace, (703) 548-7641,
Virginia

English Setter Association of America
Lisa Boughton, home: (910) 381-4013,
work: (910) 297 5022, fax: (910)
297-5023, North Carolina

*English Springer Spaniel Field Trial
Association*
Dick and Sue Burgess, (800) 377-
3824, Arizona

English Toy Spaniel Club of America
Mrs. Mary Hoagland, (609) 397-3148,
New Jersey

Field Spaniel Society of America
Patricia Ramsey, (619) 245-7346,
California

Finnish Spitz Club of America, Inc.
Cindy Goodman, (919) 661-8803,
North Carolina,
CYNDAGO@aol.com

*Flat-Coated Retriever Society of
America*
Joyce Rein, (616) 846-0773, Michigan

American Fox Terrier Club, Inc.
Mrs. Winifred H. Stout, 1-800-FOX-
TERR, Rhode Island,
wstout@rockyhill.org (work),
wstout@edgenet.net (home)

French Bulldog Club of America
Brenda Buckles, (913) 383-1377,
Kansas

*German Shepherd Dog Club of
America*
Linda Kury, (408) 247-1272, California

*German Shorthaired Pointer Club of
America*
Nancy Campbell, (203) 938-8048,
Connecticut
Bonnie Wilcox, DVM, (309) 787-4266,
Illinois

*German Wirehaired Pointer Club of
America*
Linda Strothman, (978) 861-0820,
Massachusetts

Giant Schnauzer Club of America
Carolyn Janak, (303) 988-6564,
Colorado

Golden Retriever Club of America
National Rescue Hotline, (281) 861-
0820, Texas

Gordon Setter Club of America
Tom DePotty, (612) 413-0612,
Minnesota

Great Dane Club of America
Eleanor Evans, (760) 722-1037,
California

*The Great Dane Club of Western
Pennsylvania*
Erin McGlynn, (412) 434-6326,
Pennsylvania

Great Pyrenees Club of America
Janet Ingram, (540) 731-0229, Virginia

*Greater Swiss Mountain Dog Club of
America*
DeAnne Gerner, (610) 779-9217,
Pennsylvania
Sharyl Mayhew, (703) 754-0158,
Virginia
Kathy Caslin, (309) 334-2883, Illinois

Greyhound Club of America
Cheryl Reynolds, (805) 684-4914,
California
Lois Bires, (412) 935-3276,
Pennsylvania

National Greyhound Adoption
Network, (800) 446-8637

Harrier Club of America, Inc.
Donna K. Smiley-Auborn, (619) 377-
4758, California

*Ibizan Hound Club of the United
States*
John O'Malley, (806) 746-5521, Texas

Irish Setter Club of America
Marilee Larson, (209) 295-1666,
California

Irish Terrier Club of America
Nancyanne Bruner, (423) 538-8648,
Tennessee

Irish Water Spaniel Club of America
Carolyn Lathrop, (301) 724-9162,
Maryland

Irish Wolfhound Club of America
Jean A. Minnier, (609) 268-9373,
New Jersey

Italian Greyhound Club of America
Michelle Popka, (219) 922-8147,
Indiana

*Jack Russell Terrier Association of
America*
Kelly D. Meeks-Childs, (804) 469-4744
(phone and fax), Virginia

Japanese Chin Club of America
Mimi Stauffer, (918) 225-7374,
Oklahoma

Keeshond Club of America
Tawn Sinclair, (310) 457-3569,
California

United States Kerry Blue Terrier Club
Joanne Schindler, (513) 742-3745,
Ohio

Komondor Club of America
Sandy Hanson, (414) 594-3374,
Wisconsin

Kuvasz Club of America
Michele Valesano, (707) 994-4746,
California

Labrador Retriever Club of America
Luanne Lindsey, (512) 259-3645, fax
(512) 259-5227, Texas

*Golden Gate Labrador Retriever
Rescue, Inc.*
Hotline Number: (650) 361-0261,
California

*Lab Rescue of the Labrador Retriever
Club of the Potomac, Inc.*
Diane Gildersleeve, (301) 299-6756,
Virginia

United States Lakeland Terrier Club
Bonnie Guzman, (303) 733-4220,
Colorado

American Lhasa Apso Club
Mary Schroeder, (800) 699-3115,
Colorado

American Manchester Terrier Club
Patricia Hall, (215) 957-0109,
Pennsylvania

Mastiff Club of America
National Director: Gloria Cuthbert,
(440) 639-1160, Ohio
Paul and Misty Shearon, (360) 832-
7245, WA Northwestern Region
Karen Flocker, (520) 779-0473, AZ,
Western Region
Debbie Greiner, (773) 763-7793, IL,
Midwestern Region
Janet Powell, (214) 342-3763, TX,
Mid-Southern Region
Gina Anelli, (860) 283-6278, CT,
Northeastern Region
Deborah Martin, (919) 556-0206, NC,
Southeastern Region

Miniature Bull Terrier Club of America
Kathy Brosnan, (603) 642-5355, New
Hampshire

Miniature Pinscher Club of America
Glory Ann Pigarut, (301) 868-2997,
Maryland

American Miniature Schnauzer Club
Mrs. Bolivia Powell, (214) 363-5630,
Texas

Newfoundland Club of America
Mary L. Price, (608) 437-4553,
Wisconsin

*Norwich & Norfolk Terriers Club of
America*
Susan M. Ely, (908) 766-5429, New
Jersey

*Norwegian Elkhound Association of
America*
Ruth Ness, (301) 942-3763, Maryland

Old English Sheepdog
Christine Bunsick and Jane Dempsey,
(805) 821-0416, California

Otterhound Club of America
Betsy Conway, (914) 245-6354, New
York
Betty Smith, (601) 634-0199,
Mississippi

Papillon Club of America
Diana Fuchs, (850) 875-1422, Florida

Pekingese Club of America
Dr. Claudia Covo, (212) 362-3229,
New York

*Pembroke Welsh Corgi Club of
America*
Millie Williams, (616) 625-2560,
rescue@pembrokecorgi.org,
Michigan

*Petit Basset Griffon Vendeen Club of
America*
Sherry Thommen, (505) 983-3648,
New Mexico

Pharaoh Hound Club of America
Celaine Burns, (305) 246-9598,
 rakapharo@aol.com, Florida
Pam Haig, (702) 782-6542,
 MIAPHARAOH@aol.com, Nevada
Marie Henke, (219) 336-3118,
 mhenke4950@aol.com, Ohio

American Pomeranian Club
Linda Brogoitti, (602) 979-5336,
 Arizona

Poodle Club of America
Helen Taylor, (409) 321-0132, Texas

*Portuguese Water Dog Club of
 America*
Mary Harkins, (610) 346-9370,
 Pennsylvania

Pug Dog Club of America
Maryanne Johnson, (320) 485-2876,
 Minnesota

Puli Club of America
Betty O'Donnell, (207) 283-3528,
 Maine

*Rhodesian Ridgeback Club of the
 United States*
Barbara Sawyer-Brown, (773) 281-
 5569, Illinois

American Rottweiler Club
Gwen Cheaney, (330) 722-3682, Ohio

Saint Bernard Club of America
Carol Varner Beck, (541) 878-8281,
 Oregon

Saluki Club of America
Cloris Costigan, (908) 257-9134, New
 Jersey

Samoyed Club of America
Janet White, PO Box 212, Divide, CO
 80814, tsuki@usa.net

Schipperke Club of America
Shirley Smith, (716) 985-4137, fax
 (716) 661-3437, New York

Scottish Deerhound Club of America
Virginia Cioffletti, (608) 877-4140,
 Wisconsin

Scottish Terrier Club of America
Daphne and Marshall Branzell, (210)
 653-3723, Texas

American Sealyham Terrier Club
Barbara Carmany, (330) 239-1498,
 Ohio

*American Shetland Sheepdog
 Association*
Dorothy Christiansen, (815) 485-3726,
 Illinois

American Shih Tzu Club
Phyllis Celmer, (760) 942-0874,
 California

Siberian Husky Club of America
Gerry Dalakian, (908) 782-2089, New
 Jersey

Silky Terrier Club of America, Inc.
Dr. Braden Wolf, (253) 756-5457,
 Washington

Skye Terrier Club of America
Anne Brown, (803) 726-3237 (home),
 (803) 726-6678 (fax/answering
 machine), South Carolina

Staffordshire Bull Terrier Club
Tony George, (718) 898-0298, New
 York

Standard Schnauzer Club of America
Judith Legan, (714) 551-0136,
 California

Tibetan Spaniel Club of America
Shirley Howard, (630) 231-3087,
 Illinois

Tibetan Terrier Club of America
Brenda Brown, (304) 755-2681, West
 Virginia

Vizsla Club of America
Stephen Shlyen, (610) 294-8020,
 Pennsylvania

Weimaraner Club of America
Rebecca Weimer, (618) 236-1466,
 Illinois

*Welsh Springer Spaniel Club of
 America*
Peggy Ruble, (316) 244-3782, Kansas

Welsh Terrier Club of America
Ward and Carolyn Morris, (404) 351-
 1330, Georgia
Debi Jamison, (408) 725-0424,
 California

*West Highland White Terrier Club of
 America*
Judith White, (301) 271-3380,
 Maryland

American Whippet Club
Peggy Bush, (214) 337-1758, Texas

*American Wirehaired Pointing Griffon
 Association*
Kyle Miller, (609) 265-9195,
 Kylem64@aol.com, New Jersey

Yorkshire Terrier Club of America
Suzette Heider, (407) 725-8821,
 Florida

Web Sites

There are a great number of quality Web sites available on the World Wide Web. However, there's also a lot of dreck! Although not all of the best sites can be listed, the ones below are an excellent representation of products and services available out in cyberspace. For a much more definitive listing of all of the best dog-related Web sites, you need to run out and buy *Dogs on the Web*, by Audrey Pavia and Betsy Sikora Siino (MIS Press, 1997). Pavia's and Siino's book contains more than 500 quality Web sites, listing the most serious to the most frivolous, with extensive review coverage of each site. It's both a time saver and a listing of sites you might never find on your own. A must for Webheads.

General

BreederLink Homepage
http://www.breederlink.com/index.htm

Dog Breeders Online Directory
http://www.doggies.com/index.html

Canine Connections Breed Rescue Information
http://www.cheta.net/connect/canine/Rescue/

Canine.Net
http://www.canine.net/

Dog Fancy Magazine
http://www.petchannel.com/dogs/index.html

Dog Owner's Guide
http://www.canismajor.com/dog/guide.html

Dogs On-Line
http://www.dogsonline.com

Greyhound Rescue and Adoption
http://206.160.225.6/greyhound/

Pro Dog Breed Rescue Network
http://www.prodogs.com/frmst5.htm

Project Breed
http://www.tezcat.com/~emiller/ProjectBreed.html

Organizations

All Breed Rescue Alliance
http://www.breeders.com/html/rescue/abra/info.htm

American Kennel Club
http://www.akc.org

American Rare Breeds Association
http://www.arba.org

American Society for the Prevention of Cruelty to Animals
http://www.aspca.org/

Bide-A-Wee
http://www.inch.com/~bideawee/index.html

Canadian Kennel Club
http://www.pagemake.com/~garland/homepage/ckc/firstpg.html

Crufts Dog Show
http://www.crufts.org.uk/home.htm

Dog Writer's Association of America
http://www.prodogs.com/dwaa/contents.htm

Federation Cynologique International
http://www.bestdogs.com/FCI/Default.htm

Humane Society of the United States
http://www.hsus.org

The Kennel Club
http://www.the-kennel-club.org.uk/

Training and Behavior

American Dog Trainers Network
http://www.inch.com/~dogs/

Campbell's Pet Behavior Resources
http://www.Webtrail.com/petbehavior/index.html

Dog Obedience and Training Page
http://www.dogpatch.org/obed.html

National Association of Dog Obedience Instructors
http:www.kimberly.uidaho.edu/nadoi/

Obedience Homepage
http://www.princeton.edu/~nadelman/obed/obed.html

Raising Your Dog with the Monks of New Skete
http://www.dogsbestfriend.com/

Health
AVMA (American Veterinary Medical Association)
http://www.avma.org

FDA Center for Veterinary Medicine
http://www.cvm.fda.gov/

Heinz Pets Unleashed
http://www.heinzpet.com/main/index.htm

Iams Company Homepage
http://www.iamsco.com/

National Animal Control Poison Center
http://www.prodogs.com//chn/napcc/index.htm

PennHip Method of Diagnosing Hip Dysplasia
http://www.canismajor.com/dog/pennhip1.html

Purina Pet Care Center
http://www.purina.com/

Waltham World of Pet Care
http://www.waltham.com

Activities
American Rescue Dog Association
http://www.ardainc.org

American Herding Breed Association
http://www.primenet.com/~joel/ahba/

Flyball Homepage
http://www.cs.umn.edu/~ianhogg/flyball.html

Guide Dog Association
http://www.world.net/Business/Charity/
    guide-dogs/welcome.html

Guiding Eyes for the Blind
http://www.guiding-eyes.org/

Lure Coursing
http://www.clak.net/pub/bdalzell/lure/lure coursing.faq.12/html

Mushing
http://www.readysoft.es/mushing/INGLES/HOME.HTM

Police Dog Homepage
http://www.best.com/~policek9/k9home.htm

Police K-9 Homepage
http://www.navisoft.com/k9officer/my-page.htm

Shutzhund.Com
http://www.shutzhund.com

United Shutzhund Clubs of America
http://www.igateway.net/~usagsdog/

Catalog/Resource
Flying Dog Press
http://www.flyingdogpress.com/articles.htm

Dog Lover's Bookshop
http://www.dogbooks.com

Index

EVERYTHING

The Everything Bird Book
by Tershia d'Elgin

Trade paperback, 288 pages
1-58062-061-2, $12.95

The Everything Bird Book is the only guide you'll ever need to learn about our feathered friends. It contains information on bird identification, bird evolution , what to do if your bird is sick, what are the 50 birds you are most likely to see, and much more. *The Everything Bird Book* has the fascinating answers to all your questions about the wonderful world of birds.

The Everything Cat Book
by Steve Duno

Trade paperback, 312 pages
1-55850-710-8, $12.95

Have you ever wondered how to tempt your finicky cat to eat? And how to put the fat cat on a proper diet? What's the best way to keep kitty from eating your house plants? Should you declaw your kitty, or not? You'll find the answers to theses and many other perplexing questions in *The Everything Cat Book*. From practical considerations like choosing a veterinarian and basic first-aid to fascinating cat lore and trivia. *The Everything Cat Book* offers everything you need to know about living with your favorite feline friend.

Available Wherever Books Are Sold

If you cannot find these titles at your favorite retail outlet, you may order them directly from the publisher. BY PHONE: Call 1-800-872-5627. We accept Visa, Mastercard, and American Express. $4.95 will be added to your total order for shipping and handling. BY MAIL: Write out the full titles of the books you'd like to order and send payment, including $4.95 for shipping and handling, to: Adams Media Corporation, 260 Center Street, Holbrook, MA 02343. 30-day money-back guarantee.

We Have EVERYTHING

More bestselling Everything titles available from your local bookseller:

Everything **After College Book**
Everything **Astrology Book**
Everything **Baby Names Book**
Everything® **Bartender's Book**
Everything **Bedtime Story Book**
Everything **Beer Book**
Everything **Bicycle Book**
Everything **Bird Book**
Everything **Casino Gambling Book**
Everything **Cat Book**
Everything® **Christmas Book**
Everything **College Survival Book**
Everything **Crossword and Puzzle Book**
Everything **Dessert Book**
Everything **Dog Book**
Everything **Dreams Book**
Everything **Etiquette Book**
Everything **Family Tree Book**
Everything **Fly-Fishing Book**
Everything **Games Book**

Everything **Get Ready For Baby Book**
Everything **Golf Book**
Everything **Guide to Walt Disney World®, Universal Studios®, and Greater Orlando**
Everything **Home Buying Book**
Everything **Home Improvement Book**
Everything **Internet Book**
Everything **Jewish Wedding Book**
Everything **Low-Fat High-Flavor Cookbook**
Everything **Money Book**
Everything **Pasta Book**
Everything **Pregnancy Book**
Everything **Study Book**
Everything **Trivia Book**
Everything® **Wedding Book**
Everything® **Wedding Checklist**
Everything® **Wedding Etiquette Book**
Everything® **Wedding Organizer**
Everything® **Wedding Vows Book**
Everything **Wine Book**